MORE THAN 400,000 COPIES SOLD

The BOOK of U.S. GOVERNMENT JOBS

WHERE THEY ARE, WHAT'S AVAILABLE and HOW TO COMPLETE A FEDERAL RÉSUMÉ

11th EDITION

DENNIS V. DAMP

Bookhaven Press LLC
McKees Rocks, Pennsylvania

ISSN 2158-7698

The Book of

U.S. GOVERNMENT JOBS

Where They Are, What's Available, and How to Complete a Federal Résumé

By Dennis V. Damp

BOOKHAVEN PRESS LLC
249 Field Club Circle
McKees Rocks, PA 15136
info@BookhavenPress.com, www.BookhavenPress.com, www.federaljobs.net

First Edition 1986. Eleventh Edition / Twenty-seventh Printing 2011, Completely Revised
Printed in the United States of America

Disclaimer of All Warranties and Liabilities

Publisher's Cataloging-in-Publication
(Provided by Quality Books, Inc.)

Damp, Dennis V.
    The book of U.S. Government jobs: where they are,
what's available, and how to complete a federal resume /
Dennis V. Damp. -- 11th ed.
      p. cm.
      Includes bibliographical references and index.
      ISBN-13: 978-0-943641-29-4
      ISBN-10: 0-943641-29-2
      1. Civil service positions --United States.
I. Title: II: Book of US government jobs.
III. Title: Book of United States government jobs.
JK716D36 2011   331.12'4135173
LCCN: 2011903343   QBI11-600022

For quantity discount rates, telephone 412/494-6926. Distributed to the trade by Midpoint Trade Books, 27 West 20th Street, Suite 1102, New York, NY 10011, Tel: 212-727-0190.

Table of Contents

CHAPTER THREE
What Jobs Are Available.............................. 47

CHAPTER FOUR
The Interview Process............................ 69

CHAPTER TWELVE

- Apply Early 236
- Your Application and Résumé 236
- Apply Frequently 237
- Getting in the Front Door 239
- Locate All Job Vacancies 239
- Training and Experience 240
- Networking 241
- Keys to Success 241

Visit www.federaljobs.net for updates.

About the Author

DENNIS DAMP is an author, retired federal manager, business owner, career counselor and veteran. Damp's *The Book of U.S. Government Jobs* was a three-time finalist for *"Best Career"* title by the Benjamin Franklin Awards Committee and a finalist for *"Best Career & Reference"* title in 2008 by Foreword Magazine.

Damp is the author of 25 books and a recognized employment expert. He retired in 2005 at age 55 with 35 years of government service. Dennis has been a guest on hundreds of radio talk shows and on CNN Cable TV. He developed and produced Internet Web sites and training videos, and has written numerous articles for national magazines, newspapers and Internet sites. His books have been featured in the *Wall Street Journal, Washington Post, New York Times* and *U.S. News & World Report*. The previous edition of this book was in the top 20 most checked out career guides at libraries in 2009 as reported by Library Journal.

Dennis joined the Air Force in 1968 and spent over three years on active duty and an additional seven years with the Air National Guard. He was hired by the Department of Defense (DOD) after leaving active duty and transferred to the Federal Aviation Administration (FAA) in 1975. He spent the remainder of his career in various positions with the FAA.

While employed with the FAA, Dennis worked as an electronics technician, training instructor, project engineer, computer-based instruction administrator, training program manager, program support manager, and environmental health and safety program manager. Dennis held numerous supervisory and management positions and was responsible for recruiting, rating and interviewing applicants, outreach and hiring. His last government position was technical operations manager at the Pittsburgh International Airport's air traffic control tower.

Damp's books are based on his many years in management where he was responsible for recruitment, outreach, retention and career development. His books present an insider's view of what it takes to go from job hunter to hired employee, and everything in between, to improve a job hunter's chances of landing a high-paying government job.

Foreword

First of all, I would like to thank Dennis Damp for his wonderful work over the years on *The Book of U.S. Government Jobs*, and for asking me to write the foreword for the 11th Edition. I am honored to be a part of this project, and truly appreciate this book's role in keeping the public up to date. As President and CEO of Career Pro Global, Inc., I have been observing and adjusting to federal hiring practices for more than 20 years.

We all know that the past couple of years have been extremely challenging for the American economy and job landscape. During this period, the federal government has changed many hiring practices, and jobseekers have had to adjust accordingly. This updated 11th edition features the many changes that the current Administration implemented since the previous edition was released.

On May 11, 2010, President Barack Obama issued an Executive Order to implement a sweeping reform of the federal hiring process. Perhaps the most obvious (and significant) change is this: federal agencies have been challenged to reduce overall hiring time and improve the way they notify jobseekers of their application status. Effective as of November 1, 2010, hiring reform is still in process and has already created a number of important changes for jobseekers.

For example, applicants should not be required to respond to essay-style questions (frequently known as Knowledge, Skills and Abilities, or KSAs) when submitting their initial application materials. Regardless of what an agency calls them (KSAs, supplemental questions, occupational questionnaires, etc), you still need the tools to provide well-written, relevant examples in response to these types of questions. This issue is discussed in more detail in Chapter Six.

Another major change hiring reform has created involves using a "category rating" rather than the traditional "Rule of 3" approach, which forced managers to select only from among the three highest-scoring applicants. Using category rating, hiring managers can select from among a larger number of qualified applicants.

Amid all of these changes, some things remain constant. You need to know how to write a strong, accomplishment-based résumé, and relevant, concise responses to occupational questions. Moreover, you need to know how to "fit" your application materials into the various online application systems used throughout the federal government. This book will empower you to do exactly that by providing a wealth of resources and sharing best practices from some of the career industry's best organizations.

Another constant is that the federal government is still a great career choice. For one thing, the U.S. government is the largest employer in the in the United States, hiring approximately 2 percent of the nation's civilian workforce. From October of 2009 through June 2010, agencies hired 212,188 new employees to fill critical vacancies nationwide. Likewise, federal employment increased dramatically over the past 2 years compared to the private sector where unemployment hovers in the high single digits. The two-year federal pay freeze that was implemented starting in 2011 will have little impact on total compensation growth considering that a federal employee's annual step increases, promotions, and pay for performance incentives are still permitted.

The average annual salary for all pay plans increased from $67,186 in 2005 to $82,883 in 2010. Federal employees earned an average annual compensation of $123,049 including pay and benefits in 2010 compared to just $61,051 in the private sector according to the United States Bureau of Economic Analysis. New hires in the federal government can receive student loan payoff and relocation assistance plus cash incentives for hard-to-fill positions — and the benefits package is exceptional. Federal workers' average annual benefits alone now exceed $41,791.

Even amid such challenging economic times, the federal government has remained one of the most reliable options out there for jobseekers. Many additional opportunities will be created as those who are at or beyond retirement age opt to retire. Many retirements are projected as each day 10,000 baby boomers turn age 65 for the next 19 years! Hiring will be driven by retirements and the need to staff over 100 new agencies and regulatory organizations due to the healthcare and banking legislation passed in 2010. Translation: over 40 percent of the total federal workforce is eligible for regular or early retirement!

This bears repeating: the federal government is the largest employer in the United States… and it is not going anywhere. If you are looking for a position with good pay and excellent benefits, you should consider the high-paying and secure federal job market. The federal government offers a wide range of positions in a broad variety of career fields, is currently trying to improve hiring practices and hire more veterans, and offers challenging assignments both stateside and overseas. Remember, the average pay for full-time employees in 2010 was $82,883!

Finally, I congratulate you on choosing this 11th Edition of *The Book of U.S. Government Jobs*. You obviously want the best information and resources available to aid in your job search, and you have found both in this book. This edition will help you land a high-paying, benefit-loaded, and secure government job.

Barbara A. Adams

President and CEO of Career Pro Global, Inc.

Acknowledgments

First and foremost I must thank Barbara Adams, President and owner of Career Pro Global and her staff: Lee Kelley, Patricia Duckers, and Nancy H. Segal. They devoted an inordinate amount of time updating Chapter Six to incorporate hiring reform initiatives and provided résumé samples and succinct application guidance. Barbara is a consummate professional who has helped thousands apply for federal employment.

I must also thank Linda Duncan, a federal HR specialists with over 16 years experience, who knows the federal system from the inside out. She provided insight into hiring reform initiatives and edited the content for this new edition. Our other contributors include: Robert A. Juran, copy editor; Chuck Jumpeter, a federal retiree with over 40 years of service; and George Foster, our cover designer.

My son, Dennis Damp Jr., updated this edition's directories and contact information, and my daughter, Sabrina Damp, proofreads all of our manuscripts. Without my wife's dedication, none of this would be possible; her patience, encouragement, and understanding are the keys to this and all of my books' and projects' successes.

Others include: Kate Bandos, our publicist who always goes the extra yard to get each new book off on the right track, and our distributor, Midpoint Trade Books; especially Chris Bell, and Margaret Queen. Many of my former associates and friends contributed over the years as I either relied on their counsel and guidance or participated with them on various panels, interviews, and committees.

I haven't cited all the sources and authorities that were consulted in the preparation of this guide. The list would include numerous federal departments and human resource specialists, system specialists, federal job seekers I've interviewed along the way, and librarians.

I wish to sincerely thank all who contributed. Without their input, counsel, and guidance over the years this book could not have been written.

CHAPTER ONE
Introduction to
Government Employment

F ederal employment increased dramatically over the past two years compared to the private sector, where unemployment hovers in the high single digits. From October 2009 through June 2010, agencies hired 212,188 new hires. Total employment, including the Postal Service, was 2,850,280 as of September 2010.[1]

The average annual salary now exceeds $81,186.

Many retirements are projected as each day 10,000 baby boomers turn age 65 for the next 19 years! Hiring will be driven by retirements and the need to staff over 100 new agencies and regulatory organizations due to the healthcare and banking legislation passed in 2010.

There are many reasons to consider federal employment. The average annual federal worker's compensation, pay plus benefits, is **$123,049** compared to just **$61,051** for the private sector.[2] Average salary is **$81,258** and new hires can receive student loan payoff assistance, relocation and cash incentives for hard-to-fill positions, and the benefits package is exceptional. A larger percentage of professionals and fewer service and clerical positions contribute to higher average salaries.

Objectives are listed for key elements included in each chapter. The image to the right is used throughout this book to highlight points of interest.

CHAPTER OBJECTIVES

✎ Understanding the opportunities

✎ Determining the nature of federal employment, working conditions, occupations, training, outlook, pay and benefits

✎ What benefits to expect including retirement

✎ How to develop your career and get promoted

---

[1] Central Personnel Data File 9/2010 and the 2010 Comprehensive Statement of Postal Operations

[2] Bureau of Economic Analysis, National Income & Product Account Tables 6.2D and 6.5D, 2010.

It is difficult to imagine just how large the federal job market is until you compare it to its closest private-sector rival. Wal-Mart is the largest company worldwide, with annual sales of $530 billion and 2.1 million workers. Uncle Sam employs 750,000 more workers than Wal-Mart. Over the past two years alone over 200,000 new workers were hired to fill critical vacancies nationwide. The average annual salary for all pay plans increased from $67,186 in 2005 to $81,258 in 2010. The U.S. government is the largest employer in the United States, hiring approximately 2 percent of the nation's civilian workforce.

Job hunters will find helpful information and resources in this book to research employment options, locate job vacancies, understand the federal job market, and apply for federal jobs. Numerous programs, options, and resources are reviewed and explained in detail, including:

✓ How to approach the federal sector and identify available recruitment incentives including the student loan repayment and relocation payments that are offered for hard-to-fill vacancies.

✓ The latest federal hiring reform and federal-style résumé guidance from Barbara Adams, President and CEO of CareerPro Global, Inc. CPG combines several decades of industry-writing experience from entry-level to Senior Executive Service (SES), within or aspiring to work within the federal government.

✓ How to evaluate job announcements, answer occupational questionnaires, obtain a "Best Qualified" rating, and write Knowledge, Skills, and Abilities (KSAs) statements that are still used in various forms for some positions.

✓ Most non-Postal Service federal jobs, over 80 percent, don't require written exams. Determine whether your occupation requires a written entrance exam and if one is required how to prepare for it.

✓ Over a thousand resources are listed, including interactive employment Web sites, an agency directory, occupation lists, skills index, and contact numbers for personnel specialists.

✓ You will learn about student employment programs, veterans preference, hiring opportunities for the disabled, law enforcement and overseas job opportunities, Post Office jobs, and much more.

✓ Prepare for interviews, learn about the generous pay and benefits, networking techniques, and how to locate and apply for jobs stateside and overseas.

You need to know how to take
advantage of the federal hiring system
and recent changes to successfully land
the job you want in government.

Excellent job opportunities are available for those who know how to tap this lucrative job market. All government hiring is based on performance and qualifications regardless of your gender, race, color, creed, religion, disability, or national origin. Where else can you apply for a high-paying entry-level job that offers employment at thousands of locations internationally, excellent career advancement opportunities, and careers in hundreds of occupations?

Government hired over a million part time workers in 2010 for the US. Census alone and continues to hire hundreds of thousands of full time workers each year. Other vacancies exist in the legislative and judicial branches. Numerous job opportunities are available for those willing to seek them out.

> Many opportunities will be created as over 637,000 federal employees will become eligible for retirement in 2011 according to *OPM's Analysis of Federal Employee Retirement Data Report*, Table 2.

The following statistical analysis will help you focus on just where the greatest opportunities are. The largest agencies are featured and their employment trends analyzed. Large agencies hire a broad spectrum of workers in hundreds of occupations. It's best to expand your search to as many agencies as possible to improve your chances.

Six agencies, including the Postal Service, employ approximately 75 percent of the workforce, or 2,137,710 employees. Of the 89,204 overseas jobs 62,838 were U.S. citizens. The remaining overseas employees are foreign nationals. The changes from September of 2006 to September 2010 in Table 1-1 show that all agencies except the Postal Service increased employment, some substantially. The Department of Defense increased by 76,555 employees. Overall, the total employment increased by 7 percent while the Judicial branch essentially stayed the same and the Legislative branch employment increased by 4 percent. The second largest increase was in Veterans Affairs; their employment increased 27 percent, an increase of 65,569 workers.

```
┌─────────────────────────────────────────────────────────────┐
│                                                               │
│                        TABLE 1-1                              │
│             The Six Largest Federal Departments               │
│                                                               │
│     Total Workforce          2,850, 280        100 %          │
│                                                               │
│     Legislative branch          30,859         1.10 %         │
│     Judicial branch             33,754         1.20 %         │
│     USPS & PRC *               671,687        23.60 %         │
│     Executive (non-postal)   2,113,980        74.10 %         │
│                                                               │
│       ❶ Defense                764,299                        │
│       ❷ Veterans Affairs       308,814                        │
│       ❸ Homeland Security      188,983                        │
│       ❹ Justice                109,900                        │
│       ❺ Treasury               116,901                        │
│                                                               │
│                                                               │
│   Reference: Federal Civilian Workforce Statistics – September 2010   │
│                                                               │
│   * The United States Postal Service (USPS) and the Postal Rate Commission (PRC).   │
│                                                               │
└─────────────────────────────────────────────────────────────┘
```

TABLE 1-1		
The Six Largest Federal Departments		
Total Workforce	**2,850, 280**	**100 %**
Legislative branch	30,859	1.10 %
Judicial branch	33,754	1.20 %
USPS & PRC *	671,687	23.60 %
Executive (non-postal)	2,113,980	74.10 %
❶ Defense	764,299	
❷ Veterans Affairs	308,814	
❸ Homeland Security	188,983	
❹ Justice	109,900	
❺ Treasury	116,901	

Reference: Federal Civilian Workforce Statistics – September 2010

* The United States Postal Service (USPS) and the Postal Rate Commission (PRC).

NATURE OF FEDERAL EMPLOYMENT

The federal government's essential duties include defending the United States from foreign aggression and terrorism, representing U.S. interests abroad, enforcing laws and regulations, and administering domestic programs and agencies.[3] U.S. citizens are particularly aware of the federal government when they pay their income taxes each year, but they usually do not consider the government's role when they watch a weather forecast, purchase fresh and uncontaminated groceries, travel by highway or air, or make a deposit at their bank. Workers employed by the federal government play a vital role in these and many other aspects of our daily lives.

This book describes federal government civilian career opportunities, including jobs with the Postal Service (an independent agency of the federal government). Armed forces career opportunities are described in the current edition of the Occupational Outlook Handbook.

---

[3] The 2010-2011 Career Guide to Industries, U.S. Department of Labor

Over 200 years ago, the founders of the United States gathered in Philadelphia to create a Constitution for a new national government and lay the foundation for self-governance. The Constitution of the United States, ratified by the last of the 13 original states in 1791, created the three branches of the federal government and granted certain powers and responsibilities to each. The legislative, judicial, and executive branches were created with equal powers but very different responsibilities that act to keep their powers in balance.

The legislative branch is responsible for forming and amending the legal structure of the nation. Its largest component is Congress, the primary U.S. legislative body, which is made up of the Senate and the House of Representatives. This body includes senators, representatives, their staffs, and various support workers. The legislative branch employs only about 2 percent of federal workers, nearly all of whom work in the Washington, D.C. area.

The judicial branch is responsible for interpreting the laws that the legislative branch enacts. The Supreme Court, the nation's definitive judicial body, makes the highest rulings. Its decisions usually follow the appeal of a decision made by the one of the regional Courts of Appeal, which hear cases appealed from U.S. District Courts, the Court of Appeals for the Federal Circuit, or state Supreme Courts. U.S. District Courts are located in each state and are the first to hear most cases under federal jurisdiction. The judicial branch employs about the same number of people as does the legislative branch, but its offices and employees are dispersed throughout the country.

Of the three branches, the executive branch — through the power vested by the Constitution in the office of the president — has the widest range of responsibilities. Consequently, it employed 97 percent of all federal civilian employees (excluding Postal Service workers) in 2010. The executive branch is composed of the Executive Office of the President, 15 executive Cabinet departments, including the recently created Department of Homeland Security, and nearly 90 independent agencies, each of which has clearly defined duties. The Executive Office of the President is composed of several offices and councils that aid the president in policy decisions. These include the Office of Management and Budget, which oversees the administration of the federal budget; the National Security Council, which advises the president on matters of national defense; and the Council of Economic Advisers, which makes economic policy recommendations.

Each of the 15 executive Cabinet departments administers programs that oversee an aspect of life in the United States. The highest departmental official of each Cabinet department, the secretary, is a member of the president's Cabinet. The 15 departments, listed by employment size, are listed below with a brief description and total employment.

Defense: (664,299) Manages the military forces that protect our country and its interests, including the Departments of the Army, Navy, and Air Force and a number of smaller agencies. The civilian workforce employed by the Department of Defense performs various support activities, such as payroll and public relations.

Veterans Affairs: (308,814) Administers programs to aid U.S. veterans and their families; runs the veterans hospital system, and operates our national cemeteries.

Homeland Security: (188,983) Works to prevent terrorist attacks within the United States; reduce vulnerability to terrorism; and minimize the damage from potential attacks and natural disasters. Conceived after the September 11, 2001 attacks and officially established in early 2003. There are four major directorates.

Treasury: (109,900) Regulates banks and other financial institutions, administers the public debt, prints currency, and collects federal income taxes.

Justice: (116,901) Enforces federal laws, prosecutes cases in federal courts, and runs federal prisons.

Agriculture: (108,291) Promotes U.S. agriculture domestically and internationally, manages forests, researches new ways to grow crops and conserve natural resources, ensures safe meat and poultry products, and leads the Federal anti-hunger programs, such as the Supplemental Nutrition Assistance Program (formerly known as the Food Stamp program) and the National School Lunch Program.

Interior: (79,048) Manages Federal lands, including the national parks, runs hydroelectric power systems, and promotes conservation of natural resources.

Health and Human Services: (83,202) Sponsors medical research; approves use of new drugs and medical devices; runs the Public Health Service; and administers Medicare.

Transportation: (57,947) Sets national transportation policy; plans and funds the construction of highways and mass transit systems; and regulates railroad, aviation, and maritime operations.

Commerce: (49,162) Forecasts the weather; charts the oceans; regulates patents and trademarks; conducts the Census; compiles statistics; and promotes U.S. economic growth by encouraging international trade.

State: (11,890) Oversees the nation's embassies and consulates; issues passports; monitors U.S. interests abroad; and represents the United States before international organizations.

Labor: (16,640) Enforces laws guaranteeing fair pay, workplace safety, and equal job opportunity; administers unemployment insurance; regulates pension funds; and collects and analyzes economic data through its Bureau of Labor Statistics.

Energy: (16,625) Coordinates the national use and provision of energy; oversees the production and disposal of nuclear weapons; and plans for future energy needs.

Housing and Urban Development: (10,041) Funds public housing projects; enforces equal housing laws; and insures and finances mortgages.

Education: (4,536) Provides scholarships, student loans, and aid to schools.

There are numerous independent agencies that perform tasks which fall between the jurisdictions of the executive departments, or that are more efficiently executed by an autonomous agency. Some smaller but well-known independent agencies include the Peace Corps, the Securities and Exchange Commission, and the Federal Communications Commission. Although the majority of these agencies are fairly small, employing fewer than 1,000 workers (many employ fewer than 100 workers), some are quite large. The largest independent agencies are:

- *Social Security Administration:* Operates various retirement and disability programs and Medicare.

- *National Aeronautics and Space Administration:* Oversees aviation research and conducts exploration and research beyond the Earth's atmosphere.

- *Environmental Protection Agency:* Runs programs to control and reduce pollution of the nation's water, air, and lands.

- *Tennessee Valley Authority:* Operates the hydroelectric power system in the Tennessee River Valley.

- *General Services Administration:* Manages and protects federal government property and records.

- *Federal Deposit Insurance Corporation:* Maintains stability of and public confidence in the nation's financial system, by insuring deposits and promoting sound banking practices.

WORKING CONDITIONS

Due to the wide range of federal jobs, working conditions are equally variable. While most federal employees work in office buildings, hospitals, or laboratories, a large number also can be found at border crossings, airports, shipyards, military bases, construction sites, and national parks. Work environments vary from comfortable and relaxed to hazardous and stressful, such as those experienced by law enforcement officers, astronauts, and air traffic controllers.

The vast majority of federal employees work full time, often on flexible or "flexi-time" schedules that allow workers more control over their work schedules. Some agencies also offer telecommuting or "flexi-place" programs, which allow selected workers to perform some job duties at home or from regional centers.

Some federal workers spend much of their time away from the offices in which they are based. Inspectors or compliance officers, for example, often visit businesses and work sites to ensure that laws and regulations are obeyed. Some federal workers frequently travel long distances, spending days or weeks away from home. Auditors, for example, may spend weeks at a time in distant locations.

EMPLOYMENT

The federal government, including the U.S. Postal Service, employs about 2.7 million civilian workers, or about 2 percent of the nation's workforce. The federal government is the nation's single largest employer. Because data on employment in certain agencies cannot be released to the public for national security reasons, this total does not include employment for the Central Intelligence Agency, National Security Agency, Defense Intelligence Agency, and National Imagery and Mapping Agency.

The federal government makes an effort to have a workforce as diverse as the nation's civilian labor force. The federal government serves as a model for all employers in abiding by equal employment opportunity legislation, which protects current and potential employees from discrimination based on race, color, religion, gender, national origin, disability, or age. The federal government also makes an effort to recruit and accommodate persons with disabilities.

Even though most federal departments and agencies are based in the Washington, D.C., area, fewer than 15 percent of federal employees worked in the vicinity of the nation's capital in 2010. In addition to federal employees working throughout the United States, about 3 percent are assigned overseas, mostly in embassies or defense installations.

OCCUPATIONS

Although the federal government employs workers in every major occupational group, workers are not employed in the same proportions in which they are employed throughout the economy as a whole (Table 1-2). The analytical and technical nature of many government duties translates into a much higher proportion of professional, management, business, and financial occupations in the federal government, compared with most industries. Conversely, the government sells very little, so it employs relatively few sales workers. A complete occupations list is included in Appendix C and a Skills to Hiring Agency listing is available in Appendix D.

Table 1-2

Percent distribution of employment in the federal government
and the private sector by major occupational group

Occupational Group	Federal Government	Private Sector
Total	*100*	*100*
Professional and related	33.2	20.9
Management, business, and financial	33.7	9.2
Office and administrative support	13.2	17.0
Service	8.2	19.7
Installation, maintenance, and repair	4.6	3.9
Transportation and materiel moving	2.9	6.7
Production	1.5	7.0
Construction and extraction	1.6	4.6
Sales and related	0.4	10.2
Farming, fishing and forestry	0.4	0.7

Source: BLS National Employment Matrix 2008-18

Professional and related occupations accounted for about one third of federal employment in 2010. The largest group of professional workers worked in life, physical, and social science occupations, such as biological scientists, conservation scientists and foresters, environmental scientists and geoscientists, and forest and conservation technicians. They do work such as determining the effects of drugs on living organisms, preventing fires in the national forests, and predicting earthquakes and hurricanes. The Department of Agriculture employed the vast majority of life scientists, but physical scientists were distributed throughout a variety of departments and agencies.

Many health professionals, such as licensed practical and licensed vocational nurses, registered nurses, and physicians and surgeons, were employed by the Department of Veterans Affairs (VA) in VA hospitals.

Large numbers of federal workers also held jobs as engineers, including aerospace, civil, computer hardware, electrical and electronics, industrial, mechanical, and nuclear engineers. Engineers were found in many departments of the executive branch, but they most commonly worked in the Department of Defense, the National Aeronautics and Space Administration, and the Department of Transportation. In general, they solve problems and provide advice on technical programs, such as building highway bridges or implementing agency-wide computer systems.

Computer specialists — primarily computer software engineers, network and computer systems analysts, and computer systems administrators — are employed throughout the federal government. They write computer programs, analyze problems related to data processing, and keep computer systems running smoothly. Many health professionals, such as registered nurses, physicians and surgeons, and licensed practical nurses are employed by the Department of Veterans Affairs (VA) in one of many VA hospitals.

Management, business, and financial workers made up about 34 percent of federal employment and were primarily responsible for overseeing operations. Managerial workers include a broad range of officials who, at the highest levels, may head federal agencies or programs. Middle managers, on the other hand, usually oversee one activity or aspect of a program. One management occupation — legislators — are responsible for passing and amending laws and overseeing the executive branch of the government. Within the federal government, legislators are entirely found in Congress.

Management, business, and financial workers made up about 34 percent of federal employment.

Others occupations in this category are accountants and auditors, who prepare and analyze financial reports, review and record revenues and expenditures, and investigate operations for fraud and inefficiency. Purchasing agents handle federal purchases of supplies. Management analysts study government operations and systems and suggest improvements. These employees aid management staff with administrative duties. Administrative support workers in the federal government include secretaries and general office clerks. Purchasing agents handle federal purchases of supplies, and tax examiners, collectors, and revenue agents determine and collect taxes.

Compared with the economy as a whole, workers in service occupations were relatively scarce in the federal government. About seven out of 10 federal workers in service occupations were protective service workers, such as detectives and criminal investigators, police and sheriff's patrol officers, and correctional officers and jailers. These workers protect the public from crime and oversee federal prisons.

Federally employed workers in installation, maintenance, and repair occupations include aircraft mechanics and service technicians who fix and maintain all types of aircraft. Also included are electrical and electronic equipment mechanics, installers, and repairers, who inspect, adjust, and repair electronic equipment such as industrial controls, transmitters, antennas, radar, radio, and navigation systems.

The federal government employed a relatively small number of workers in transportation; production; construction; sales and related; and farming, fishing, and forestry occupations. However, they employ almost all air traffic controllers in the country and a significant number of agricultural inspectors and bridge and lock tenders.

TRAINING AND ADVANCEMENT

In all but a few cases, applicants for federal jobs must be U.S. citizens. Applicants who are veterans of military service may also be able to claim veterans' preference status over other candidates with equal qualifications. For an increasing number of jobs requiring access to sensitive or classified materials, applicants must undergo a background investigation in order to obtain a security clearance. This investigation covers an individual's criminal, credit, and employment history, as well as other records. The scope of the investigation will vary, depending on the nature of the position in the government and the degree of harm that an individual in that position could cause.

In all but a few cases, applicants for federal jobs must be U.S. citizens.

The educational and training requirements for jobs in the federal government mirror those in the private sector for most major occupational groups. Many jobs in professional and related occupations, for example, require a four-year college degree. Some, such as engineers, physicians and surgeons, and biological and physical scientists, require a bachelor's or higher degree in a specific field of study. Because managers usually are promoted from professional occupations, most have at least a bachelor's degree. However, registered nurses and many technician occupations may be entered with two years of training after high school. Office and administrative support workers in the government usually need only a high school diploma, although any further training or experience, such as a junior college degree or a couple of years of relevant work experience, is an asset. Most federal jobs in other occupations require no more than a high school degree, although most departments and agencies prefer workers with vocational training or previous experience.

Once the person is employed, each federal department or agency determines its own training requirements and offers workers opportunities to improve job skills to advance to other jobs. These may include technical or skills training, tuition assistance or reimbursement, fellowship programs, and executive leadership and management training programs, seminars, and workshops. This training may be offered on the job, by another agency, or at local colleges and universities.

Advancement for most workers in the federal government is currently based on a system of occupational pay levels, or "grades," although more departments and agencies are being granted waivers to experiment with different pay and promotion strategies. Workers typically enter the federal service at the starting grade for an occupation and may be promoted throughout their careers while others begin a "career ladder" of promotions until they reach the full-performance grade for that occupation. This system provides for a limited number of noncompetitive promotions, which usually are awarded at regular intervals, assuming job performance is satisfactory. The exact pay grades associated with a job's career track depend upon the occupation.

Typically, workers without a high school diploma who are hired as clerks start at grade 1 unless they have 6 months of general experience to qualify for a GS-03. High school graduates with no additional training hired at the same job start at grade 2 or 3. Entrants with some technical training or experience who are hired as technicians may start at grade 4. Those with a bachelor's degree generally are hired in professional occupations, such as economist, with a career ladder that starts at grade 5 or 7, depending on academic achievement. Entrants with a master's degree or Ph.D. may start at grade 9. Individuals with professional degrees may be hired at the grade 11 or 12 level. Those with a combination of education and substantive experience may be hired at higher grades than those with education alone.

New employees usually start at the first step of a grade (defined on page 16); however, if the position in question is difficult to fill, entrants may receive somewhat higher pay or special rates. Physicians and engineer positions are paid on a special pay table.

Federal workers usually receive periodic step increases within their grade if they are performing their job satisfactorily. They must compete for subsequent promotions, and advancement becomes more difficult. At this point, promotions occur as vacancies arise, and they are based solely on merit. In addition to within-grade longevity increases, federal workers are awarded bonuses for excellent job performance.

Workers who advance to managerial or supervisory positions may receive within-grade longevity increases, bonuses, and promotions to higher grades. The top managers in the federal civil service belong to the Senior Executive Service (SES), the highest positions that federal workers can reach without being specifically nominated by the president and confirmed by the U.S. Senate. Relatively few workers attain SES positions, and competition is intense. Bonus provisions for SES positions are even more performance-based than are those for lower-level positions. Because it is the headquarters for most federal agencies, the Washington, D.C. metropolitan area offers the best opportunities to advance to upper-level managerial and supervisory jobs.

OUTLOOK

Wage and salary employment in the federal government is projected to increase by 10 percent over the 2008-18 period. There will be a substantial number of job openings as many federal workers are expected to retire over the next decade, although job prospects are expected to vary by occupation.

Wage and salary employment in the federal government, except Post Office, is expected to increase by 10 percent over the coming decade, which is close to the 11 percent growth rate for all industries combined. Staffing levels in federal government can be subject to change in the long run because of changes in public policies as legislated by the Congress, which affect spending levels and hiring decisions for the various departments and agencies. In general, over the coming decade, domestic programs are likely to see an increase in employment.

While there will be growth in many occupations over the coming decade, demand will be especially strong for specialized workers in areas related to public health, information security, scientific research, law enforcement, and financial services. As a larger share of the U.S. population enters the older age brackets, demand for healthcare will increase. This will lead to a substantial number of new jobs in federal hospitals and other healthcare facilities for registered nurses and physicians and surgeons. In addition, as cyber security becomes an increasingly important aspect of national defense, rapid growth will occur among information technology specialists, such as computer and information research scientists, who will be needed to devise defense methods, monitor computer networks, and execute security protocol. Furthermore, as global activity in scientific development increases, the federal Government will add many physical science, life science, and engineering workers to remain competitive. Aside from these specific areas, numerous new jobs in other occupational areas will arise as the diverse federal workforce continues to expand.

As financial and business transactions face increased scrutiny, a substantial number of compliance officers and claims adjusters, examiners, and investigators will be added to federal payrolls. In addition, as the population grows and national security remains a priority, many new law enforcement officers, such as detectives and criminal investigators will be needed.

Job prospects in the federal government are expected to vary by occupation. Over the next decade, a significant number of workers are expected to retire, which will create a large number of job openings. This may create favorable prospects in certain occupations, but jobseekers may face competition for positions in occupations with fewer retirements, or for popular jobs that attract many applicants.

Competition for federal positions can increase during times of economic uncertainty, when workers seek the stability of federal employment. In general, employment in the federal government is considered to be relatively stable because it is less susceptible than private industries to fluctuations in the economy.

GETTING STARTED

The Book of U.S. Government Jobs walks you through the federal hiring process. This book steers readers to highly informative government and private sector internet web sites, self-service job information centers, and telephone job hotlines, and it explores all facets of the federal job market.

Readers will find up-to-date information on how the federal employment system works from an insider's perspective, how to locate job announcements through various methods, and guidance on how to complete a federal application package that will get the attention of rating officials. You'll learn about special hiring programs for the physically challenged, veterans, and students. Thousands of job opportunities, Civil Service Exam requirements, overseas jobs, Postal Service jobs, how to complete your employment application, and much more. The Job Hunter's Checklist in Appendix A offers a comprehensive checklist that will take you through the entire federal employment process. Use Appendix A throughout your job search. Visit http://federaljobs.net, this book's companion web site, for book updates, valuable links, résumé and KSA writing services, qualification standards for all occupations, and for links to tens of thousands of job announcements.

The five appendices include an easy-to-use federal job check list, complete lists of federal occupations, comprehensive agency summaries, an agency skills index, and contact lists including employment office addresses and phone numbers.

This book will guide you step-by-step through the federal employment process, from filling out your first employment application to locating job announcements, networking resources, and hiring agencies. Follow the guidelines set forth in this book to dramatically improve your chances of landing a federal job.

PAY AND BENEFITS

Job security, good pay, and an excellent retirement system are just a few of the top reasons most people seek federal employment. Others consider government careers because of desirable travel opportunities, training availability, diverse occupations, and the ability to locate jobs nationwide and overseas.

In an effort to give agencies more flexibility in how they pay their workers, there are several different pay systems in effect or planning to be implemented over the next few years. The Federal Aviation Administration (FAA) uses a core compensation pay band system. Their system incorporates fewer, but wider pay bands, instead of grade levels. Pay increases, under these systems, are almost entirely based on performance, as opposed to length of service.

A number of agencies like the Federal Aviation Administration implemented core compensation pay band systems as early as 1995.

There are eight predominant pay systems. Approximately half of the workforce is under the General Schedule (GS) pay scale, 20 percent are paid under the Postal Service rates, and about 10 percent are paid under the Federal Wage System (FWS). The remaining pay systems are for the Executive Schedule, Foreign Service, Special Salary Rates, and Nonappropriated Fund Instrumentalities pay scales, and Veterans Health Administration.

It is the case, however, that the majority of professional and administrative federal workers are still paid under the General Schedule (GS). The General Schedule, shown in Table 1-3, has 15 grades of pay for civilian white-collar and service workers, and smaller within-grade step increases that occur based on length of service and quality of performance. New employees usually start at the first step of a grade. In an effort to make federal pay more responsive to local labor market conditions, federal employees working in the U.S. receive locality pay. The specific amount of locality pay is determined by survey comparisons of private sector wage rates and federal wage rates in the relevant geographic area. At its highest level, locality pay can lead to an increase of as much as 26 percent above the base salary. A January pay adjustment tied to changes in private sector pay levels is divided between an across-the-board pay increase in the General Schedule and locality pay increases in most years.

In January 2011 the average wage for full-time workers paid under the General Schedule was $82,883. For those in craft, repair, operator, and laborer jobs, the Federal Wage System (FWS) is used to pay these workers. This schedule sets federal wages so that they are comparable to prevailing regional wage rates for similar types of jobs. As a result, wage rates paid under the FWS can vary significantly from one locality to another.

In addition to base pay and bonuses, federal employees may receive incentive awards. These one-time awards, ranging from $25 to $10,000, are bestowed for a significant suggestion, a special act or service, or sustained high job performance. Some workers also may receive "premium" pay, which is granted when the employee must work overtime, on holidays, on weekends, at night, or under hazardous conditions.

The *2011* "Base Rate" General Schedule (GS) pay chart is presented in this chapter. Updated GS pay tables including all 36 Locality Pay Tables are posted on visit www.federaljobs.net — select "Pay Schedules" on the main menu. This site is the companion Web site for *The Book of U.S. Government Jobs* and many of this book's resources and Web links are listed on this site to assist you with your job search. On September 30, 2010, OPM published an Interim Rule in the Federal Register making Alaska and Hawaii separate whole State locality pay areas and including the other non-foreign areas as defined in 5 CFR 591.205 in the Rest of U.S. locality pay area.

General Schedule (GS) base pay varies from the GS-1 level at $17,803 per annum to $129,517 per annum at step 10 of the GS-15 grade, not including locality pay adjustments. The Senior Executive Service salary tops out at $179,700 per annum. The average annual salary for full-time non-postal employees increased to just over $82,883 in 2010. Starting pay depends on the level of experience, education and complexity of the position applied for.

Each GS grade has 10 pay steps. Currently, a GS-9 starts at $41,563 for step 1 and reaches $54,028 per year at step 10 (not including locality pay adjustments). At the GS-9 grade, each pay step adds $1,385 to the annual salary. Pay steps are earned based on time in service and the employee's work performance. General

Schedule employees are referred to as white-collar workers under the federal classification system. There are 36 locality pay areas. Visit www.federaljobs.net for specific locality pay information for your area. All of the 36 locality pay areas adjust the base salary in a range from 9.44% to 35.15%.

TABLE 1-3
Annual Salary Base Rates (Without Locality)
2011 General Schedule (GS)

General Schedule (GS) Step Increases 1-10 in Dollars									
GS	1	2	3	4	5	6	7	8	9	10
1	17,803	18,398	18,990	19,579	20,171	20,519	21,104	21,694	21,717	22,269
2	20,017	20,493	21,155	21,717	21,961	22,607	23,253	23,899	24,545	25,191
3	21,840	22,568	23,296	24,024	24,752	25,480	26,208	26,936	27,664	28,392
4	24,518	25,335	26,152	26,969	27,786	28,603	29,420	30,237	31,054	31,871
5	27,431	28,345	29,259	30,173	31,087	32,001	32,915	33,829	34,743	35,667
6	30,577	31,596	32,615	33,634	34,653	35,672	36,691	37,710	38,729	39,748
7	33,979	35,112	36,245	37,378	38,511	39,644	40,777	41,910	43,043	44,176
8	37,631	38,885	40,139	41,393	42,647	43,901	45,155	46,409	47,663	48,917
9	41,563	42,948	44,333	45,718	47,103	48,488	49,873	51,258	52,643	54,028
10	45,771	47,297	48,823	50,349	51,875	53,401	54,927	56,453	57,979	59,505
11	50,287	51,963	53,639	55,315	56,991	58,667	60,343	62,019	63,695	65,371
12	60,274	62,283	64,292	66,301	68,310	70,319	72,328	74,337	76,346	78,355
13	71,674	74,063	76,452	78,841	81,230	83,619	86,008	88,397	90,786	93,175
14	84,697	87,520	90,343	93,166	95,989	98,812	101,635	104,458	107,281	110,104
15	99,628	102,949	106,270	109,591	112,912	116,233	119,554	122,875	126,196	129,517

Approximately 10 percent of total federal non-postal employment is classified under the Wage Grade (WG) blue-collar pay schedules. Wage Grade workers are placed in a five step pay system and the pay is based on competitive rates that are established by an annual wage survey. The Department of Defense employs the largest number of Wage Grade workers.

Sample of Wage Grade (WG) Occupations

WG-2502 Telephone Mechanic WG-4204 Pipefitting
WG-2892 Aircraft Electrician WG-4417 Offset Press Operating
WG-3314 Instrument Making WG-4754 Cemetery Caretaking
WG-3502 Laboring WG-5220 Shipwright
WG-3703 Welding WG-5788 Deckhand
WG-3919 Television Equip. WG-7304 Laundry Working
WG-4102 Painting WG-7404 Cooking

See Appendix D for a complete list of WG occupations.

There are a number of special compensation systems that augment the general schedule. Physicians receive signing bonuses for a one-year continued-service agreement and additional bonuses for two years. The Federal Aviation Administration pays employees in safety-related careers under a "Core Compensation" multi-pay band system. Organizations such as the General Accounting Office (GAO), NASA, and the Commerce Department's National Institute of Standards and Technology either are exempt from or have exceptions to the GS pay system.

The SES is a corps of men and women, composed of those who administer public programs at the top levels of federal government. Some positions include additional recruitment incentives. The SES programs and application guidance are included in Chapter Six.

Structure of the SES Pay System	Minimum	Maximum
Agencies with a Certified SES Performance Appraisal System	$119,544	$179,700
Agencies without a Certified SES Performance Appraisal System	$119,544	$165,300

Pay reform has been implemented to offset competitive hiring pressures from private industry and local governments. Agencies can now offer allowances and bonuses when recruiting, match salary within certain limits, and are authorized to pay interview travel expenses under certain circumstances.

Table 1-4

Average annual 2009 salaries for GS full-time workers

Occupations *(Selected occupations)*	Salary
All Occupations	$74,403
General attorney	128,422
Financial management	119,671
General engineer	114,839
Air Traffic Controller	109,218
Economist	108,010
Chemistry	101,687
Computer science	100,657
Microbiology	97,264
Architecture	94,056
Criminal investigating	93,897
Customs & border protection	92,558
Statistics	92,322
Accounting	91,541
Information technology management	91,104
Librarian	84,796
Ecology	84,283
Human resource management	81,837
Budget analysis	80,456
Nurse	77,166
Chaplain	75,485
Mine safety and health	75,222
Engineering technical	69,092
Medical technologist	64,774
Border patrol agent	59,594
Correctional Officer	53,459
Police	52,058
Legal assistance	48,668
Fire protection and prevention	48,166
Secretary	46,384
Tax examining	42,035
Human resource assistant	40,334

SOURCE: U.S. Office of Personnel Management, 2009 & CBO Report

VACATION AND SICK LEAVE

All employees receive 10 paid holidays, 13 days of vacation for the first three years service, 20 days of vacation with three to 15 years of service, and 26 days after 15 years. Additionally, 13 sick days are accrued each year regardless of length of service and employees can carry over any sick leave accumulation to the next year. Many federal employees accrue sick leave balances of a year or more during their career. The author had 2100 hours of sick leave, just over one year, accumulated when he retired in 2005. He was able to exchange his sick leave balance for an increase in his annuity payment. Military time may be creditable for annual leave and retirement benefits. For example, if you have three years of military service, you could earn 20 vacation days per year rather than 13 like most first time Federal employees. Military service may also be creditable toward your Federal retirement is a deposit is made. For additional information on military deposits visit http://federalretirement.net/militarybuyback.htm.

HEALTH AND LIFE INSURANCE

Medical health plans and the Federal Employees' Group Life Insurance (FEGLI) programs are available to most employees. The Federal Employees Health Benefits (FEHB) plan is an employee-employer contribution system and includes fee-for-service, consumer-driven, point-of-service, and HMO options. The costs are reasonable and the coverage excellent.

The federal government offers low cost comprehensive dental and vision care under the Federal Employees Dental & Vision Insurance Program (FEDVIP). Coverage is available from a number of healthcare providers and is competitively priced with standard and high options. The FEGLI program offers low-cost term life insurance for the employee and basic coverage for the family. FEGLI offers up to five times the employee's salary in death benefits.

One of the primary benefits of federal employment is the satisfaction you experience from working in a challenging and rewarding job. Positions are available with the level of responsibility and authority that you desire. The average benefits package for a federal employee exceeds $41,000 annually.

RETIREMENT

The federal retirement system is based on Social Security contributions, a Federal Employees Retirement System (FERS) annuity, and the Thrift Savings Plan (TSP); an employee contribution system fashioned after a 401k defined contribution plan. You can elect to contribute up to maximum allowable into the (TSP) savings plan. FERS employees receive 1 percent automatically and the government matches the next 3 percent contributed by the employee and 50 cents per dollar for the next 2 percent contributed. Therefore, if you contribute a minimum of 5 percent Uncle Sam matches 5 percent. New hires should consider contributing a minimum of 5 percent to receive a 5 percent match from the government.

New hires should consider contributing a minimum of 5 percent to receive a full match from the government.

Contributions are tax-deferred and reduce taxable income by the amount contributed. The retirement benefit is determined by the amount accumulated during the employee's career. This includes the interest earned and capital gains realized from the retirement fund. Visit www.federaljobs.net/retire, our retirement planning Web site, for complete information and details about the federal retirement system.

There are many withdrawal options, including lump sum and various fixed term annuities. The TSP plan contribution payout is in addition to your federal retirement annuity and Social Security benefits that you will be eligible for at retirement.

CAREER DEVELOPMENT

Each department and agency determines required training and offers workers opportunities to improve job skills and gain knowledge to be successful in their careers. Career development training includes technical or skills training, tuition assistance or reimbursement, fellows programs outlined in Chapter Three, and executive leadership and management training programs, seminars, and workshops. Training may be offered on the job, by another agency, or at local colleges and universities. Visit www.fedcareer.info for detailed information on the government's *"Individual Development Plan"* program.

Visit www.fedcareer.info
for career development guidance

Today there are many diverse opportunities for self-development and one of the major initiatives is online and computer-based instruction. Most agencies offer extensive online courses for skills improvement and career development. I encourage all federal employees to take advantage of these programs to enhance their promotion potential and to improve their skills. Some courses are required by the position. However, most are designed to improve job performance.

I encourage all federal employees to take advantage of these programs to enhance their promotion potential and to improve their skills.

Starting in my early thirties I took advantage of many agency-sponsored training programs that helped me prepare — and eventually be selected for — supervisory and management positions. I completed evening college courses receiving reimbursement for up to 50 percent of my tuition, attended seminars, signed up for agency correspondence courses, and volunteered for temporary and lateral assignments throughout my 35-year career. I used the courses to improve my writing, automation, organizational, and interpersonal skills. When I was assigned to complete a course project, I developed the project around an actual work issue and eventually presented the project plans to management in the form of proactive work improvement plans and suggestions.

The improvement plans and suggestions attracted the attention of upper management, and I believe this is why I was selected for my first supervisory position at the early age of 35. I was selected from a group of applicants who were older and had considerably more experience.

At each juncture of my career I used career development training to improve productivity, soft skills such as interpersonal behavior and management skills, and technical expertise. I developed comprehensive Individual Development Plans (IDPs) shortly after reporting for my first job with the Federal Aviation Administration in 1975 and revised my plan annually throughout my career. I believe this is why I was successful in working my way up through the ranks from a GS-0856-07 step 1 grade to my final senior management position when I retired in 2005 from the Federal Aviation Administration (FAA). My last position was air traffic control tower technical operations manager at the Greater Pittsburgh International Airport. Learn more about the IDP process at www.fedcareer.info and my book, the second edition of *Take Charge of Your Federal Career*.

You will find extensive leadership programs in the form of conferences, seminars, residential courses, general coursework, developmental assignments, coaching initiatives, distance learning, lectures, mentoring , workshops, on-the-job training and much more. The programs are offered either to federal employees from specific agencies or to all federal employees, and there are opportunities for non-federal employees as well.

TYPES OF TRAINING

- Orientation Training (New Employees)
- Technical and Administrative Skills Training
- Professional Training
- Supervisory Training
- Executive and Management Training
- Career Development Training
- Required training for safety or EEO

Career development programs are offered by most agencies for target positions and personal long term career goals. Each agency offers its own unique programs. However, they are all authorized by the same federal regulations and many similarities exist between agencies. The following is a sampling of currently offered career development programs.

*A*ppendix B provides a comprehensive federal agency and department directory.

WHERE THE JOBS ARE

Fifteen Cabinet departments and more than 100 independent agencies compose the federal government system. These departments and agencies have offices in all corners of the world. The size of each agency varies considerably. The larger the agency, the more diverse the opportunities. Appendix B provides a comprehensive federal agency directory and Appendix D offers a cross reference of your skills and education to specific hiring agencies.

Agencies are like corporations in the sense that each agency has a headquarters office, typically located in Washington D.C., regional offices located around the country to manage large geographic areas, and many satellite offices to provide public services and to perform agency functions. A good example is the Social Security Administration, which has offices in most areas to administer the Social Security program; manage disability claims, sign up those who retire at 62 and again at age 65 when they are required to elect Medicare options, etc.

Jobs can be found in all parts of the country and overseas — even in places you might never imagine. Don't exclude any location regardless of size. In 1975 I was hired by the FAA to work at the Philipsburg Airport in central Pennsylvania. Philipsburg is a small town of 3,056 and I maintained navigational aids and communications facilities at the airport and State College. One of the main reasons I was hired was that few bid on these remote-location jobs. If you want to be successful in your job search, expand your area of consideration. It took me three years to get trained and transfer back to my home town.

If you want to be successful in your job search, expand your area of consideration.

To locate potential employers and federal offices in your area, check the blue pages in your phone book, and start networking as described in Chapter Four using the informational interview process. A comprehensive agency directory is available in Appendix B. Locate the agencies in your area to find out what jobs may be available or soon become available. Visit www.federaljobs.net and follow the links to 141 federal personnel offices and agency employment sites to explore available careers and locate job vacancies. Chapter Three will show you how to find job vacancies and what jobs are available.

If you desire to travel, the government offers abundant opportunities to relocate within the 50 states and overseas. Chapter Eight provides information on overseas employment opportunities including qualifications, hiring agency contact information, and much more. Twelve federal agencies and departments offer employment abroad for more than 89,204 workers. The Department of Defense Dependent Schools system employ hundreds of teachers for military dependent schools overseas.

The state with the largest number of employees is California with 356,545 and Delaware the least with 3,270. All of the 315 Metropolitan Statistical Areas (MSA) in the U.S. and Puerto Rico have federal civilian employment as listed in the Central Personnel Data File. Small towns and rural areas outside of MSAs have approximately 18 percent of total non-postal federal workers.[4] The actual number of federal civilian employees is greater than the above figures. The Defense Intelligence Agency, Central Intelligence Agency, and the National Security Agency do not release their data. Chapter Three provides job resources to help you find jobs.

EDUCATION REQUIREMENTS

In the federal government, 55 percent of all workers do not have a college degree. The level of required education is dependent upon the job applied for. Each job announcement lists needed skills and abilities including education and work experience. However, the more education and work experience you have, the more competitive you will be when ranked against other applicants. A sample qualification statement is presented in Chapter Two for administration and management positions. The majority of positions within the government have a published qualifications standard similar to the provided example.

You can review and download a specific qualification standard online at www.federaljobs.net. You can often substitute work experience for a college degree in many fields. Refer to the qualification standard in Chapter Two, you will find that you can substitute three years, one year equivalent to at least a GS-4, of general work experience for a four-year course of study leading to a bachelor's degree. Many look at the job announcement and see *"Bachelor's Degree"* and pass up the job not knowing that three years general experience could qualify them for the position. Read the entire job announcement, front to back, before eliminating the job from consideration.

Many look at the job announcement and see "Bachelor's Degree" and pass up the job not knowing that three years of general experience could qualify them for the position.

CIVIL SERVICE EXAM INTRODUCTION

Over 80 percent of all jobs do not require a written entrance exam. Uncle Sam rates most applicants through an extensive review of their work experience and/or education that is stated on their application or federal style résumé. Tests are required for specific groups including secretarial/clerical, air traffic control, law enforcement and certain entry level jobs. However, there are exceptions to those occupations as well. For example, if you apply for clerical positions with many agencies, they often waive the entrance exam and require you to fill out a comprehensive *"Occupational Questionnaire"* and you may also be able to self-certify your typing speed.

Chapter Five provides sample test questions and offers detailed testing information and guidance. You will also be able to determine if the occupation that you are applying for requires a written entrance exam.

---

[4] Federal Civilian Employment by State & Metropolitan Areas (CPDF)

TABLE 1-5

FEDERAL EMPLOYMENT BY STATE — SEPTEMBER 2010

Non-Postal

STATE	TOTAL	STATE	TOTAL
Alabama	36,634	Nevada	10,944
Alaska	13,833	New Hampshire	4,193
Arizona	41,229	New Jersey	28,496
Arkansas	13,954	New Mexico	26,433
California	158,635	New York	61,010
Colorado	38,195	North Carolina	40,549
Connecticut	8,128	North Dakota	6,536
Delaware	3,270	Ohio	48,402
Florida	82,356	Oklahoma	38,650
Georgia	75,123	Oregon	21,750
Hawaii	25,056	Pennsylvania	61,587
Idaho	10,280	Rhode Island	6,860
Illinois	43,006	South Carolina	20,871
Indiana	23,522	South Dakota	8,672
Iowa	8,688	Tennessee	27,298
Kansas	16,587	Texas	127,859
Kentucky	25,499	Utah	29,226
Louisiana	19,935	Vermont	4,406
Maine	10,866	Virginia	135,298
Maryland	106,391	Washington	54,852
Massachusetts	26,296	Washington, D.C.	128,324
Michigan	27,693	West Virginia	15,620
Minnesota	17,653	Wisconsin	14,830
Mississippi	18,052	Wyoming	6,568
Missouri	33,178	Overseas	89,204
Montana	11,770	*Unspecified	39,980
Nebraska	10,359		

OPM Employment Statistics, September 2010

CHAPTER TWO
Hiring Reform and
the Recruitment Process

Hiring reform is creating significant changes to the federal recruitment process that will be phased in gradually across all agencies over time. Applicants can be expected to encounter a mix of the old and new systems until agencies are able to implement the new procedures. The key for applicants is to read the job announcement thoroughly, complete, and submit **ALL** required documentation including a federal style résumé, by the closing date of the job announcement.

The new hiring process is based on category ratings rather than a point system that was used by many agencies for decades. Applicants are placed in one of several categories; *typically, Best Qualified, Highly Qualified*, or *Qualified*. Agencies may use different category titles. The federal government provides fair and equitable opportunities for all applicants regardless of race, national origin, gender, age or religious beliefs. The system is designed to reduce and eliminate, wherever possible, outside influence such as nepotism and political affiliation to level the playing field.

Barbara Adams, President and CEO of CareerPro Global, Inc., has several decades of federal résumé writing experience. She contributed updated application guidance and résumé examples for this new edition to help readers submit professional applications that conform to the new requirements. Barbara knows the system from the inside out and fully understands the constantly changing federal application process.

CHAPTER OBJECTIVES

✎   Understand federal recruitment reforms and category ratings

✎   Determine your eligibility and how to apply

✎   Determine if civil service exams are required

✎   Identify recruitment incentives

✎   Discover typical federal employee characteristics *(Table 2-4)*

HIRING REFORM

On May 11, 2010, President Barack Obama issued an Executive Order resulting in sweeping reform of the federal hiring process. Federal hiring reform, effective November 1, 2010, requires federal agencies to:

- Eliminate any requirement that applicants respond to essay-style questions (frequently known as Knowledge, Skills and Abilities, or KSAs) when submitting their initial application materials;

- Allow individuals to apply for federal employment by submitting résumés and cover letters or completing simple, plain-language applications;

- Provide for selection from among a larger number of qualified applicants by using the "category rating" approach, rather than the "Rule of 3" approach, under which managers may only select from among the three highest-scoring applicants;

- Notify applicants of the status of their application at key points in the process; and

- Reduce hiring time.

While this may not sound like much in the way of change, it is quite significant for applicants seeking federal jobs. Although applying for a federal job sounds like it will now parallel the private-sector process, it is still complicated; as always, you will need to carefully analyze job announcements and fully detail your skills and experience in your résumé and cover letter in a way the government understands. In addition, if you are a veteran of military service, and meet the appropriate criteria, you will still receive preference in hiring.

Applying for a federal job requires a strategic approach, a strong application package, and patience. You will maximize your opportunities for success if you apply for positions for which you are truly qualified, have an application package that incorporates the keywords, qualifications, and KSAs required of the position and understand that, even though the process has been simplified, obtaining a federal job still takes longer than obtaining a private-sector one. The federal hiring process is evolving and by following the application guidance outlined in Chapter Six you will have a much better chance of landing a federal job.

THE FEDERAL HIRING PROCESS IS CHANGING

Officials have backed off the President's deadline of November 1, 2010, stating that only some agencies are ready to change. Some include Departments of Commerce, Defense, and Veterans Affairs (DOC, DOD, VA). The National Aeronautics and Space Administration (NASA) has also moved toward the change, while other agencies have begun the lengthy conversion process, which could take years to complete the transformation, according to the Office of Personnel Management (OPM).

CATEGORY RATING

One of the major hiring reform changes is the requirement to utilize the category rating approach to refer candidates. In the past, applicant's résumés were scored with a numerical rating; a hiring manager could select from only among the top three highest-scoring applicants and could not "pass over" a veteran to select a non-veteran. This was known as the "Rule of 3."

Under category rating, applicants are put into categories and do not receive a specific numeric score. Hiring managers may select anyone in the top category as long as they do not select a non-veteran if there are veterans in the same category. The purpose of category rating is to increase the number of qualified applicants while preserving Veterans' Preference rights. The category rating approach gives agencies the flexibility to assess and select from among applicants in the highest quality category without regard to the "Rule of 3."

"The Presidential Memorandum – Improving the Federal Recruitment and Hiring Process," issued on May 11, 2010, requires agencies to use the category rating approach to assess and select job applicants for positions filled through Competitive Examining. Agencies are required to evaluate candidates' applications and place them into two or more predetermined quality categories. Quality categories are defined by Human Resources (HR) with the assistance of Subject Matter Experts (SMEs) through job analysis prior to the posting of an announcement. The categories are written to reflect the requirements to perform the job successfully and to distinguish differences in the quality of candidates' job-related competencies or Knowledge, Skills, and Abilities (KSAs). Some factors considered when creating categories include:

- Breadth and scope of competencies/KSAs;
- Increased levels of difficulty or complexity of competencies/KSAs;
- Successful performance on the job; and
- Level of the job.

The highest quality category definition is written to identify the "Best Qualified" individuals for the position.

> **Example:** Agency uses two quality categories: Highly Qualified and Qualified. In filling an HR Specialist, GS-201-14, policy position, the agency might define the Highly Qualified category as experience in a senior-level HR position writing regulations or agency policy or providing guidance to an agency on staffing, downsizing, realignment, classification, or compensation. The Qualified category might include senior-level HR operations experience in staffing, downsizing, realignments, classification, or compensation.

The quality categories are defined prior to a position being posted. The announcement will contain information about how many categories an agency is using and how Veterans' Preference is applied; the announcement will not, however, disclose scoring keys or define the quality categories.

Those preference eligibles that meet the qualification requirements for the position and have a compensable service-connected disability of at least 10% are listed in the highest quality category (except in the case of scientific or professional positions at the GS-9 level or higher). Preference eligibles receive Veterans' Preference by being listed ahead of non-preference eligibles within the same quality category in which they are placed. No preference points (e.g., 5 or 10 points) are added to the preference eligibles' rating, and any preference eligible may be selected. Refer to Chapter Seven for preference eligibility guidance.

Hiring managers make selections from within the highest quality category, regardless of the number of candidates (i.e., the Rule of 3 does not apply). However, preference eligibles receive absolute preference within each category. If a preference eligible is in the category, an agency may not select a non-preference eligible unless the agency requests to pass over the preference eligible and the request is approved.

Additionally, hiring managers are not required to interview everyone within a category. All candidates within a category are considered equally qualified. However, the hiring manager may interview one or more applicants and some agency and union contracts have specific interview requirements.

As was the case before hiring reform, you may request reconsideration of your rating. The agency must explain to you, upon request, why you were placed in a particular category. Contact the person listed on the announcement for additional information about requesting reconsideration.

Adding further confusion to the recruitment process is the fact that government personnel specialists do not have the time to counsel the hundreds of thousands who apply for federal jobs each year. There are too many questions and too few counselors to answer them. This is why I wrote the first edition of this book in 1985. I was a federal manager and too many applicants didn't understand what was needed to successfully approach the federal sector, and more important, land a job.

```
                         ┌──────────────────────────────────┐
                         │          Good to Know            │
                         │                                  │
                         │  ■  Hiring reform provides managers with a
                         │     larger pool of eligible candidates from which
                         │     to make a selection through the use of
                         │     category rating.
                         │  ■  Veterans' Preference is still absolute in
                         │     category rating.
                         └──────────────────────────────────┘
```

Barbara Adams and her federal résumé writing staff from CareerPro Global (CPG) compiled the following list of the top ten hiring reform findings resulting from their extensive work in this area.

TEN MAJOR FINDINGS RELATED TO HIRING REFORM:

1.   Some agencies have completely eliminated KSAs.

2.   In other agencies, KSAs have been eliminated in the initial application process, but can still be requested later in the screening process if the applicant is considered "Best Qualified."

3.   Many applications may list KSAs and then state, "DO NOT REPLY TO THESE KSAs." However, while completing the application online, you will notice textboxes with up to 8,000 character limits that are titled "Online Assessments and/or Essay Questions" that require a candidate to write a summary in support of KSAs. In our opinion, these "essays" are simply KSAs in a different form. We recommend going through a trial run before submitting an application to determine what is actually required.

4.   Specialized experience may be included in the vacancy announcement and MUST be addressed within the body of the résumé. We recommend utilizing 150 to 200 words to support your experience relevant to the specialized experience required within the body of your federal résumé.

5.   Occupational questionnaires are still a viable part of the application. When multiple-choice or Yes/No questions are asked, in some cases, there is a follow-up essay question required to support or expand a candidate's response.

6.   KSAs to be addressed within the body of the résumé. Some vacancy announcements request that KSAs be addressed within the résumé itself. CPG suggests writing short versions of accomplishments that address the

applicant's knowledge, skills, and abilities in the respective position performed.

7.   Cover letters – a new part of the federal application. CPG recommends that a candidate address the specialized experience and a brief summary of his/her accomplishments related to the experience or KSAs specified in the vacancy announcement. Submit a cover letter only if the vacancy announcement requests one.

8.   Shorter vacancy closing dates are being found in some applications to reduce the number of applications received and decrease hiring times. In many cases, CPG is finding three to five-day openings. CPG suggests preparing in advance by having your résumé ready for a specific job series or title; the résumé can then be tweaked, as necessary, when a specific vacancy opens.

9.   Category ratings. Hiring managers no longer score applicants using a numerical system, but instead assess their overall qualifications in their résumé, KSAs, and occupational questionnaires to place applicants into categories: Veterans Preference, Highly Qualified, Qualified and Not Qualified.

10. Shorter federal applications with great concise content are better in most cases. CPG recommends that you focus on your accomplishments, specialized experience, KSAs, and exactly what is required in the first paragraph of the job description of the vacancy announcement. Targeting your federal application to specific series, grades, and vacancies combined with the aforementioned content will substantially increase your chances in earning a "Best Qualified" rating.

Federal agencies are changing their application methods almost daily to find the best way to select the "Best Qualified" candidates. The federal application process will continue to evolve as each agency adopts its own process to comply with OPM requirements and federal hiring reform.

CPG highly recommends that you read the entire federal vacancy announcement prior to applying for a position. Follow the specific application requirements exactly; do not deviate in any way. Submit documents only if they are requested by the announcement.

COMPETITIVE SERVICE

Approximately 50 percent of civilian jobs are in the *competitive service*, which means that people applying for them must be evaluated by the Office of Personnel Management (OPM) either directly or through agency personnel offices that are delegated direct-hire or case-hire authority.

Candidates are chosen from an applicant pool based on their qualifications and how closely they meet the desired knowledge, skills, abilities, and competencies stated in the vacancy announcement.

Read the job announcement throughly to determine all requirements. Chapter Six shows you how to evaluate job announcements and complete a professional federal style résumé to improve your chances. Only U.S. citizens are eligible for positions in the Competitive Service.

EXCEPTED SERVICE

Excepted Service positions are "excepted" by law because the agencies offering these types of positions have direct ties to national security and/or intelligence functions, or are otherwise inappropriate for competitive examining.

Examples of positions that fall under Excepted Service include attorneys, chaplains, and medical doctors; for these types of jobs, it is difficult to use standard qualification requirements such as what's used in competitive jobs for Human Resources (HR) to rate applicants. Examples of agencies that fill the bulk of their vacancies via Excepted Service include the Central Intelligence Agency (CIA), the Department of State (DOS), the National Security Agency, and the Federal Bureau of Investigation (FBI).

Excepted Service positions are not required by law to be posted on USAJobs.gov. Candidates who are interested in these types of positions should consult the official websites of the agencies that offer this type of employment opportunity. Excepted service job benefits, pay, etc. are identical in most cases to competitive service positions.

EXAMINATIONS

Hiring for federal jobs is generally through a competitive examination. Don't be intimidated by the word "examination." The majority — approximately 80 percent — of government jobs are filled through a competitive examination of your background, work experience, and education, as listed on your application not through a written test. There are exceptions to this rule, and noncompetitive appointments are available for certain veterans, the physically challenged or disabled, and other groups. All hiring is based on the ability to perform the work advertised in the job announcement.

Approximately 80 percent of government jobs are filled through a competitive examination of your background, work experience, and education, not through a written test.

DETERMINING YOUR ELIGIBILITY

Eligibility is determined through the evaluation of an applicant's related education **AND/OR** work experience. For example, an entry level radio operator would start at a GS-2 pay grade, $20,017 per year, if he or she was a high school graduate **OR** had at least three months of general experience. That same radio operator could start at a GS-4, $24,518 per year, if he or she had six months of general experience and six months of specialized experience, **OR** two years of education above high school with courses related to the occupation. You would add 9 to 35 percent to the base pay salary figures for a specific *"Locality Pay"* area, or use the specific locality pay chart for the official duty location of the position.

College degree requirements can in many cases be substituted for work experience. Refer to the Job Qualification Standard for Administrative and Management Positions presented in this chapter. Applicants for jobs in this group can substitute three years of general experience for a four year bachelor's degree. Many job hunters without degrees see Bachelor's Degree listed as required in the job announcement, stop reading and look elsewhere. If they had read the entire job announcement they would have realized that work experience could be substituted for this degree requirement. Many highly qualified applicants miss out on lucrative jobs because of this one fact.

College degree requirements, in many cases, can be substituted for work experience.

General Experience

This is any type of work which demonstrates the applicant's ability to perform the work of the position, or any experience which provides a familiarity with the subject matter or process of the broad subject areas of the occupation. Specialized experience can be substituted for general experience.

Specialized Experience

This is experience which is in the occupation of the position to be filled, in a related occupation, or in one of the specialized areas within that occupation, which has equipped the applicant with the particular *knowledge, skills, abilities, and other characteristics* (KSAOs) to perform the duties of the position.

Written Tests

An examination announcement (job opening notice) may or may not require a written test. In many cases the examination consists of a detailed evaluation of your work experience, education, and schooling listed on your employment application. The Office of Personnel Management (OPM) eliminated the reliance on a written test as a single examining method and now provides agencies with additional examining options. Under this program, applicants apply for specific vacancies rather than broad occupational groups. While written tests will continue to be used for some jobs, taking a test is no longer the compulsory first step in the hiring process.

It should be noted that if a written test is required, many agencies allow applicants to bypass the written test for select occupations by completing an "Occupational Questionnaire." This is a series of questions, often 30 to 75 or more, that you have to answer in detail, often online. Occupational questionnaires are not KSAs. Many applicants confuse them for KSA statements. If KSAs are required, the

Don't confuse Occupational Questionnaires with KSA statements.

job announcement will identify them as such. See Chapter Six for additional guidance in this area.

Applicants must complete a federal style résumé or the Optional Application for Employment (OF-612 form) in some cases. Read the job announcement to determine the required format. Most agencies accept applications online. It is best to compile your federal style résumé off line and then copy and paste it into the online application. OPM or the hiring agency then evaluates the applicants' responses to determine the most highly qualified candidates. Hiring offices receive a list of the qualified applicants from either OPM or the agency's human resource department for each vacancy. Agencies may require qualified applicants to take a written test for specific occupations. Applicants apply for job openings posted on www.USAJOBS.gov or on individual agency sites.

The federal government evaluates each candidate on his/her ability to perform the duties of the position. Ability is obtained through education AND/OR experience. Even engineering positions are rated this way. There are several alternative non-degree paths that allow applicants to rate as eligible for engineering positions. OPM qualifications for engineering positions require either a four-year engineering degree OR four-year college level education, and/or technical experience. Chapter Three provides specific details on the Engineering Conversion Program.

JOB SERIES

There are over 900 job series — occupations — to choose from. Each job announcement describes the required experience, education, job location, pay and miscellaneous details needed to apply for a position within a *job series*. A complete occupational job series listing is provided in Appendix C. These series are from the General and Wage Grade Schedules in the competitive service. Excepted service job series are designated with different alpha characters; however, most follow the General Series Qualification Standards.

JOB SERIES EXAMPLES
General Schedule

TITLE	SERIES
Accountant	GS-0510
Secretary	GS-0318
Engineer-Electrical	GS-0801
Computer Specialist	GS-0334
System Specialist	GS-2101

Wage Grade

Equipment Mechanic	WG-5800
Laboring	WG-3502

EXAMINATION ANNOUNCEMENTS

Examination announcements, most often referred to as job announcements, are issued by the Office of Personnel Management and by individual agencies that have direct hire or case examining authority. The Office of Personnel Management (OPM) operates an extensive Internet Web site at www.usajobs.gov that you can use to locate federal job announcements for job vacancies. OPM does not advertise jobs for all agencies. To locate all available jobs, contact individual agencies in your area. A list of federal agency employment sites is available on www.federaljobs.net. Refer to Chapter Three to locate Internet sites, job hotlines, and other services that offer federal job listings. A sample job announcement is presented in Chapter Six.

Visit www.federaljobs.net for direct links
to over 140 agency recruiting sites.

Examination announcements are advertised for periods from several days to continuously open depending on the agency's critical needs. Exceptions to these rules apply to Veteran Recruitment Appointments (VRA) and recently discharged veterans, disabled veterans, and the disabled. You must obtain examination announcements through the resources mentioned above and in Chapter Three.

Case Examining

The Office of Personnel Management implemented case examining hiring procedures to assist agencies that have critical hiring needs. Agencies conduct targeted recruitment, issue a job announcement for the immediate filling of specific jobs, and close a case file when the selection process is completed. Applicants can apply direct to agencies with case examining authority for targeted positions. The announcements issued list the title, series and grade of the position, opening/closing dates and duty location; provide information concerning the duties, responsibilities and qualification requirements of the position; and provide the name and phone number of a contact person in the recruiting agency. To obtain announcements, applicants must visit the agency's Web site or contact the agency where the vacancy exists.

Over 80 percent of all job vacancies are now advertised through either case examining or direct hire authority.

The agency reviews the applicant's basic eligibility. The final ratings are completed by OPM and the candidates are ranked accordingly. OPM maintains a centralized listing of open case examinations through USAJOBS. Case examining procedures involve a one-time-only action with no expectation of filling other vacancies at a later date.

Direct Hire Authority

Direct hire authority is granted to agencies with specific hiring needs in one or several job series. The Office of Personnel Management allows agencies with this Delegated Examining Authority — often referred as Direct Hire Authority — to advertise job openings, rate applicants, establish their own eligibility lists and registers, conduct interviews and hire. Unlike case examining, which is a one-time action, Delegated Examining Authority grants agencies to conduct competitive examinations for all positions in the competitive service, except for administrative law judge positions.

Job seekers can locate individual agency positions on their Web site or you can subscribe to one of several private companies' federal jobs listing services that are listed in Chapter Three. OPM is encouraging agencies to list their job openings on USAJOBS (see Chapter Three resources).

APPLYING FOR FEDERAL JOBS

It is important to remember that you must submit all required information and forms. You have the option of using a federal style résumé format, the OF-612 Optional Application for Federal Employment, or online applications that most agencies now use. If you don't include all required information as presented in Chapter Six, your application may be rejected, or at the very least you may not be rated in the top rated category if key data is missing.

There are vast differences between industry's standard brief résumé format and the detailed information you must supply on the federal style résumé format. The résumé most people are accustomed to is a short one to two page introduction. Uncle Sam's federal style résumé must be highly structured with specific data or it may not be considered. The federal style résumé is probably your best bet because of your ability to send it as hard copy or copy and paste the federal style résumé into an online application. I suggest using the federal style résumé format presented in Chapter Six to guide you when completing your application.

Inadequately prepared applications and résumés prevent many highly qualified candidates from making the best qualified list.

The federal government rates applicants on their work experience and education. Prior to hiring reform, a personnel specialist rated your application. Under the new system managers and subject matter experts participate in the process, a much improved rating method.

Federal Qualification Standards specify qualifying work experience and education and these documents will help you determine whether or not you meet the basic qualifications for a desired position. (See a sample qualification standard in this chapter.) These standards break most job series down to general and specialized qualifying work experience and required education. You must have at least the amount of education or experience (general or specialized) as specified in the OPM qualification standards for the grade and series of the position you are applying for to meet the basic qualifications. Past work experience and training must be noted in detail on your application. The selecting official can consider any candidate in the top rated category with some exceptions for Veterans Preference. Interviews are optional. Refer to Chapter Six for guidance on how to complete your application.

LITTLE KNOWN FACTS

If you visit USAJOBS online search through their current list of job vacancies, the list may not be all-inclusive. Agencies in your area may have direct hire or case hiring authority for specific job skills, and excepted agencies are not required to post their vacancies on USAJOBS..

To locate other potential job openings and networking resources, contact individual agency personnel or human resource departments where you wish to work. Appendix B lists agency contact information and the companion web site for this book at www.federaljobs.net offers comprehensive federal job searches and related private sector jobs by occupation and/or agency listings.

Review the blue pages in your white page telephone directory. Blue pages list government agencies in your area. The yellow pages also offer comprehensive government listings.

To obtain information about a particular agency, refer to Appendix B for contact information, addresses, Web sites, and a brief agency description. You can also explore over 140 federal agencies and departments online from links posted on www.federaljobs.net/federal.htm.

Don't overlook your local state employment office. The Office of Personnel Management supplies current employment lists to all state employment offices, and direct hire agencies may forward their lists to state agencies.

HOW JOBS ARE FILLED

Selecting officials can fill positions through internal promotions or reassignments, re-employing former employees through reinstatement, using special noncompetitive appointments such as the Veterans Recruitment Act, or by appointing a new employee through a vacancy announcement.

NONCOMPETITIVE APPOINTMENTS

Noncompetitive appointments are special hiring authority for special emphasis hiring programs such as the Veterans Recruitment Program discussed in Chapter Seven and special hiring practices for people with physical or mental disabilities covered in Chapter Ten.

Agencies evaluate their attrition, projected retirements, and staffing allowances throughout the year. However, they may hold off hiring until close to the end of the fiscal year on September 30 because of budgetary concerns. Agencies are able to use the funds they save for positions that go unfilled for that fiscal year. However, they must be staffed at 100 percent by September 30 or they risk losing that funding next fiscal year. Therefore, one of the best times of the year to look for employment is July through September.

Adding to the confusion, many federal employees are eligible to retire at age 55 to 57 with 30 years service or at age 60 with 20 years service. Some job series offer early retirement with as little as 20 years service. Many opt to remain long after their eligibility date. After retirement eligibility is reached, agencies don't know when employees will elect to retire; one day agencies are fully staffed and the next day they could have 50 people submit their retirement paperwork. Hundreds of thousands of federal workers are now eligible for retirement.

All this uncertainty causes agencies to go begging for new employees at or close to the end of the fiscal year, September 30. Unfortunately, if agencies advertise through the Office of Personnel Management or initiate hiring actions through delegated hiring authority it can take from several weeks to months before the job is advertised, the applicants rated, and the selection made.

Federal managers fear that if they don't hire up to their authorized employment ceiling in the current fiscal year, Congress will, with the stroke of a pen, reduce their employment ceiling next year.

Noncompetitive appointments including former employees with reinstatement rights can be selected and hired the same day. If you qualify for noncompetitive appointments, multiply your chances by contacting agencies in your area. Send them a federal style résumé or the OF-612 form, and write a cover letter explaining who you are, what program you qualify under, and when you can start working. Be tactful and don't demand employment. Agencies don't have to hire anyone noncompetitively if they choose not to, or if prohibited by internal rules.

The term "noncompetitive" is misleading. Individuals within noncompetitive groups do compete for jobs. If there are three Veterans Recruitment Appointment (VRA) candidates vying for the same position, the best qualified candidate will be selected from this group, generally through the interview process.

REINSTATEMENT

Reinstatement is the noncompetitive re-entry of a former federal employee into the competitive service. Formal federal employees are not required to compete with applicants for federal employment. Reinstatement is a privilege accorded in recognition of former service and not a "right" to which the former employee is entitled. Reinstatement is completely at the discretion of the appointing agency.

Career status is obtained when an employee works for three full years with the federal government in a career position. Former employees entitled to veterans preference who served, or who were serving, under appointment that would lead to career status and non-veteran employees with career tenure may be reinstated regardless of the number of years since their last appointment.

Former non-veteran career-conditional employees, those who worked less than three years with the federal government, may be reinstated only within three years following the date of their separation. Certain types of service outside the competitive service may be used to extend this limit. Employees seeking reinstatement should apply directly to the personnel office of the agency where they wish to work.

SAMPLE QUALIFICATION STANDARD

The following qualification standard example will give you an idea of what a rater looks for and how all job series standards are written:

GROUP COVERAGE QUALIFICATION STANDARD FOR ADMINISTRATIVE AND MANAGEMENT POSITIONS

This qualification standard covers positions in the General Schedule that involve the performance of two-grade interval administrative and management work. It contains common patterns of creditable education and experience to be used in making qualifications determinations. Section IV-B of the Qualification Standard Handbook contains individual occupational requirements for some occupations that are to be used in conjunction with this standard. Section V identifies the occupations that have test requirements.

A list of the occupational series covered by this standard is provided on pages IV-A-13 and IV-A-14 of the Qualification Standard Handbook. This standard may also be used for two-grade interval positions other than those listed if the education and experience pattern is determined to be appropriate.

EDUCATION AND EXPERIENCE REQUIREMENTS

Table 2-1 on the next page shows the amount of education and/or experience required to meet the basic qualifications for positions covered by this standard.

		EXPERIENCE	
GRADE	EDUCATION	GENERAL	SPECIALIZED
GS-5	4-year course of study to a bachelor's degree	3 years, 1 year equivalent to at least GS-4	None
GS-7	2 full years of graduate level education or superior academic achievement	None	1 year equivalent to at least GS-5
GS-9	2 full years of progressively higher level graduate education or master's or equivalent graduate degree (such as an LL.B. or J.D.)	None	1 year equivalent to at least GS-7
GS-11	3 full years of progressively higher education or Ph.D. or equivalent doctoral degree	None	1 year equivalent to at least GS-9
GS-12 & above	None	None	1 year equivalent or at least next grade level

TABLE 2-1

EDUCATION OR EXPERIENCE

Some of the occupational series covered by this standard include both one-and two-grade interval work. The qualification requirements described in this standard apply only to those positions that typically follow a two-grade interval pattern. While the levels of experience shown for most positions covered by this standard follow the grade level progression pattern outlined in the table, users of the standard should refer to the "General Policies and Instructions" (Section 11 of the Qualifications Handbook) for guidance on crediting experience for positions with different lines of progression.

Undergraduate Education: Successful completion of a full four-year course of study *in any field* leading to a bachelor's degree, in an accredited college or university, meets the GS-5 level requirements for many positions covered by this standard. Others have individual occupational requirements in Section IV-B that specify that applicants must, in general, (1) have specific course work that meets the requirements for a major in a particular field(s), or (2) have at least 24 semester hours of course work in the field(s) identified. Course work in fields closely related to those specified *may* be accepted if it clearly provides applicants with the background of knowledge and skills necessary for successful job performance. One year of full-time undergraduate study is defined as 30 semester hours or 45 quarter hours, and is equivalent to nine months of general experience.

Superior Academic Achievement: The superior academic achievement provision is applicable to all occupations covered by this standard. See the "General Policies and Instructions" for specific guidance on applying the superior academic achievement provision.

Graduate Education: Education at the graduate level in an accredited college or university in the amounts shown in the table meets the requirements for positions at GS-7 through GS-11. Such education must demonstrate the knowledge, skills, and abilities necessary to do the work.

One year of full-time graduate education is considered to be the number of credit hours that the school attended has determined to represent one year of full-time study. If that information cannot be obtained from the school, 18 semester hours should be considered as satisfying the one year of full-time study requirement.

Part-time graduate education is creditable in accordance with its relationship to a year of full-time study at the school attended.

For certain positions covered by this standard, the work may be recognized as sufficiently technical or specialized that graduate study alone may not provide the knowledge and skills needed to perform the work. In such cases, agencies may use selective factors to screen out applicants without actual work experience.

General Experience: For positions for which individual occupational requirements do not specify otherwise, general experience is three years of progressively responsible experience (one year of which was equivalent to at least GS-4) that demonstrates the ability to:

1. Analyze problems to identify significant factors, gather pertinent data, and recognize solutions;

2. Plan and organize work; and

3. Communicate effectively orally and in writing.

Such experience may have been gained in administrative, professional, technical, investigative, or other responsible work. Experience in substantive and relevant secretarial, clerical, or other responsible work may be qualifying as long as it provided evidence of the knowledge, skills, and abilities (KSAs) necessary to perform the duties of the position to be filled. Experience of a general clerical nature (typing, filing, routine procedural processing, maintaining records, or other non-specialized tasks) is not creditable. Trades or crafts experience appropriate to the position to be filled may be creditable for some positions.

For some occupations or positions, applicants must have had work experience that demonstrated KSAs in addition to those identified above. Positions with more specific general experience requirements than those described here are shown in the appropriate individual occupational requirements.

Specialized Experience: Experience that equipped the applicant with the particular knowledge, skills, and abilities to perform successfully the duties of the position, and that is typically in or related to the work of the position to be filled. To be creditable, specialized experience must have an equivalent to at least the next lower grade level in the normal line of progression for the occupation in the organization. Applicants who have the one year of appropriate specialized experience, as indicated in the table, are not required by this standard to have general experience, education above the high school level, or any additional specialized experience to meet the minimum qualification requirements.

Combining Education and Experience: Combinations of successfully completed post-high school education and experience may be used to meet total qualification requirements for the grade levels specified in the table. They may be computed by first determining the applicant's total qualifying experience as a percentage of the experience required for the grade level, then determining the applicant's education as a percentage of the education required for the grade level, and then adding the two percentages. (See examples below.) The total percentages must equal at least 100 percent to qualify an applicant for that grade level. Only graduate education in excess of the amount required for the next lower grade level may be used to qualify applicants for positions at grades GS-9 and GS-11. (When crediting education that requires specific course work, prorate the number of hours of related courses required as a proportion of the total education to be used.)

The following are examples of how education and experience may be combined. They are examples only, and are not all-inclusive.

1) The position to be filled is a Quality Assurance Specialist, GS-1910-5. An applicant has two years of general experience and 45 semester hours of college that included nine semester hours in related course work as described in the individual occupational requirements in Section IV-B. The applicant meets 67 percent of the required experience and 38 percent of the required education. Therefore, the applicant exceeds 100 percent of the total requirement and is qualified for the position.

2) The position to be filled is a Management Analyst, GS-343-9. An applicant has six months of specialized experience equivalent to GS-7 and one year of graduate level education. The applicant meets 50 percent of the required experience but none of the required education, since he or she does not have any graduate study beyond that which is required for GS-7. Therefore, the applicant meets only 50 percent of the total requirement and is not qualified for the position. (The applicant's first year of graduate study is not qualifying for GS-9.)

3) The position to be filled is a Music Specialist, GS-1051-11. An applicant has nine months of specialized experience equivalent to GS-9 and 2 ½ years of creditable

graduate level education in music. The applicant meets 75 percent of the required experience and 50 percent of the required education, i.e., the applicant has ½ year of graduate study beyond that required for GS-9. Therefore, the applicant exceeds the total requirement and is qualified for the position. (The applicant's first two years of graduate study are not qualifying for GS-11.)

SELECTIVE FACTORS FOR COVERED POSITIONS

Selective factors must represent knowledge, skills, or abilities that are essential for successful job performance and cannot reasonably be acquired on the job during the period of orientation/training customary for the position being filled. For example, while the individual occupational requirements for Recreation Specialist provide for applicants to meet minimum qualifications on the basis of education or experience in any one of a number of recreational fields, a requirement for knowledge of therapeutic recreation may be needed to perform the duties of a position providing recreation services to persons with physical disabilities. If that is the case, such knowledge could be justified as a selective factor in filling the position.

FEDERAL STUDENT LOAN REPAYMENT PROGRAM

The federal government has paid over $248 million in student loan repayment incentives to new hires and current employees since the program's inception in 2002. Student loan repayment is intended to be a tool for agencies to use when necessary to help them achieve their recruitment and retention goals.[1] The federal student loan repayment program authorizes agencies to repay federally insured student loans as a recruitment or retention incentive for candidates or current employees of the agency.

The program authorizes agencies to set up their own student loan repayment programs to attract or retain highly qualified employees.[2] Any employee is eligible, except those occupying a position excepted from the competitive civil service because of their confidential, policy-determining, policy-making, or policy-advocating nature (e.g., Schedule C appointees).

Although the student loan is not forgiven, agencies may make payments to the loan holder of up to a maximum of $10,000 for an employee in a calendar year and a total of not more than $60,000 for any one employee.

Employees that accept loan payment are required to sign a service agreement to remain in the service of the paying agency for a period of at least three years. Employees must reimburse the paying agency for all benefits received if he or she is separated voluntarily or separated involuntarily for cause or poor performance. In

The federal government has paid over $248 million in student loan repayment incentives to new hires and current employees since its inception.

---

[1] Fiscal Year 2009 Federal Student Loan Repayment Program Report to Congress

[2] Authorized per 5 U.S.C. 5379, employee defined by U.S.C. 2105

addition, an employee must maintain an acceptable level of performance in order to continue to receive repayment benefits.

One word of caution. When you accept student loan reimbursement the payments sent to your loan holder are included in the employee's gross income and in wages for federal employment tax purposes. Therefore, your actual payment will be reduced by the taxes incurred.

Table 2-2

Student Loan Repayment Program Statistics

	2002	2003	2004	2005	2006	2007	2008	2009
Participating Agencies	16	24	28	30	34	33	35	36
Employees Benefiting	690	2,077	2,945	4,409	5,755	6,619	6,879	8,454
Amount of Benefits in Millions	$3.2	$9.2	$16.4	$28	$36	$42	$52	$62

Job Classifications

Agencies may choose to provide student loan repayment benefits to recruit or retain employees across all job series, or target the incentive to a particular occupation or set of occupations. Table 2-3 lists the occupations that agencies used student loan repayments most often.[3] Don't be discouraged if your occupation is not on this list. Employees from a diverse cross section of occupations (42.7 percent of all incentives awarded) have received tuition reimbursement and the list ranges from secretary, chemists, and program analysts to IT specialists, nurses, office managers and scientists and everything in between.

Agencies may use student loan repayment benefits to recruit or retain employees across all job series, or target the incentive to a particular occupation or set of occupations.

[3] OPM's *Fiscal Year 2009 "Federal Student Loan Repayment Program" Report to Congress.*

Table 2-3

2009 Student Loan Occupational Summary

Occupation	Employee Count	% of Total
Attorney	810	9.6
Criminal Investigator	748	8.8
Miscellaneous Administrative	542	6.4
Intelligence	456	5.4
Contract Specialist	435	5.2
GAO Analyst	364	4.3
Management and Program Analysis	345	4.1
Nurse	255	3.0
Business and Industry	228	2.7
Mechanical Engineer	208	2.4
Financial Administration and Program	197	2.3
General Engineer	175	2.1
Nuclear Engineer	168	2.0
Information Technology Management	163	1.9
Accounting	157	1.9
Inspection, Investigation, and Compliance	150	1.8
Human Resource Specialist	145	1.7
Miscellaneous Clerk & Assistant	131	1.6
All Other Occupations	2,777	32.0
TOTAL	**8,454**	**100.00**

You might not receive an offer **UNLESS YOU ASK!** If you are selected for a position and no incentives are offered don't hesitate to ask if the agency will pay your student loans if you accept the position. Be tactful, agency don't have to pay incentives; they do it to meet their recruitment goals and they want to attract qualified employees in a highly competitive market. The next section will discuss other incentives that you must often ask for, such as pay matching.

Visit OPM's Web site at http://opm.gov/oca/PAY/StudentLoan/index.asp for additional information on this subject. You can also find current information and updated statistics at http://federaljobs.net.

RECRUITMENT, RELOCATION, AND RETENTION INCENTIVES

A recruitment incentive may be paid to an eligible individual who is appointed to a General Schedule (GS), senior-level (SL), scientific or professional (ST), Senior Executive Service (SES), Federal Bureau of Investigation and Drug Enforcement Administration (FBI/DEA) SES, Executive Schedule (EX), law enforcement officer, or prevailing rate position. OPM may approve other categories for coverage upon written request from the head of the employing agency.

*A*sk hiring agencies to match your previous salary **BEFORE** you accept the position.

Recruitment incentives may not be paid to presidential appointees; noncareer appointees in the Senior Executive Service; those in positions excepted from the competitive service by reason of their confidential, policy-determining, policy-making, or policy-advocating natures; agency heads; or those expected to receive an appointment as an agency head.

Agencies may pay a recruitment incentive to an employee newly appointed to a position that is likely to be difficult to fill in the absence of an incentive. Recruitment incentive pay may not exceed 25 percent of the employee's annual rate of basic pay in effect at the beginning of the service period multiplied by the number of years in the service period, not to exceed four years, Agencies may also pay a relocation incentive to a current employee who must relocate to accept a position in a different geographic area that is difficult to fill. Employees who accept incentives must sign an agreement to fulfill a period of service with the agency. An agency may decide to use different payment options.

Payment options — Recruitment and relocation incentives may be paid:

✓ As an initial lump-sum payment at the beginning of the service period;

✓ In equal or variable installments throughout the service period;

✓ As a final lump-sum payment on completion of the service period; or

✓ In a combination of these methods.

Retention Incentives

Agencies may pay a retention incentive to a current employee if they determine the unusually high or unique qualifications of the employee or a special need of the agency for the employee's service makes it essential to retain the employee and the employee would likely leave federal service without this incentive. Retention incentives may not exceed 25 percent of an employee's rate of basic pay. These incentives can also be awarded for a group or category of employees not to exceed 10 percent of the employee's rate of basic pay.

Ask if they are offering recruitment incentives prior to accepting a position. If they aren't offering recruitment incentives, ask if they will at least match your previous employer's salary. Many accept their first position at less salary than what they were earning in the private sector. Ask the hiring agency to match your previous salary (before you accept the position) and you could end up starting at other than a step 1 in your pay grade. You will have to provide copies of your most recent pay stubs and you have to request this **PRIOR** to accepting a position. Agencies can't match salary after you accept the initial offer. Salary matches are used to attract new hires when filling critical positions. It never hurts to ask.

*You might not receive an offer **UNLESS YOU ASK!***

TABLE 2-4
The "Typical" Federal Civilian Employee

INDIVIDUAL CHARACTERISTICS	2000	2008
Average Age	46.3	46.8
Average Length of Service	17.1	15.5
Retirement Eligible		
CSRS	17.0%	45.7%
FERS	11.0%	13.0%
College Educated	41%	44.3%
Gender		
Men	55%	56.6%
Women	45%	44.3%
Race & National Origin		
Minority Total	30.4%	33.0%
Black	17.1%	17.3%
Hispanic	6.6%	7.6%
American Indian/Alaska Native	4.5%	2.1%
Asian/Pacific Islander	4.5%	5.4%
Disabled	7.0%	7.0%
Veterans Preference	24.0%	22.4%
Vietnam Era Veterans	14.0%	19.0%
Retired Military	3.9%	6.0%
Retired Officers	0.5%	1.2%

Source: "Profile of Federal Civilian Non-Postal Employees, September 30, 2008"

CHAPTER THREE
What Jobs Are Available

The United States (U.S.) government regularly lists more than 20,000 vacancies per day in all disciplines and locations, including both the homeland and overseas. There is something for everyone, no matter what his/her experience or educational level. If job seekers are flexible in terms of the location and federal agency in which they are willing to work, they gain the extra advantage of being able to select a broader range of vacancy announcements to which they can apply.

There are three excellent sources where you can find and apply for federal jobs: USAJobs.gov, Agency Direct, and FederalJobs.Net.

*Visit, federaljobs.net to link to hundreds of agency employment sites to find **ALL** available jobs.*

USAJobs.gov

This is the official employment website of the federal government. In January 2010, the Office of Personnel Management (OPM), the agency behind www.USAJobs.gov, launched a streamlined design of the USAJobs website to make it easier to find jobs according to user-input search criteria, as well as to apply for these jobs with just a few keystrokes, in most cases.

OPM's new site allows visitors to register and set up a personalized account to compile an online résumé and to receive e-mail alerts for job vacancies. Not all agencies use OPM's services; however, you might start out on USAJobs.gov and be redirected to an agency's specific application system.

CHAPTER OBJECTIVES

✎ Find federal job vacancies in your area

✎ How to improve your chances

✎ Discover useful & productive job resources *(periodicals, hotlines, web sites, directories, books, services & agency phone numbers)*

✎ Learn how former employees can be reinstated

✎ Explore student employment opportunities

For example, the Army uses Civilian Personnel Online (CPOL) to fill its civilian vacancies and the Federal Aviation Administration (FAA) uses Automated Staffing Application Program (ASAP) to fill its openings.

Every system requires a separate account; again, it's important to read the announcement and to ensure you set up an account on the corresponding system(s) once you have identified the agency(ies) in which you have an interest in gaining employment.

> Applicants who are recent college graduates or entry-level applicants may also want to establish a search agent on www.studentjobs.gov.

Job seekers can also call OPM's **USAJOBS** hot-line for updated job information at 1-703-724-1850, TTY 978-461-8404. The USAJOBS jobs hotline is menu driven, and you can search jobs by answering specific questions using your telephone keypad. The phone prompts help you select jobs and salary ranges of interest. The online search is much easier, if you don't have access to a computer visit your local library to explore the easy to use referenced Web sites.

Using Agency Direct

This simply means that you visit the official website of the agency(ies) in which you have an interest. While the vast majority of the agencies list their vacancies through USAJobs.gov (and, as such, their employment links will redirect you to this site), there are some agencies that fall under the "Excepted" hiring category; this means that they are not required by law to list certain positions on USAJobs.gov (though more and more agencies are recognizing the value of including their vacancies on USAJobs.gov). For a master list with links to 141 federal agency web sites visit www.federaljobs.net/federal.htm.

Visit Chapter Three to better understand the differences between the two primary job categories: Competitive and Excepted Service.

FederalJobs.Net

The site www.federaljobs.net provides easy to find information about all aspects of federal employment and expanded centralized job listings for federal agencies and related private sector jobs. The job search feature compiles its listings from all agencies across the Internet and provides easy-to-use searches by occupation and /or agency. The real benefit is that all searches are geographically targeted to your area and include related private sector jobs to provide access to the largest pool of available jobs for your area and expertise.

Use the site's search feature to find needed information and the resources section provides abundant outlets for your job search. Many of the links referenced in this book are available on this site.

Many resources are available to locate job announcements including agency sponsored job hot lines, Internet Web sites, employment services, directories, and periodicals. These resources are listed in this chapter under Common Job Sources. Specific hiring programs such as student hiring, employee reinstatement, and engineering conversion paths are discussed following the job resource listings.

Individual agency personnel offices can also be contacted to obtain job announcements and to find out about the agencies' recruitment plans. An agency directory is included in Appendix C and a consolidated listing of Washington, D.C. federal personnel departments is provided in this chapter. If an agency has direct hire or case examining authority, and many do today, they advertise jobs independently from the Office of Personnel Management. OPM does not list job vacancies for all agencies that have direct hire job authority. Occasionally OPM conducts job fairs throughout the country and they are announced on its USAJOBS Web site.

Chapter Seven explains the Veteran Recruitment Appointment (VRA) Program and Veterans Preference. Postal Service jobs are covered separately in Chapter Nine. The U.S. Postal Service (USPS) doesn't advertise job openings through OPM. Opportunities for people with disabilities are in Chapter Ten and law enforcement including Homeland Security and airport screener's jobs are featured in Chapter Eleven. If you are interested in overseas jobs, review Chapter Eight.

IMPROVING YOUR CHANCES

The more contacts you make, the greater your chances. **Don't get lost in the process.** Too many job seekers pin all their hopes on one effort. They find an open announcement, send in an application, then forget about the process until they receive a reply. Federal jobs are highly competitive and the more jobs you apply for the better your chances.

Good things come to those who wait,
as long as they work like hell while they wait.

Content, proper spelling, and grammar counts when sending in your application forms and/or federal style résumé. Complete your application and résumé using the procedures outlined in Chapter Six. Most agencies require online applications and prefer the federal style résumé format. The standard private sector résumé is not sufficient to apply for a federal job, it's too brief and lacks the detail necessary to be properly rated. You can download free fill-in Microsoft Word OF-612 forms at www.federaljobs.net if you prefer this format over a résumé.

I participated in many selection panels during my 35 years of government service and was a certified rating official for the Federal Aviation Administration (FAA). I also coordinated and/or conducted hundreds of job interviews for our organization. The first impression that a rating official has of a new applicant is reflected by his or her application package. I can tell you that many of the applications that I reviewed during my career lacked attention to detail and the spelling and grammar left much to be desired. Half the time the applications didn't get a high enough rating to be considered.

Don't make this same mistake — take the time to draft a coherent, clear, error free, and concise federal style résumé as outlined in Chapter Six. With today's word processors and spell check functions there isn't any reason to submit an application with misspelled words, and the word processor grammar check functions are also very helpful. If you don't have the inclination or time to do it right, hire a service such as CareerPro Global to assist you with your federal style résumé. Notice that I say, assist you with your federal style résumé; it takes a lot of time and work for both the résumé service and client to complete a federal style résumé that will get you hired. So even if you hire a service to complete yours, understand that you will have to provide considerable input and devote time to reviewing drafts to get it right. Only the highest rated applicants are referred for interviews and eventually selected for a job.

Take the time to draft a coherent, clear, error free, and concise application.

If you need assistance writing your application request a free initial consultation from CPG by mentioning that you heard about their services in *The Book of U.S. Government Jobs*. Call 1-800-471-9201 to talk with a consultant.

One Size Doesn't Fit All

Too many applicants make the mistake of submitting the exact same résumé for all jobs they apply for. There can be significantly different duties and responsibilities for the same job series with other organizations, and you must address those differences in the application package. Tailor your federal style résumé, as described in Chapter Six, for each job that you bid on to improve your chances.

Use the list of job resources listed in this chapter to improve your chances. If you're willing to relocate, search for job announcements from other areas and apply for as many jobs in similar or related occupations that you qualify for. One other word of advice: highlight the key duties and responsibilities listed in the job announcement and then use those exact terms in your work descriptions and application package as described further in Chapter Six. Don't forget to use the *"Job Hunter's Checklist"* in Appendix A to steer you through the entire process.

Use the "job Hunter's Checklist in Appendix A to steer you through the entire process.

The informational interviewing methods presented in Chapter Four will help you develop agency contacts that may be able to help you land a job with Uncle

Sam. You aren't locked into the first job or location that you are originally selected for. Once hired, you'll have ample opportunities to bid for jobs in-house.

I accepted my first federal civil service position after discharge from active military duty in Topeka, Kansas, and was able to transfer to my home town in less than a year. Several years later, I applied to the competitive service and accepted a position in a small town of 3,056 in central Pennsylvania and was able to transfer back to Pittsburgh, my home town, for a second time three years later. Many agencies have offices at hundreds of locations and you can bid to any one of those locations for future promotions or to enter a related field. Check with employing agencies to see if they have offices located in or close to the area where you want to relocate. If so, you will more than likely have an opportunity to bid on future openings as long as they employ your specialty at that location.

> *Our business in life is not to get ahead of others,
> but to get ahead of ourselves — to break our own
> records, to outstrip our yesterdays by our today.*
>
> **Susan B. Johnson**

COMMON JOB SOURCES

This section presents resources that can be used to locate federal job announcements. After reviewing the listed resources, refer to Appendix C for a complete list of federal occupations. Appendix B lists agency contact information. A number of the periodicals and directories listed in this chapter are available at public libraries.

Resource headings include job openings, Internet Web sites, directories, and general information. Job openings include publications with job ads and job hotlines. The general information section lists related books, pamphlets, informational services, and brochures. All job sources are listed alphabetically.

JOB OPENINGS

Periodicals and Newspapers with Federal Job Ads

Equal Opportunity Publications — 445 Broad Hollow Road, Suite 425, Melville, NY 11747; 631-421-9421, e-mail info@eop.com. This company publishes a number of excellent publications including **Minority Engineer, Woman Engineer, Equal Opportunity, CAREERS & The disABLED, Hispanic Career World** and **African–American Career World** magazines. Display ads feature national employers, including the federal government, seeking applicants for many varied fields. Each issue offers a dozen to 60 or more display job ads. Call for subscription rates or visit the Web site at www.eop.com/.

Federal Career Opportunities — Federal Research Service, PO Box 1708, Annandale, VA 22003; 1-800-822-5027 or 703-914-JOBS. You can e-mail question to info@fedjobs.com. Federal job listings, $9.95 per month, $19.95 for a three month subscription. Includes federal and private sector job listings. The vacancy listings are available online at www.fedjobs.com. Other job hunting resources are available.

Federal Jobs Digest — P.O. Box 89, Edgemont, PA 19028; 610-725-1769, www.jobsfed.com; publishes online database job listings and bi-monthly subscription to Federal Jobs Digest. Visit site for details and pricing.

Federal Times — 6883 Commercial Dr., Springfield, VA 22159; 1-800-368-5718, www.federaltimes.com, weekly subscription available. Call for rates. Publishes some vacancies with brief descriptions starting at the GS-7 level and provides abundant information about federal employment.

Federal Practitioner — Quadrant Health Com, Inc.,7 Century Drive, Suite 302, Parsippany, NJ 07054-4609, published monthly. Call Fax: (973) 206-9251 for subscription rates. Generally includes up to a dozen or so ads for Veterans Administration hospital nurses and physicians under the *"Career Center"* section. Visit their Web site at www.fedprac.com or email fedprac@qhc.com.

The Black Collegian Magazine — Black Collegiate Services, 140 Carondelet St., New Orleans, LA 70130; phone 504-523-0154, published semiannually. Visit the Web site at www.black-collegian.com. Free copies are sent to over 800 schools. Search job listings online.

Federal Job Hotlines

USAJOBS Automated Telephone System — Federal government jobs national hotline, 703-724-1850, TTY 978-461-8404. If you have a problem with an announcement, first call the contact number listed on the job announcement. This service is operated by the Office of Personnel Management. The hotline phone answers 24 hours a day and provides federal employment information for most occupations. Callers can leave messages to receive forms and announcements by mail. Requested job announcements and applications are mailed within 24 hours. Online voice prompts and voice commands allow access with any touchtone or rotary dial telephone. **Note** — Not all job vacancies are listed on this service. Excepted agencies and agencies with direct hire authority announce vacancies through their individual human resources departments. Their web site at www.usajobs.gov is much easier to use and you can access it online at your local library if you don't have a computer at home.

WEB SITES

Many Web sites are available to assist you with your job search. Agencies have searchable online job databases available or they use OPM's USAJOBS Web site to post job vacancies. You can review job vacancy announcements and apply for vacancies nationwide online in most cases.

Federal Jobs Network — (www.federaljobs.net) This career center will assist you with your federal government job search and guide you step-by-step through the process. Search this site for key words and phrases. Includes a listing of over 141 federal agency employment Web sites that you can visit for up-to-date job listings and agency information. You will also find current pay scales and up-dates to the 11th Edition of *The Book of U.S. Government Jobs*. Visit this site often for updated information.

Federal Online Job Search by FRS — (www.fedjobs.com) Federal Research Service, Inc.,PO Box 1708, Annandale, VA 22003; 1-800-822-5027 or 703-914-JOBS; e-mail *info@fedjobs.com*. A searchable database of thousands of federal job vacancies updated each weekday. Search job vacancies by GS series, grade, location, eligibility, agency or any combination of the above. Subscriptions are available. Call or visit the Web site for rates.

Federal Web Locator — (www.lib.auburn.edu/madd/docs/fedloc.html) The Federal Web Locator is a service provided by the Villanova Center for Information Law and Policy and is intended to be the one-stop shopping point for federal government information on the Internet.

Student Jobs — (www.studentjobs.gov) Use this site to explore student job vacancy announcements and draft your résumé. This excellent site also provides active links to agencies that recruit students.

USA.gov — (www.usa.gov) This site is the U.S. government's official Web portal and makes it easy for the public to get U.S. government information and services on the Web. There are five major channels to search; Citizens, Business and Nonprofits, Federal Employees, Government to Government, and Visitors to the U.S. Click on the Federal Employees link to learn about benefits and pay, policies and practices. A great place to look for government-specific information.

USAJOBS — (www.usajobs.gov) Operated by the Office of Personnel Management (OPM). This site provides access to the national federal jobs database; full text job announcements; answers to frequently asked employment questions; and access to electronic and hard copy application forms. Listings are divided into professional career, entry level professional, senior executive, worker-trainee, clerical and technician, trades and labor, and summer positions. An e-mail job notification feature is available, and registered users can create and store up to three searches on this service. When jobs are announced you will be notified by e-mail.

This site offers a résumé builder that you can use to create a federal style résumé that can be printed, saved, and edited.

Federal Department Internet Web Sites

Generally you can link to individual agencies of each department from the listed home page. For example, when you visit the Department of Transportation's Web site you will find links to the Federal Aviation Administration and other agency links. Visit www.federaljobs.net/federal.htm for a comprehensive agency web site list.

Appendix C includes Web addresses for most agencies and major departments.

Executive Departments:

Agriculture	www.usda.gov
Commerce	www.commerce.gov/
Defense	www.defense.gov/
Education	www.ed.gov
Energy	www.energy.gov
Health & Human Services	www.hhs.gov
Homeland Security	www.dhs.gov/
Interior	www.doi.gov
Justice	www.justice.gov
Labor	www.dol.gov
State	www.state.gov
Transportation	www.dot.gov
Treasury	www.treasury.gov
Veterans Affairs	www.va.gov
White House	www.whitehouse.gov

Independent Establishments and Government Corporations:

Central Intelligence Agency	www.cia.gov
Environmental Protection Agency	www.epa.gov
Federal Communications Commission	www.fcc.gov
Office of Personnel Management	www.opm.gov
U. S. Postal Service	www.usps.gov

DIRECTORIES

Federal Employees Almanac — (Published in January of each year), 1105 Media, Inc, PO Box 3167, Carol Stream, IL, 60132, 1-800-989-3363. A comprehensive guide to federal pay, benefits, retirement and more. Includes pay scales, detailed information about special emphasis hiring programs, veterans benefits, with detailed contact information. Visit www.federaldaily.com for more information.

Federal Personnel Guide — (Published February 1 every year) - LRP Publications, 360 Hiatt Drive, Palm Beach Gardens, FL 33418; 800-341-7848, annual guide, 300 pages, $19.95 plus shipping. This guide is a useful, accurate, time-saving source of valuable information on government organization, compensation, promotion, retirement, insurance, benefits, and other important and interesting subjects for Civil Service, Postal Service, and all other employees of the federal government. Available in print, CD and online at www.fedguide.com/.

Federal Yellow Book: Who's Who in Federal Departments and Agencies — Leadership Directories Inc., 104 Fifth Ave, New York, NY 10011; 212-627-4140, quarterly. The Federal Yellow Book is a comprehensive directory of individuals within the executive branch of the federal government located within the Washington, D.C. metropolitan area. All of the information listed in the Federal Yellow Book is verified directly with each organization listed. Includes thousands of e-mail and fax numbers. This is an expensive guide and you may find a copy at your local library. Web site at www.leadershipdirectories.com/.

Military Installation Directory — A free military installation guide is available at www.military.com, click on *"Military Bases"* in the left border. This comprehensive guide allows you to browse by service, location or alphabetically. It includes a phone directory, medical services, community listings, employment and school information. Use this guide to find installations in your area that may be hiring civilian support personnel

The United States Government Manual — Current year edition, 700 pages, $30. Order by phone at 1-866-512-1800, 202-512-1530 (D.C. Metro area) or online at www.bookstore.gpo.gov/. Available at many libraries. The official handbook of the federal government provides comprehensive information on all agencies of the legislative, judicial, and executive branches. The manual also includes information on quasi-official agencies; international organizations in which the United States participates; and boards, commissions, and committees.

A typical agency description includes a list of principal officials, a summary statement of the agency's purpose and role in the federal government, a brief history of the agency, including its legislative or executive authority, a description of its programs and activities, and a "Sources of Information" section. This last section provides information on consumer activities, contracts and grants, employment, publications, and many other areas of public interest.

GENERAL INFORMATION

Books, Services, and Software

Military to Federal Career Guide; Federal Résumé Writing for Veterans — by Kathryn Kramer Troutman, 136 pages with CD, $18.95. This military transition book is a comprehensive guide for military personnel seeking federal employment. It takes readers through the critical steps including networking, federal benefits for veterans, writing your résumé, determining where you fit in, understanding vacancy announcements, searching for jobs, and interview preparation. The accompanying CD provides abundant resources and sample résumés for various military specialties. Order by calling 1-800-782-7424 (answers 24/7) or online through www.federaljobs.net.

Post Office Jobs — (5th Edition) by Dennis V. Damp, 256 pages, $24.95. The USPS employs over 600,000 workers in 300 job categories for positions at 39,000 post offices, branches, stations, and community post offices throughout the United States. This book includes sample tests to help you pass the 470 Battery Exam, prepares you for the interview, and shows you how to apply. Available at bookstores nationwide or order by calling 1-800-782-7424 (answers 24/7) or online through www.postalwork.net.

SES Monthly Column by Barbara Adams - SES Exclusive, a column that focuses on the Senior Executive Service (SES). This column will provide insight into obtaining an SES position and maintaining and succeeding in an SES career with tips from Barbara. Available online at www.fedmanager.com/partners.php.

Take Charge of Your Federal Career — (2nd Edition June 2010) by Dennis V. Damp, 216 pages, $29.95. Call 1-800-782-7424 to order. An updated and practical, action-oriented career management workbook for federal employees. Packed with proved tips and valuable assessment and evaluation tools, this unique workbook provides federal workers with the know-how and guidance they need to identify, obtain, and successfully demonstrate the skills and experience required to qualify for new and better federal jobs.

Services

Résumé Writing Service — Visit www.federaljobs.net/applyfor.htm and click on *"Federal Résumé and KSA Writing Service."* CareerPro Global offers expert federal résumé, KSA, and federal application writing services. Receive a free initial consultation by mentioning that you heard about their service in *The Book of U.S. Government Jobs*, call 1-800-471-9201 to talk with a consultant about having them write a professional federal style résumé for you.

TABLE 3-1
WASHINGTON, D.C. AGENCY
OFFICE NUMBERS (February 2010)

TDD (Telephone Device for the Deaf)
Main office number ● *Job Hotline* ■ *Personnel Office*

References: Government Manual 2010-2011/ The Federal phone listings at
http://www.info.gov/phone.htm

Agriculture Department	202/720-4623	Fish & Wildlife Service	■ 703/358-1743
Rural Development	202/720-4323	Mineral Mgmt. Service	202/787-1000
Food/Safety	301/344-4755	National Parks Service	■ 202/208-6843
Farm & Foreign Service	202/720-7115	U.S. Geological Survey	■ 703/648-7405
Forest Service	202/205-1661		
Graduate School	888/744-4723	**Justice Dept.**	● 202/514-3397
		Attorney Applications	■ 202/514-1432
Commerce Department	■ 202/482-2000	Bureau of Prisons	■ 202/307-3082
Economics & Statistics	202/606-9900		● 800/995-6423
International Trade	202/482-3917	Drug Enforcement Admin.	202/305-8600
Nat'l Oceanic & Admin.	202/482-4190	FBI	202/317-2727
Patent/Trademark Office	571/272-8400	US Marshal Service	202/307-9065
Defense Department	■ 703/545-6700	**Labor Department**	202/693-5000
Defense Logistics Agency	703/767-6200		
Dept. of the Air Force	703/697-6061	**State Department**	202/647-4000
Dept. of the Army	703/697-5081	Foreign Service	■ 202/261/8888
Dept. of the Navy	■ 703/697-7391	State Dept. Job Info	● 202/663-2176
U.S. Marine Corps	703/614-1034		
National Security Agency	301/688-6524	**Transportation**	202-366-4000
			● 800/525-2878
Education	■ 800/872-5327	Federal Aviation Admin.	202/267-3883
		Federal Highway Admin.	202/366-0534
Energy	■ 202/586-4940	Federal Transit Admin.	202/366-4043
		Maritime Administration	202/366-5807
Health & Human Services	202/619-0257		● 800/996-2723
Substance Abuse &		Surface Transportation	202/245-0230
Mental Health	240/276-2130		
Food & Drug Admin.	■ 888/463-6332	**Treasury**	202/622-2000
Indian Health Service	■ 301/443-2650	Bureau of Public Debt	■ 304/480-6144
National Inst. of Health	301/496-4000	Alcohol, Tobacco & Trade	■ 202/927-5000
Housing & Urban Dev.	■ 202/708-0980	Comptroller of Currency	■ 202/874-4700
		Engraving & Printing	■ 202/874-3733
Homeland Security	202-282-8000	Financial Mgmt. Service	■ 202/874-8090
Coast Guard	877/669-8724	IRS	■ 202/622-5000
Immigration & Customs	202-435-1000	Thrift Supervision	■ 202/906-6061
Secret Service	202-406-5800	US Mint	■ 202/354-7200
			800/872-6468
Interior	■ 202/208-3100	**Veterans Affairs**	202/273-4800
Bureau of Reclamation	■ 303/445-2684		

INDEPENDENT AGENCIES

African Development Foundation	202/673-3916
Central Intelligence Agency	703/482-0623
Commodity Trading Comm.	201/418-5080
Consumer Product Safety	301/504-7908
Defense Nuclear Facilities	202/694-7000
EEO Commission	■ 202/663-4900
Environmental Protection	■ 202/564-4355
Export-Import Bank of US	800/565-3946
Farm Credit Administration	■ 703/883-4056
Federal Communications Commission	■ 888/225-5322
Federal Deposit Ins. Corp.	202/898-6993
Federal Housing Finance	866/796-5595
Federal Labor Relations	■ 202/218-7949
Federal Maritime Comm.	■ 202/523-5725
Federal Mediation and Conciliation Service	202/606-8100
Federal Mine Safety & Health	202/434-9900
Federal Trade Commission	■ 202/326-2180
Federal Reserve System	202/942-1600
General Accounting Office	■ 202/512-6092
General Services Admin.	■ 202/501-0705
Government Printing Office	■ 202/512-1124
Inter-American Foundation	703/306-4301
Merit Systems Protection Bd.	800/209-8960
NASA	■ 202/358-0000
National Labor Relations Bd	202/273-1000
TDD	202/273-4300
National Mediation Board	202/692-5000

National Archives/Records	● 800/827-4898
TDD	314/801-0886
National Capital Planning	202/482-7200
National Credit Union Admin.	703/518-6300
National Foundation of the Arts and the Humanities	202/682-5400
National Science Foundation	■ 703/292-8180
	● 800/628-1487
National Transportation Safety Board	■ 202/314-6230
Nuclear Regulatory Comm.	301/415-7000
Occupation Safety & Health	202/606-5050
Office of Government Ethics	202/482-9300
Office of Mgmt. & Budget	202/395-7250
Office of Personnel Mgmt.	■ 202/606-1800
Peace Corps	■ 202/692-1200
	● 800/818-9579
Postal Regulatory Commission	202/789-6800
Securities & Exch. Comm.	■ 202/942-7500
Selective Service System	■ 703-605-4100
Small Business Admin.	202/205-6600
Social Security Admin.	410/965-1234
	800/772-1213
Tennessee Valley Authority	■ 865/632-3199
	202/898-2999
Trade & Development	703/875-4357
US Comm. on Civil Rights	■ 202/376-8364
US International Trade Commission	■ 202/205-2651
US Postal Service	202/268-2000
	800/275-8777

If you try a number and it has changed, go to http://www.info.gov/phone.htm to locate the new number.

TABLE 3-2
THE TYPICAL FEDERAL CIVILIAN EMPLOYEE

(NON-POSTAL EMPLOYMENT)

JOB CHARACTERISTICS	2010
Annual Base Salary	$81,258
Pay System	
General Schedule (GS)	60.2%
Wage Grade	10.5%
Other	29.2%
Occupations	
White-Collar	89.3%
Professional	24.3%
Administrative	353%
Technical & Other	29.9%
Blue-Collar	10.6%
Work Schedule	
Full-Time	93.6%
Part-Time	3.6%
Intermittent	2.7%
Service	
Competitive	69.8%
Excepted & SES*	30.1%

* The SES is the Senior Executive Service.

Source: Central Personnel Data File

EQUAL EMPLOYMENT OPPORTUNITY

The federal government is an Equal Opportunity Employer. Hiring and advancement in the government are based on qualifications and performance regardless of race, color, creed, religion, gender, age, national origin, or disability.

EMPLOYMENT OPTIONS

There are numerous employment paths available: full time, part time and job sharing positions, cooperative education hiring programs, student employment, job opportunities for veterans, and the handicapped. Military dependents and veterans can be hired under special appointment through the Family Member Preference, Military Spouse Preference Programs, or the Veterans Readjustment Appointment (VRA) Program. Military dependent and veterans' programs are explained in Chapter Seven.

The majority of applicants will seek federal employment through announcements from those listed on USAJOBS or individual agency sites. Alternate routes are categorized into special emphasis groups, such as student employment, military dependent, veteran and handicapped hiring programs. Refer to the related chapter for guidance on special emphasis hiring options.

STUDENT EMPLOYMENT OPPORTUNITIES

Major student employment program changes are planned for 2011. On December 27, 2010, President Obama signed Executive Order 13562 entitled "Recruiting and Hiring Students and Recent Graduates." The principal purpose of the order is to establish a comprehensive structure to help the Federal Government be more competitive in recruiting and hiring talented individuals who are in school or who have recently received a degree.

The Executive Order directs OPM to consolidate student and recent graduate programs into the Pathways Programs framework with three clear program paths that are tailored to recruit, train and retain well-qualified candidates:

- Internship Program. A new Internship Program will be created that is targeted towards students enrolled in a wide variety of educational institutions.

- Recent Graduates Program. This brand new program will target recent graduates of trade and vocational schools, community colleges, universities, and other qualifying institutions. To be eligible, applicants must apply within two years of degree completion (except for veterans precluded from doing so due to their military service obligation, who will have six years after degree completion). Successful applicants will be placed in a two-year career development program with a cohort of peers hired during time frames aligned with academic calendars. After successfully completing the program, participants will be considered for noncompetitive conversion to career jobs.

- Presidential Management Fellows (PMF) Program. For more than three decades, the PMF Program has been the Federal government's premier leadership development program for advance degree candidates. The Executive Order expands the eligibility window for applicants, making it more "student friendly" by aligning it with academic calendars and including those who have received a qualifying advanced degree within the preceding two years. It also directs OPM to set qualification standards, and to make changes in order to make the PMF experience more robust and substantive for participants.

The three Pathways Programs will each provide noncompetitive conversion eligibility to participants and will be used in targeted ways to develop talent for civil service careers.

Effective March 1, 2011, the Executive Order also eliminates the Federal Career Intern Program (FCIP). OPM will be proposing implementing regulations and assisting Federal agencies in adopting these reforms. Students and recent graduates can expect to see these reforms fully implemented within a year.

Under Section 8 of Executive Order 13562, prior executive orders and regulations that establish or implement Presidential Management Fellows (PMF), Student Career Experience Program (SCEP), and Student Temporary Employment Program (STEP) remain in effect, at least until such time as regulations to implement the new Internship Program and to make changes to the PMF Program become final and effective. Accordingly, agencies may continue to hire and employ people under these programs. Executive Order 13562 directs OPM to provide guidance on conducting an orderly transition from existing student and internship programs. OPM is expected to expedite the drafting of proposed regulations on all three programs.

Getting Started

Visit www.studentjobs.gov/ to start your job search and explore the site for everything from summer jobs to apprenticeships and scholarships.

Application requirements, including when to apply, will differ for each program. Programs are offered throughout the year (spring, summer, fall, and winter). Program durations vary from six weeks up to three years depending on the requirements. The different start times and length of programs provide the maximum flexibility for students and career professionals. You must read and comply with all application deadlines as specified by each program.

The following program list is featured on the site. Click on each heading to review the available programs, agency sponsors, program descriptions, and application dates. Check this site frequently for new program additions and agency job announcements. Application dates for many of the programs are fixed to specific dates each year.

Student Domestic and International Programs

- Apprenticeships
- Cooperative
- Fellowships
- Grants
- Internships
- Scholarships
- Volunteers

Job Searches

Searches for student jobs on www.studentjobs.gov can be confusing initially. I suggest just entering the location where you are looking for work from the drop-down menu, leave the *"Occupational Series"* entry blank and click *"Search For Jobs"* at the bottom of the page. This will bring up a list of ALL jobs available in your area. Click on the job vacancy of interest.

Print out and thoroughly read the job announcements. Follow the application guidance and if you have questions call or e-mail the staffing specialist listed in the announcement.

Presidential Management Fellows Program (PMF)

This program (formerly the Presidential Management Internship Program) is targeted for graduate students who would like to enter management government.

Entry into this program is considered an honor and recognized throughout government. Professional, entry-level positions are available that provide exposure to a wide range of public management issues. Fellows candidates are appointed for a two-year period and most positions are located in the Washington, D.C. area. Visit www.pmf.gov for complete information and guidance. At the end of the two-year appointment, Fellows upon program completion are converted to permanent positions as long as their performance was satisfactory.

Qualifications

Typical study areas that qualify include finance, economics, accounting, criminal justice, business administration, health administration, urban planning, social services, public administration, information systems management, law, political science, and information systems management. This list is not all-inclusive.

❶ You must be scheduled to receive or have received a graduate degree.

❷ During your studies you must have demonstrated an outstanding ability and personal interest in a government career in management of public policies and programs.

❸ You are currently a U.S. citizen or will soon become a citizen before being appointed to a PMF.

Your graduate school's dean, director, or chairperson must nominate you for the program. Nominations are made by December 1 of each year. Selections from each school are highly competitive and are based on skills, abilities, and knowledge.

The final selections from all nominees are made through a comprehensive individual and group interview, application assessment, writing samples, and a review of your school's recommendations.

Presidential Management Fellows announcements are mailed in September to graduate schools nationwide. If interested, contact your career placement and guidance office. Call the Career America Hotline for additional information and specific appointment details.

Student Volunteer Services

Students can volunteer to work with local agencies to gain valuable work experience. These jobs are not compensated. Schools coordinate participation, and high school and college students are eligible for this program. A number of colleges include volunteer service internships. Interested students can contact agencies directly.

The Student Volunteer program is an excellent path for students to develop agency contacts, work experience, and gain insight into various government careers. Often, participants receive career counseling and acquire first-hand information on upcoming paid student and full time openings.

All agencies are permitted to utilize this program. However, many don't participate for various reasons. Interested students should ask their career counselor for assistance when contacting agencies. Often, a counselor can persuade a manager to try out the program on a test basis. Student Volunteer Services is an excellent opportunity for aggressive students to get their foot in the door.

THE LARGEST OCCUPATIONS

White-collar workers are classified into 442 different occupations. Refer to Appendix D for a complete list of white-collar occupational groups and their descriptions. Average worldwide annual base salary for this group reached $81,258 in January 2010. The table on page 61 lists the 20 white-collar occupations with at least 16,000 employees.

Occupations ranged in size from several occupations with fewer than 10 employees each to 62,751 employees in the 2210 Information Technology Management job series.

TABLE 3-5

THE LARGEST WHITE-COLLAR OCCUPATIONS

SERIES	JOB TITLE	TOTAL
0301	Miscellaneous Administration	88,812
0303	Miscellaneous Clerk & Assistant	76,086
2210	Information Technology Mgmt.	68,626
0301	Nurse	60,889
1802	Compliance Inspection and Support	56,774
0343	Management & Program Analysis	55,828
1811	Criminal Investigating	41,654
0905	General Attorney	30,928
1101	General Business and Industry	29,963
1102	Contracting	29,928
1901	General Inspection, Investigation, & Comp	29,420
0105	Social Insurance Administration	27,406
0318	Secretary	27,176
0962	Contract Representative	27,043
0602	Medical Officer	26,542
0201	Human Resources Management	24,624
2152	Air Traffic Control	21,726
0501	Financial Administration and Program	21,266
0801	General Engineering	21,179
1895	Customs and Border Protection	19,629

SOURCE: U.S. Office of Personnel Management Workforce Information & Planning
Group Central Personnel Data File (CPDF) September 2010

There are 213,500 full-time blue-collar workers classified into 300 occupations and organized into 37 job family groups. Refer to Appendix D for a complete description and list of blue-collar occupational groups.

TABLE 3-6
THE LARGEST BLUE COLLAR OCCUPATIONS

SERIES	TITLE	TOTAL
3566	Custodial Worker	11,819
4749	Maintenance Mechanic	10,987
8852	Aircraft Mechanic	10,668
6907	Materials Handler	8,438
5803	Heavy Mobile Equipment Mechanic	8,005
7408	Food Service Worker	8,005
5801	Transportation/Mobile Equipment Maint	7,804
3806	Sheet Metal Mechanic	6,681
2604	Electronics Mechanic	6,331
5703	Motor Vehicle Operator	6,093
2805	Electrician	4,278
3502	Laboring	4,175
4102	Painting	4,081
7404	Cooking	3,923
3414	Machining	3,783
2610	Electronic Integrated System Mechanic	3,712
8602	Aircraft Engine Mechanic	2,940
5716	Engineering Equipment Operating	2,833
6914	Store Working	2,721
4204	Pipefitting	2,653
3703	Welding	2,293

SOURCE: U.S Office of Personnel Management Workforce Information & Planning Group Central Personnel Data File (CPDF)

Wage system pay is based on locality, and wage surveys are conducted each year by the DOD to set wage rates for all areas. Over 85 percent of all wage grade jobs are with the Departments of Defense and Veterans Affairs and 47 percent are veterans. Wage rate pay schedules are available online at http://federaljobs.net/. Click on the menu selection titled *"Pay Schedules."*

REINSTATEMENT ELIGIBILITY

If you had prior federal career or career-conditional service with the federal government you are eligible to reenter the federal competitive service workforce without competing with the public in a civil service examination.[1] You may apply for any open civil service examination, but reinstatement eligibility also enables you to apply for federal jobs open only to status candidates.

What Are the Eligibility Requirements?

If you held a career or career-conditional appointment at some time in the past there is no time limit on reinstatement eligibility for those who:

- Have veterans' preference, or
- Acquired career tenure by completing three years of substantially continuous creditable service.

If you do not have veterans' preference or did not acquire career tenure, you may be reinstated within three years after the date of your separation. Reinstatement eligibility may be extended by certain activities that occur during the three-year period after separation from your last career or career-conditional appointment. Examples of these activities are:

- Federal employment under temporary, term, or similar appointments.
- Federal employment in excepted, non-appropriated fund, or Senior Executive Service positions.
- Federal employment in the legislative and judicial branches.
- Active military duty terminated under honorable conditions.
- Service with the District of Columbia government prior to January 1, 1980 (and other service for certain employees converted to the District's independent merit system).
- Certain government employment or full-time training that provided valuable training and experience for the job to be filled.
- Periods of overseas residence of a dependent who followed a federal military or civilian employee to an overseas post of duty.

---

[1] 5 CFR Part 15.

Applying for Reinstatement?

You have to contact agencies and locate job vacancies. Reinstatement eligibility doesn't guarantee you a job. Agencies determine the sources of applicants they will consider. Individuals usually apply to agencies in response to advertised job vacancies. Some agencies accept applications only when they have an appropriate open merit promotion announcement, while others accept applications at any time. If you are seeking a higher grade or a position with more promotion potential than you previously held, generally you must apply under a merit promotion announcement and rank among the best-qualified applicants to be selected. Status applicants include individuals who are eligible for reinstatement.

To establish your reinstatement eligibility, you need a copy of your most recent SF 50, Notification of Personnel Action, showing tenure group 1 or 2, along with your application. You may obtain a copy of your personnel records from your former agency if you recently separated. Otherwise, send your request to Federal Records Center address:

FEDERAL RECORDS CENTER
National Archives and Records Administration
111 Winnebago Street
St. Louis, Missouri 63118
(314) 801-9250

Such inquiries should include your full name under which formerly employed, Social Security number, date of birth, and to the extent known, former federal employing agencies, addresses and dates of such employment. The Privacy Act of 1974 (5 USC 552a) and the Office of Personnel Management require a signed and dated written request for information from federal records. No requests for information from personnel or any other type of records will be accepted by telephone or e-mail.

Qualifications

You must meet the qualification requirements for the position. Written tests are not common, but if one is required, you must take it. You must also meet the suitability standards for federal employment. If you were removed for cause from your previous federal employment, it will not necessarily bar you from further federal service. The facts in each case as developed by inquiry or investigation will determine the person's fitness for re-entry into the competitive service.

A former employee who did not complete a required probationary period during previous service under the appointment upon which his/her eligibility for reinstatement is based is required, in most cases, to serve a complete one-year probationary period after reinstatement.

ENGINEERING CONVERSIONS

Many professional engineering jobs are open to non-degree applicants who meet the Office of Personnel Management's Engineering Conversion criteria. This is good news to those who have over 60 semester hours of college in specific areas of study. Federal regulations state that to qualify for professional engineering positions, GS-5 through GS-15, a candidate must meet basic requirements for all professional engineering positions. The GS-800 Engineering Position Qualification Standard provides an alternate and primary conversion path. A copy is available at www.federaljobs.net/quals2.htm.

Primary Path

The primary path consists of having an engineering degree from a four-year accredited college. The curriculum must be accredited by the Accreditation Board for Engineering and Technology (ABET) or include the specific courses and five of the specific study areas listed in Note 1 below.

Alternate Paths

Alternate paths are available to those without a four-year engineering degree but have the specific knowledge, skills, abilities, and work experience for an engineer position. Four years of college level education, training, and/or technical experience is required and can be obtained through the following paths:

1) Professional Engineering Registration Exam
2) Engineering-in-Training Examination
3) 60 semester hours in an accredited college including the courses and areas of study listed in Note 1 below
4) A degree in related curriculum

The first three alternate paths require appropriate training and work experience. If an applicant has the engineering experience and completed A, B, or C above, OPM will rate them as Professional Engineers.

The fourth alternate path is a related degree. For example, applicants who have a four-year degree in civil engineering and bid on a mechanical engineering job can be rated eligible if they have at least one year of experience under a professional mechanical engineer.

NOTE 1. Curriculum must include differential and integral calculus and courses (more advanced than first year physics and chemistry) in five of the seven areas including statics and dynamics, strength of materials, fluid mechanics, hydraulics, thermodynamics, electrical fields and circuits, nature and properties of materials, and other fundamental engineering subjects including optics, heat transfer, and electronics.

CHAPTER FOUR
The Interview Process

There are two primary interview types that you will encounter during your job search—the *informational interview* and the *employment interview*. The informational interview—initiated by the job seeker—is a valuable networking tool used to explore job opportunities. Employment interviews are initiated by prospective employers to assess your ability and weigh your strengths and weaknesses with other applicants. The person with acceptable qualifications and the ability to impress the interview panel gets the job.

Even under the best of conditions, interviews are often intimidating, and going to an interview without knowing the "rules" can be downright frightening. Understanding the interview process will help you throughout your career and just knowing what to expect will improve your mental stability as well. Before discussing interview specifics I'll introduce you to the interview process through an associate's true story. I changed the names to protect their privacy.

It was May 1969, and our main character — let's call him Tony — had recently been discharged from the Army. He decided to continue his college education and enrolled at a university in Pennsylvania. Shortly after Tony's discharge, he went on an ***informational interview*** — more on this type of interview later — at the Tobyhanna Army Depot, looking for any available position within his chosen electronics field.

CHAPTER OBJECTIVES

✎   Locate job prospects through informational interviews

✎   Prepare for the job interview

✎   Review commonly asked interview questions

✎   What to do after the interview

✎   Follow the "Interview Checklist" on page 86

He was informed that no opportunities were currently available; however, the Federal Aviation Administration (FAA) might be looking for someone with his electronic background that he could submit a "package" to the Office of Personnel Management (OPM) in New York to determine his qualifications. That application package was nearly 100 pages thick. It questioned every aspect of Tony's background and knowledge. He completed the "package," made a copy for himself, and mailed it off to this thing called OPM, not knowing what to expect. Months later Tony received a letter from OPM advising him that he was qualified and an ***employment interview*** (more on this later, too) was scheduled with the FAA. He was given a phone number and told to contact the FAA for the exact date, time, and location for his interview. The interview would be in just three weeks. Tony was as excited as he was nervous. What was the FAA? What did they do? What were they looking for? Shouldn't they be calling him rather than vice versa? Lots of questions — few answers. How did Tony prepare for this interview? What was the outcome?

In 1969, information was not nearly as available as it is today. The Internet was a figment of our imagination and learning about the FAA was not easy. A trip back to Tobyhanna helped Tony find out some basic information about the FAA and what the different General Schedule (GS) levels were. Apparently they were just like ranks in the service and determined your salary and status. Tony then pulled out the copy of his "package" and began to study what he had submitted. Finally, he wrote down some key questions for which he needed answers. Here are his questions:

1. What is the FAA and exactly what does it do?
2. What is the mission of the FAA?
3. How does someone with my credentials (microwave radio equipment repairman) fit in with this agency's mission and goals?
4. Where is the job located?
5. What additional training will I need, if any?
6. What is my career development potential?

Tony then called the number and scheduled his interview for January 10, 1970 at the New York Air Route Traffic Control Center (ARTCC) — whatever that was — on eastern Long Island, N.Y. He made sure he got clear directions on how to get to the location and that he knew the full names of those he was to contact upon arrival. He then went back to reviewing his package and determined how he would answer questions testing his knowledge of all the skills he had listed. He also identified what he would take along with him. Since the ARTCC was nearly 200 miles from his home, Tony took along a friend, Frank — nice to have someone you know for moral support on those long drives — a change of clothes (since Tony didn't know the exact nature of the positions available, he chose a suit and tie for the interview — better to dress up than to dress down, he surmised) in case there might be a delay and the interview would be postponed, a copy of his "package" and a notepad with his questions written on it. Apparently Tony had also been a Boy Scout and knew that being prepared was the key to any successful venture.

The big day came, and Tony arrived at his destination about 30 minutes prior to his interview. Nancy, the receptionist, greeted Tony and his friend at the entrance, showed them into the facility and told them where they could freshen up. She showed Frank to the cafeteria and said he could wait there for Tony.

Tony straightened his tie, brushed out the wrinkles, splashed a bit of water on his face and then took a seat and waited for his interview. Nancy was very helpful and conveyed a sense of informality and ease. Tony noted that this wasn't a "stiff upper lip" kind of environment and that the atmosphere was relaxed. Clearly a very professional environment, but most of the staff seemed comfortable, relaxed and joked easily with one another. Tony noted these behaviors on his pad and thought, "I could like working here."

As he was reviewing his notes and questions Tony was taking slow, deep breaths, and silently repeating a positive affirmation to himself, *"I was successful in my interview because I was prepared and confident."*

Nancy's phone broke the silence. She listened for a minute, said okay, and hung up. She motioned to Tony and said, "You can go in now. Val is ready for you." "Val?" asked Tony. "Mr. Lawrence," said Nancy.

Val greeted Tony, extended his hand and announced, "Hi, I'm Val Lawrence. Welcome to the FAA." During that handshake, Tony introduced himself and said, "Mr. Lawrence, I'm glad to meet you and really appreciate your taking the time to interview me for this position." "Please call me Val," was the response. "Have a seat," Val said. As Tony sat down, he noticed that Val had a copy of his "package" on his desk.

After a few minutes of small talk about Tony's trip and the like, Val said, "Okay, let's get started." Tony agreed and asked if it would be okay if he took some notes during the interview. Val agreed and began to describe the FAA and what the work entailed. It was clear that Val had read and become familiar with Tony's background and qualifications. He asked numerous specific questions concerning the data Tony had listed in his "package" and even asked about some specific pieces of equipment that Tony had worked on while in the Army. As Val described some of the functions required for the positions available, Tony took notes on terminology, industry-specific acronyms and other items with which he was not familiar.

During the interview Tony asked for clarification on all the notes he had taken. After about an hour of this give-and-take, Val took Tony and Frank on a tour of the facility. This tour answered numerous questions and Tony began to see what would be involved with the job and to realize this would be a great place to work. When they returned to Val's office, Fred, one of the supervisors, was waiting for them. Val introduced them and told Fred of Tony's qualifications and that he might be a candidate for employment. Fred pointed to a piece of sophisticated-looking electronic equipment in the corner of Val's office and asked Tony if he knew what it was. There sat a small piece of waveguide with a small dent in one side. Tony had worked with lots of waveguide in the Army and had noted that in his package.

Clearly, Fred was not just a casual observer in this process. It was obvious that he, too, had read Tony's "package" and this was a serious test. Tony realized that any dents in waveguide made it inoperative and said, "Hmm, looks like a piece of broken waveguide to me." Fred said, "Well I'll be damned!" nodded to Val and left. Tony realized that he had passed the test.

Val shook Tony's hand, and said, "I don't know what the outcome will be right now; however, I think you will fit in here just fine. Someone will get back to you within two weeks and let you know."

Tony thanked Val again for his time and for the tour and asked if he should call if he didn't hear anything within those two weeks. Val said, "Sure, but don't worry, you'll hear from us."

Tony and Frank left the facility and returned home. A week later, Tony received a telegram from the FAA offering him a job starting at the highest pay grade for which he qualified. On February 16, 1970, Tony began his career with the FAA. On June 3, 2006, he retired from that same FAA.

As you read through the remainder of this chapter and learn more about the interviewing process, refer to this story and see how Tony addressed the concerns and challenges of the different types of interviews. Then ask yourself, "How would I respond to these challenges? What would my questions be?" Once you find and document those answers, you, too, will be prepared for whatever comes your way, and using your newfound information and skills, you will be able to find a long and successful career as did Tony. Good luck!

INFORMATIONAL INTERVIEWS

The first step is to call agencies in your area and ask to talk with a supervisor who works in your specialty, e.g, administration, technical, computer operations, etc. If an immediate supervisor isn't willing to talk with you in person, ask to talk with someone in the human resources department. Briefly explain to this individual that you are investigating government careers and ask if he/she would be willing to spend 30 minutes talking with you in person about viable federal career paths with the agency.

If you're uncertain whether or not your job skills are needed by an agency, contact the personnel or human resources department.

If an informational interview is granted, take along a signed copy of your employment application or federal résumé and a cover letter describing your desires and qualifications. The informational interview will help you investigate available employment opportunities in many diverse agencies. You will need to identify persons to interview through the methods mentioned above. You don't have to limit your informational interviews strictly to supervisors. Any individual currently employed in a position you find attractive can provide the necessary information. The outcome of these interviews will help you make an objective career decision for specific positions. There is one key element you must stress when requesting an informational interview:

***When asking for the interview, make them aware that you
only desire information and
are not asking for a job.***

This should be brought to their attention immediately after requesting an interview. Many supervisors and employees are willing to talk about their job even when no vacancies exist. These interviews often provide insight into secondary careers and upcoming openings that can be more attractive than what you were originally pursuing.

Place a time limit on the interview. When contacting supervisors, request the interview by following the above guidelines but add that you will only take 30 minutes of their time. Time is a critical resource that must be respected and used wisely. When going for the interview you should be prepared to ask specific questions that will get the information you need. The following questions will help you prepare:

INFORMATIONAL INTERVIEW QUESTIONS

Experience and Background

1. What are the training and educational requirements of this position?

2. How would you suggest that I prepare for a career in this field?

3. What experience is absolutely essential?

4. How did you get started?

5. What do you find most and least enjoyable about this work?

Credentials

How would you rank these items with respect to their importance concerning a position with your agency?

1. Education

2. Special skills

3. Former work experience

4. Personality

5. Organizational knowledge

6. Other (name specific skills)

General Questions

1. What advice would you give to someone interested in this field?

2. How do I find out about available jobs and how they are advertised?

3. Does this agency hire from regional offices or does it hire through the Office of Personnel Management (OPM)?

4. Does this position have career development potential, and if so, what is the highest grade achievable?

5. What are the travel requirements of the job?

6. Is shift work a requirement? If yes, what are the shifts?

Referral

1. As a result of our conversation today, who else would you recommend I speak with?

2. May I use your name when I contact them?

If an interview is not granted: Ask permission to send a résumé or the new optional application forms for their prospective employee file. In many cases agencies do not have direct hire authority. However, if upcoming positions open they can notify you when the job will be advertised. Positions created through these methods bring aboard highly desirable employee prospects under future competitive announcements.

Certain agencies do have direct hire authority. To determine if an agency has this ability you must contact its regional HR or personnel department. Send direct hire agencies a cover letter and application for the prospective employment file. Office addresses and phone numbers can be obtained by calling local area agency offices and asking for the address and phone number of that agency's regional office. You can also use the Agency Directory in Appendix C.

It is hard to imagine the diversity of jobs needed by most agencies. Don't exclude any agency in this process. Most agencies hire a broad spectrum of skills and professions. When going for the interview, dress appropriately for the position applied for. You can expect numerous rejections while pursuing these methods. Don't become discouraged. Good managers, in industry as well as the federal government, are always on the lookout for qualified employees. If you present yourself in a professional manner, demonstrate a good work ethic, and have the appropriate educational background, you will make a connection. Persistence pays off when dealing with the government. Many promising candidates give up prematurely before giving their efforts a chance to work. You must realize that it may take some time for a desirable position to become available.

Most government job openings are first advertised within the agency, and current employees have the first chance to bid for a higher-paying position. If the job can't be filled in-house it is advertised in the private sector by the Office of Personnel Management or in certain cases by the agency itself. These are the jobs you will be bidding on. The reason for going to the private sector is that no qualified in-house bidders applied for the available positions.

EMPLOYMENT INTERVIEWING

There are several different types of interviews you may encounter. You probably won't know in advance which type you will be facing. Below are descriptions of the different types of interviews and what you can expect in each of them.[1]

Types of Interviews

- **Screening Interview**. A preliminary interview either in person or by phone, in which an agency or company representative determines whether you have the basic qualifications to warrant a subsequent interview.

- **Structured Interview**. In a structured interview, the interviewer explores certain predetermined areas using questions which have been written in advance. The interviewer has a written description of the experience, skills and personality traits of an "ideal" candidate. Your experience and skills are compared to specific job tasks. This type of interview is very common and most traditional interviews are based on this format.

- **Unstructured Interview**. Although the interviewer is given a written description of the "ideal" candidate, in the unstructured interview the interviewer is not given instructions on what specific areas to cover.

- **Multiple Interviews**. Multiple interviews are commonly used with professional jobs. This approach involves a series of interviews in which you meet individually with various representatives of the organization. In the initial interview, the representative usually attempts to get basic information on your skills and abilities. In subsequent interviews, the focus is on how you would perform the job in relation to the company's goals and objectives.

  After the interviews are completed, the interviewers meet and pool their information about your qualifications for the job. A variation on this approach involves a series of interviews in which unsuitable candidates are screened out at each succeeding level.

- **Stress Interview**. The interviewer intentionally attempts to upset you to see how you react under pressure. You may be asked questions that make you

---

[1] Excerpted from the Job Search Guide, U.S. Department of Labor.
This excellent guide is available from the Government Printing Office.

uncomfortable, or you may be interrupted when you are speaking. Although it is uncommon for an entire interview to be conducted under stress conditions, it is common for the interviewer to incorporate stress questions as a part of a traditional interview. Examples of common stress questions are provided later in this chapter.

- **Targeted Interview**. Although similar to the structured interview, the areas covered are much more limited. Key qualifications for success on the job are identified and relevant questions are prepared in advance.

- **Situational Interview**. Situations are set up which simulate common problems you may encounter on the job. Your responses to these situations are measured against predetermined standards. This approach is often used as one part of a traditional interview rather than as an entire interview format.

- **Group Interview**. You may be interviewed by two or more agency or company representatives simultaneously. Sometimes one of the interviewers is designated to ask "stress" questions to see how you respond under pressure. A variation on this format is for two or more company representatives to interview a group of candidates at the same time.

NOTE: Many agencies have initiated quality-of-work life and employee involvement groups to build viable labor/management teams and partnerships. In this environment, agencies may require the top applicants to be interviewed by three groups. There are generally three interviews in this process, one by the selection panel and the other two by peer and subordinate groups. All three interview groups compare notes and provide input to the selection committee.

The interview strategies discussed in this chapter can be used effectively in any type of interview you may encounter.

BEFORE THE INTERVIEW

Prepare in advance. The better prepared you are, the less anxious you will be and the greater your chances for success. There is an old saying in the real estate business that value is determined by three things: location, location, location. In interviewing, it's preparation, preparation, preparation.

One very important consideration in your preparation is the role that stress plays in these situations. They say that public speaking is the most stressful situation for the majority of people. Well, interviewing for a career position is a close second, so let's talk a bit about stress and what you can do to ensure that stress works for you rather than against you.

Some level of stress will keep you focused and alert, while chronic stress can be a killer. Having those "butterflies" in your stomach is not a bad thing. If you feel they are getting the best of you, try some of Tony's techniques:

- Take long, slow, deep breaths. Breathe in through your nose for a count of 10, then slowly exhale through your mouth for the same count. Do this repeatedly and watch how much you calm down.

- Repeat to yourself some positive affirmation statements. Remember Tony's? *"I was successful in my interview because I was prepared and confident."* Positive affirmation statements always focus on the outcome, not the approach.

- Stay focused in the present. Don't frighten or alarm yourself with what "might" happen.

- Get comfortable. Avoid sitting on wallets or keys.

- Engage your sense of humor. Laughing releases tension and increases chemicals in your brain that enhance well-being.

- Stay fit! Exercise and eat a healthy diet. Your body cannot cope effectively with stress if it doesn't have the tools (nutrients) it needs. Follow the food guide pyramid.

- Role play. Find someone to role play the interview with you. This person should be someone with whom you feel comfortable and with whom you can discuss your weaknesses freely. The person should be objective and knowledgeable, perhaps a business associate.

- Use a mirror or video camera when you role play to see what kind of image you project.

Assess your interviewing skills

- What are your strengths and weaknesses? Work on correcting your weaknesses, such as speaking rapidly, talking too loudly or softly, and nervous habits such as hands shaking or inappropriate facial expressions.

- Learn the questions that are commonly asked and prepare answers to them. Examples of commonly asked interview questions are provided later in this chapter. Career centers and libraries often have books which include interview questions. Practice giving answers which are brief but thorough.

- Decide what questions you would like to ask and practice politely interjecting them at different points in the interview.

Evaluate your strengths

- Evaluate your skills, abilities and education as they relate to the type of job you are seeking.

- Practice tailoring your answers to show how you meet the federal agency's needs, if you have details about the specific job before the interview.

Assess your overall appearance

- Find out what clothing is appropriate for your occupation. Although some agencies now allow casual attire, acceptable attire for most federal professional positions is conservative.

- Have several sets of appropriate clothing available, since you may have several interviews over a few days.

- Your clothes should be clean and pressed and your shoes polished.

- Make sure your hair is neat, your nails clean and you are generally well groomed.

Research the federal department and agency. The more you know about the agency and the job for which you are applying, the better you will do on the interview. Get as much information as you can before the interview. (See Chapter Three and review Appendices C and D.)

Take along extra copies of your résumé, optional forms, or other appropriate application forms in case the interviewer ask for them. Make sure you bring along the same versions that you originally sent the agency. You may refer to your federal style résumé to complete other application forms such as the OF-306.

Arrive early at the interview. Plan to arrive 10 to 15 minutes early. Give yourself time to find a restroom so you can check your appearance.

It's important to make a good impression from the moment you enter the reception area. Greet the receptionist cordially. Be confident, positive and make eye contact. Introduce yourself and identify why you are there. If you shake hands with the receptionist, provide a firm handshake (don't crush his/her hand). Use appropriate salutations, e.g., Miss Johnson, Mr. Donald, etc. You never know what influence the receptionist has with your interviewer. With a little small talk, you may get some helpful information about the interviewer and the job opening. Remember, you only get one chance to make a positive first impression. Most people — not just interviewers — form their impressions about new acquaintances within the first 30 to 60 seconds of their initial meeting. Use this minute wisely. If you are asked to fill out an application while you're waiting, be sure to fill it out completely and print the information neatly.

DURING THE INTERVIEW

The job interview is usually a two-way discussion between you and a prospective employer. The interviewer is attempting to determine whether you have what the agency needs, and you are attempting to determine if you would accept the job if offered. Both of you will be trying to get as much information as possible in order to make those decisions. Ask your interviewer if you may take notes. (I've never heard of anyone who got a no to this question.) This lets your interviewer know that you are interested in learning and connecting with the process. You will certainly hear some terms or conditions with which you are not familiar. Rather than interrupting your interviewer, jot them down so you can ask the appropriate questions at the first available opportunity.

Don't make negative comments about anyone or anything, including former employers.

The interview that you are most likely to face is a structured interview with a traditional format. It usually consists of three phases. The introductory phase covers the greeting, small talk and an overview of which areas will be discussed during the interview. The middle phase is a question-and-answer period. The interviewer asks most of the questions, but you are given an opportunity to ask questions as well. The closing phase gives you an opportunity to ask any final questions you might have, cover any important points that haven't been discussed and get information about the next step in the process.

Introductory Phase

This phase is very important. You want to make a good first impression and, if possible, get additional information you need about the job and the agency.

- Make a good impression. You only have a few seconds to create a positive first impression which can influence the rest of the interview and even determine whether you get the job.

The interviewer's first impression of you is based mainly on non-verbal clues. The interviewer is assessing your overall appearance and demeanor. When greeting the interviewer, be certain your handshake is firm and that you make eye contact. Address your interviewer by name and thank him/her for the opportunity. Your initial conversation might go something like this: *"Thank you, Miss Henderson, for taking time from your schedule to interview me. I am very interested in learning...(more about your company, this position, etc)...and how I might be able to help you achieve your goals."* Wait for the interviewer to signal you before you sit down.

Once seated, your body language is very important in conveying a positive impression. Find a comfortable position and relax. Lean forward slightly and maintain eye contact with the interviewer. This posture shows that you are interested in what is being said. Smile, nod, and use active listening skills appropriately. There are numerous books available in local libraries on active listening and it would be advisable to do some research in this area. Some of the most common, and most effective, of these skills are quite simple. Saying *"uh-huh," "yes," "I see," "interesting,"* and other acknowledgments let your interviewer know that you are hearing what he/she is saying and are staying "connected" with the flow of the interview.

The use of paraphrasing, at appropriate times, also lets your interviewer know that you are truly hearing what is being discussed. Paraphrasing is another active listening technique where you repeat what you just heard, but put it in your own words. For example, your interviewer may mention that their organization has its technical training facility in Oklahoma City. You might respond with, *"So, I heard you say that based on my skill level, I may have to attend some technical school training courses at your Oklahoma City location?"* This may also generate some additional questions concerning things like the length of training courses, travel reimbursements, etc. Show that you are open and receptive by keeping your arms and legs uncrossed. Avoid keeping your briefcase or your handbag on your lap. Pace your movements so that they are not too fast or too slow. Remain relaxed and confident.

- Get the information you need. If you weren't able to get complete information about the job and the agency or department in advance, you should try to get it as early as possible in the interview. Be sure to prepare your questions in advance. Knowing the following things will allow you to present those strengths and abilities that the employer wants.

- ✎   Why does the company need someone in this position?
- ✎   Exactly what would they expect of you?
- ✎   Are they looking for traditional or innovative solutions to problems?

■ **When to ask questions.** The problem with a traditional interview structure is that your chance to ask questions occurs late in the interview. How can you get the information you need early in the process without making the interviewer feel that you are taking control?

Deciding exactly when to ask your questions is the tricky part. Timing is everything. You may have to make a decision based on intuition and your first impressions of the interviewer. Does the interviewer seem comfortable or nervous, soft-spoken or forceful, formal or casual? These signals will help you to judge the best time to ask your questions.

The sooner you ask the questions, the less likely you are to disrupt the interviewer's agenda. However, if you ask questions too early, the interviewer may feel you are trying to control the interview.

Try asking questions right after the greeting and small talk. Since most interviewers like to set the tone of the interview and maintain initial control, always phrase your questions in a way that leaves control with the interviewer. Perhaps say, *"Please tell me a little more about the job so that I can focus on the information that would be most important to the agency."* If there is no job opening but you are trying to develop one or you need more information about the agency, try saying, *"Please share your insight as to where the company is going so I can focus on those areas of my background that are most relevant."*

You may want to wait until the interviewer has given an overview of what will be discussed. This overview may answer some of your questions or may provide some details that you can use to ask additional questions. Once the middle phase of the interview has begun, you may find it more difficult to ask questions.

Middle Phase

During this phase of the interview, you will be asked many questions about your work experience, skills, education, activities and interests. You are being assessed on how you will perform the job in relation to the agency objectives.

All your responses should be concise. Use specific examples to illustrate your point whenever possible. Although your responses should be prepared in advance so that they are phrased well and effectively, be sure they do not sound rehearsed. Remember that your responses must always be adapted to the present interview. Incorporate any information you obtained earlier in the interview with the responses you had prepared in advance and then answer in a way that is appropriate to the question.

The following are some typical questions, with possible responses:

Question: *"Tell me about yourself."*

Reply:

Briefly describe your experience and background. If you are unsure what information the interviewer is seeking, say, "Are there any areas in particular you'd like to know about?"

Question: *"What is your weakest point?"* (A stress question)

Reply: Mention something that is actually a strength. Some examples are:

   "I'm something of a perfectionist."

   "I'm a stickler for punctuality."

   "I'm tenacious."

Give a specific situation from your previous job to illustrate your point.

Question: *"What is your strongest point?"*

Reply:

   "I work well under pressure."

   "I am organized and manage my time well."

If you have just graduated from college you might say,

   "I am eager to learn, and I don't have to unlearn old techniques."

Give a specific example to illustrate your point.

Question: *"What do you hope to be doing five years from now?"*

Reply:

   "I hope I will still be working here and have increased my level of responsibility based on my performance and abilities."

Question: *"Why have you been out of work for so long?"* (A stress question)

Reply:

   "I spent some time re-evaluating my past experience and the current job market to see what direction I wanted to take."

   "I had some offers but I'm not just looking for another job; I'm looking for a career."

Question: *"What do you know about our agency? Why do you want to work here?"*

Reply:

This is where your research on the agency will come in handy.

"You are a small/large agency and a leading force in government."

"Your agency is a leader in your field and growing."

"Your agency has a superior reputation."

"Your agency has a vision to provide superior service to its customers through teamwork and collaboration, and that matches my value system perfectly. I know that I can help you ensure that vision is a reality."

You might try to get the interviewer to give you additional information about the agency by saying that you are very interested in learning more about its mission, vision, philosophy, goals and objectives (MVP-GO). In doing your research on each prospective employer, find out this information, write it down and take it with you to the interview. Then keep it in your files for future reference. This will help you to focus your response on relevant areas.

Question: *"What is your greatest accomplishment?"*

Reply:

Give a specific illustration from your previous or current job where you saved the company money or helped increase profits. If you have just graduated from college, try to find some accomplishment from your school work, part-time jobs or extra-curricular activities.

Question: *"Why should we hire you?"* (A stress question)

Highlight your background based on the company's current needs. Recap your qualifications, keeping the interviewer's job description in mind. If you don't have much experience, talk about how your education and training prepared you for this opportunity.

Question: *"Why do you want to make a change now?"*

Reply:

"I want to develop my potential."

"The opportunities in my present company are limited."

Question: "Tell me about a problem you had in your last job and how you resolved it."

Reply:

The employer wants to assess your analytical, teamwork, communication and other necessary skills to determine your suitability. Think of a situation you encountered at a previous job. If your work experience is very limited, think of a personal situation. This should be a situation where you experienced a successful outcome. Describe clearly but briefly what you encountered, then describe the steps you took to resolve the problem, implement the solution, create the process, or whatever other action was required. You may need to think about this for a minute or two.

This is an important question and you should prepare for it well in advance of your interview so you are not caught off guard.

Some Questions You Should Ask

- ✎ "What are the agency's current challenges?"
- ✎ "Could you give me a more detailed job description?"
- ✎ "Why is this position open?"
- ✎ "Are there opportunities for advancement?"
- ✎ "To whom would I report?"

Closing Phase

During the closing phase of an interview, you will be asked whether you have any other questions. Check your notes and ask any relevant questions that have not yet been answered. Highlight any of your strengths that have not been discussed. If another interview is to be scheduled, get the necessary information. If this is the final interview, ask when the decision will be made and if/when you may call. As you are leaving, shake hands with your interviewer, make solid eye contact, thank the interviewer by name and say goodbye.

ILLEGAL QUESTIONS

During an interview, you may be asked some questions that are considered illegal. It is illegal for an interviewer to ask you questions related to gender, age, race, religion, national origin or marital status, or to delve into your personal life for information that is not job-related. What can you do if you are asked an illegal question? Take a moment to evaluate the situation. Ask yourself questions like:

- ✎ How uncomfortable has this question made you feel?
- ✎ Does the interviewer seem unaware that the question is illegal?
- ✎ Is this interviewer going to be your boss?

Then respond in a way that is comfortable for you.

If you decide to answer the question, be succinct and try to move the conversation back to an examination of your skills and abilities as quickly as possible. For example, if asked about your age, you might reply, "I'm in my forties, and I have a wealth of experience that would be an asset to your company." If you are not sure whether you want to answer the question, first ask for a clarification of how this question relates to your qualifications for the job. You may decide to answer if there is a reasonable explanation. If you feel there is no justification for the question, you might say that you do not see the relationship between the question and your qualifications for the job and you prefer not to answer it.

AFTER THE INTERVIEW

You are not finished yet. It is important to assess the interview shortly after it is concluded. Following your interview you should:

- Write down the name, phone number, e-mail address, and title (be sure the spelling is correct) of the interviewer.

- Review what the job entails and record what the next step will be.

- Note your reactions to the interview; include what went well and what went poorly.

- Assess what you learned from the experience and how you can improve your performance in future interviews.

Send a thank-you note within 24 hours. Your thank-you note should:

- Be hand-written only if you have very good handwriting. Most people use a word processor to prepare the thank-you note.

- Be on good quality white or cream colored paper.

- Be simple and brief.

- Express your appreciation for the interviewer's time.

- Show enthusiasm for the job.

- Get across that you want the job and can do it.

Here is a sample thank-you letter:

(Current date)

Dear Mr. Adams:

Thanks for taking the time to meet with me this afternoon. I enjoyed the interview and I am excited about the possibility of working for the Treasury Department. I believe that my military background, education, and work experience in law enforcement will be beneficial to your criminal investigation unit. I look forward to hearing from you, and if additional follow-up interviews are necessary just let me know the place and time and I will clear my schedule to attend.

As we agreed, I will call you next Thursday if I don't hear from you beforehand.

Sincerely,

PHONE FOLLOW-UP

If you were not told during the interview when a hiring decision will be made, call after one week.

At that time, if you learn that the decision hasn't been made, find out whether you are still under consideration for the job. Ask if there are other questions the interviewer might have about your qualifications and offer to come in for another interview if necessary. Reiterate that you are very interested in the job.

- If you learn that you did not get the job, try to find out why. You might also inquire whether the interviewer can think of anyone else who might be able to use someone with your abilities, either in another department or at another agency.

- If you are offered the job, you have to decide whether you want it. If you are not sure, thank the employer and ask for several days to think about it. Ask any other questions you might need answered to help you with the decision.

- If you know you want the job and have all the information you need, accept the job with thanks and get the details on when you start. Ask whether the employer will be sending a letter of confirmation, as it is best to have the offer in writing.

Who Gets Hired?

In the final analysis, the agency will hire someone who has the abilities and talents which fulfill its needs. It is up to you to demonstrate that you are the person they want by submitting a comprehensive and thorough application package and by doing well in the interview. Don't leave the interview to chance. Proper preparation can mean the difference between success and failure.

INTERVIEW CHECKLIST

Remember the three rules for a successful interview: 1) Preparation; 2) Preparation; and 3) More Preparation.

☐ Know the type of interview for which you are preparing. Is it informational or for employment?

☐ Make a list of all the questions you need to ask.

☐ Watch your time and don't abuse that privilege.

☐ Dress appropriately and err on the side of caution. It is better to be slightly overdressed than vice versa.

☐ Remember, the only information your interviewer will have about you is what you submitted in your "package." Keep a copy of this data and review it thoroughly prior to your interview.

☐ Create scenarios that you would ask yourself if you were the interviewer and prepare responses. This will prevent you from being caught off guard.

☐ Don't make stuff up! If you don't know the answer to a specific question, say so. Then, if it is an essential question, write it down and ask the interviewer if he or she needs you to call back with the answer.

☐ Incorporate positive body language such as solid eye contact, a firm handshake, proper posture and the like. This conveys a sense of confidence and maturity.

☐ Incorporate the stress management techniques identified in this chapter.

☐ Be positive, persistent and patient. It was nearly nine months from Tony's initial "informational interview" to his "employment interview" with an entirely different agency.

☐ Keep files on all your interviews. You never know when someone may call you back — even if you have already found employment with another agency. Be prepared to follow the opportunities.

☐ Re-read this chapter as often as necessary to comprehend the principles identified here.

☐ Finally, do some research. Topics like stress management, body language, dressing for success, active listening and other "soft skills" are too extensive to cover in this chapter. Numerous volumes are available on these topics in your local libraries and on the Internet. Take the time to read some of these so your tool box will be full.

Good luck, and have a long and fruitful government career.

CHAPTER FIVE
Civil Service Exams

Today, written tests are only required for specific occupations including mail handlers, certain law enforcement occupations, air traffic controllers, foreign service specialists, and a few entry level jobs. The majority — more than 80 percent — of government jobs are filled through a competitive analysis of your background, work experience, and education — not through a written exam. Read the job announcement thoroughly to determine if a test or self-certification of a skill is necessary.

Approximately 80% of government jobs are filled through a comprehensive analysis of your background, work experience, and education, not through a written test.

Mandatory testing for administrative careers was eliminated years ago. OPM and individual agencies advertise professional and administrative job vacancies and interested parties request and receive application material online. Now that most entrance written tests aren't used, applicants typically complete an occupational questionnaire and a federal style résumé or an optional application form. Most agencies want applicants to apply online.

Personnel offices rate applications and generate hiring lists within two to six weeks from the job announcement's closing date. The "Best Qualified" applicants are referred to a selection official for consideration. The occupational questionnaire is discussed in Chapter Six.

CHAPTER OBJECTIVES

✎ How to determine if an exam is required

✎ Review the list of careers with mandatory testing

✎ Understand the differences between a federal and private sector résumé

✎ Clerical and administrative support exams

Notice that I mentioned federal style résumé several times. I emphasize *"federal style"* because a resume in the federal sector is nothing like most private sector one-page résumés. A federal style résumé is highly structured and may contain 43 specific blocks of information as listed in Chapter Six, and the format is standardized. A typical federal style résumé is between three and six pages long and if Knowledge, Skills, Abilities statements are required your résumé could easily reach seven to 10 pages or more. If you submit an improperly formatted résumé it may be rejected or at the very least you may not rate "Best Qualified" for the job.

Most people who first approach the federal sector are taken aback by the amount of time, energy, and paperwork required to apply for jobs. Applicants who put the extra effort and time into compiling their own unique federal style résumé and tailor it to the job announcement are more likely to succeed.

CAREERS WITH MANDATORY TESTING

Some occupations require specialized testing and assessments. The tests are used to validate physical and mental ability and skills required for the position. The exams vary in length from several hours to half a day or more. You will find required exams in law enforcement, the Foreign Service, postal workers, air traffic control specialists, and other related occupations. See the chapters on law enforcement and the Postal Service for more information. The information listed below provides a brief summary of the major occupations that require written exams and a list of their web sites where you can go for additional information.

Air Traffic Control Specialist — www.faa.gov/training_testing/schools/

Applicants for the Federal Aviation Administration's (FAA) Air Traffic Control positions must graduate from an accredited Air Traffic Certified Training Institution (AT-CTI). AT-CTI schools send names of students enrolled in their program to the FAA. There is an AT-CTI database of names for tracking purposes until graduation and recommendation. After enrollment in an AT-CTI program, students take **FAA's authorized pre-employment test**. This test determines an individual's aptitude to become an air traffic control specialist.

Border Patrol — www.cbp.gov/

The Department of Homeland Security (DHS) employs thousands of Border Patrol agents. Applicants must pass **The U.S. Border Patrol Logical Reasoning Test** to be considered for positions. The test evaluates how well applicants can read, understand, and apply critical thinking skills to factual situations. A study guide is available at www.cbp.gov/xp/cgov/careers/study_guides/guides_bp/. Agents must read and study laws, legal commentary, and regulations. Applicants who successfully pass the entrance screening exam and are hired will receive extensive training at their Border Patrol Academy. A free 60-page study guide is available on the Web site. Border Patrol vacancies are advertised at www.usajobs.gov.

Central Intelligence Agency — www.cia.gov/careers/

All applicants must successfully complete a thorough medical and psychological exam, a polygraph interview and an extensive background investigation. U.S. citizenship is required. Other proficiency tests may be required to verify language skills, etc.

Federal Bureau of Investigation — www.fbijobs.gov/

In order to apply for a job, you must first register online. After registering, you can apply to any vacancy currently posted. When applying to a vacancy, carefully read and respond to the application questions.

The application process can take up to one year to complete depending upon an applicant's qualifications and the current hiring needs of the FBI. It includes passing a written test, interview, polygraph examination, physical fitness test, physical, and a thorough background investigation.

Foreign Service Written Exam — www.careers.state.gov/

Application procedures for employment with the Department of State vary according to your career choice. Foreign Service Officers, for example, must pass the **Foreign Service Officer Selection Process**. Students must also meet certain criteria and deadlines for the program they choose to enter.

Internal Revenue Service — www.jobs.irs.gov/

Various positions with the IRS require assessment tests. IRS agents must complete an accounting assessment process that takes approximately four to five hours. It is composed of an accounting assessment and an interview with a panel of experienced Revenue Agent managers.

Mail Handlers USPS — www.usps.com/employment

The Postal Service uses **Test 473 for Major Entry-Level Jobs** exam. The exam is also referred to as the 473 Battery Exam. All mail carriers must pass this exam with a score of 70 or higher. Check for exam dates in your area on the USPS employment Web site and use the study guide in the book titled *"Post Office Jobs,"* 5th edition.

Secret Service — www.secretservice.gov/

The Secret Service is a federal law enforcement agency with headquarters in Washington, D.C. and more than 150 offices throughout the United States. The agency is mandated by Congress to carry out dual missions: protection of the nation's leaders and extensive criminal investigations. Special Agent applicants must pass the Treasury Enforcement Agents (TEA) written examination.

Transportation Security Agency — www.tsa.gov/join/index.shtm

TSA jobs require U.S. citizenship and successful completion of a full background investigation. In addition, persons interested in security officer positions must pass a medical examination, be able to read, speak, and write English, and pass a physical ability test, a drug and alcohol screening, and an **aptitude test**.

U.S. Customs — www.ice.gov/careers/

Some Immigration and Custom Enforcement (ICE) entry-level law enforcement occupations require applicants to pass a written test as part of the application process. Two of these tests include the **ICE Immigration Enforcement Agent Test** and the **ICE Special Agent Test**. Test preparation manuals are provided on the Web site to assist prospective applicants with sample questions, test-taking tips and other guidance.

CLERICAL TESTS

Clerical and administrative support written exams were used to measure the clerical and verbal abilities needed to design, organize, and use a filing system, organize effectively the clerical process in an office, make travel, meeting and conference arrangements, locate and assemble information for reports and briefings, compose non-technical correspondence, be effective in oral communication, and use office equipment.

Most agencies choose to use the occupational questionnaire and self certification instead of the written clerical test. Clerical tests and other written exams were made optional by OPM years ago. Applicants, for the most part today, complete an occupational questionnaire, submit a federal style résumé, and self certify typing speed.

In addition to meeting experience or education requirements in Table 5-1, applicants for clerical and administrative positions must show possession of the skills listed in Table 5-2. Applicants may meet these requirements by presenting a certificate of proficiency from a school or other organization, self-certify their proficiency, or in rare cases pass the appropriate written performance test. Agencies may verify proficiency skills of self-certified applicants by administering performance tests as well.

Read the job announcement's "How to Apply" section to determine what is required and submit your application prior to the closing date. The key is to be rated "Best Qualified." Prepare a federal style résumé that rating officials can easily determine that you possess the required education, skills and work experience to be effective in the position. Follow the guidance in Chapter Six to prepare your résumé.

TABLE 5-1
QUALIFICATION REQUIREMENTS

For Clerk Typist positions:

GRADE	GENERAL EXPERIENCE		EDUCATION	PROFICIENCY
GS-2	3 months	OR	High school or equivalent	40 wpm typing
GS-3	6 months	OR	1 year above high school	40 wpm typing
GS-4	1 year	OR	2 years above high school	40 wpm typing

For Clerk Stenographer positions:

GRADE	GENERAL EXPERIENCE		EDUCATION	PROFICIENCY
GS-3	6 months	OR	High school or equivalent	40 wpm typing
GS-4	1 year	OR	2 years above high school	40 wpm typing
GS-5	2 years	OR	4 years above high school	40 wpm typing

For all other clerical and administrative support positions covered:

GRADE	GENERAL EXPERIENCE		EDUCATION
GS-2	3 months	OR	High school or equivalent
GS-3	6 months	OR	1 year above high school
GS-4	1 year	OR	2 years above high school

Some clerical and administrative support positions also require typing and/or stenography proficiency. If the title has a parenthetical of O/A or Office Automation, it will require the incumbent to type 40 WPM.

General Experience

High school graduation or the equivalent may be substituted for experience at the GS-2 level for all listed occupations except Clerk-Stenographer, where it may be substituted for experience at the GS-3 level. Equivalent combinations of successfully completed education and experience requirements may be used to meet total experience requirements at grades GS-5 and below. Table 5-3 lists the positions and grades covered under the Clerical and Administrative Support Positions test.

TABLE 5-2
PROFICIENCY REQUIREMENTS

Clerk-Typist, Office Automation Clerk/Assistant, Clerk-Stenographer, Data Transcriber, and Positions with Parenthetical Titles of (Typing), (Office Automation), (Stenography), or (Data Transcription).[1]

In addition to meeting experience or education requirements, applicants for these positions must show possession of the following skills. Applicants may meet these requirements by passing the performance test, presenting a certificate of proficiency from a school or other organization authorized by the Office of Personnel Management local office, or by self- certifying their proficiency. Performance test results and certificates of proficiency are acceptable for three years. Agencies may verify proficiency skills of self-certified applicants by administering performance test.

- Clerk-Typist, GS-2/4; Office Automation Clerk/ Assistant (any grade); (Typing) (any grade); and (Office Automation) (any grade):
  - 40 words per minute typing speed

- Data Transcriber, GS-2/4; and (Data Transcription) (any grade):
  - skill in operating an alphanumeric data transcribing machine,
  - or 20 words per minute typing speed 1 for GS-2 transcription duties
  - or 25 words per minute typing speed 1 for GS-3 and GS-4 transcription duties

- Clerk-Stenographer, GS-3/4:
  - 40 words per minute typing speed 1 and
  - 80 words per minute dictation speed 2

- Clerk-Stenographer, GS-5:
  - 40 words per minute typing speed 1 and
  - 20 words per minute dictation speed 2

- (Stenography) (any grade):
  - 40 words per minute typing speed1 and either
  - 80 words per minute dictation speed2 for GS-3 and GS-4 stenographic duties
  - 20 words per minute dictation speed2 for GS-5 stenographic duties

---

[1] Group Coverage Qualification Standards for Clerical and Administrative Support Positions

CHAPTER SIX
Completing Your Employment Application

This chapter guides you through the federal application process. Unlike the private sector, applicants must submit detailed federal-style résumés and, in some cases, include replies to occupational questionnaires, and Knowledge, Skills, and Abilities (KSA) statements.

It is misleading to assume that a standard résumé will land you a job.

Most federal applications are compiled and completed online; in fact, many agencies prefer that applicants use this method. However, some agencies will only accept hard-copy application packages by mail, fax, or in person. Each federal vacancy announcement will specify its submission requirements.

This chapter will also help individuals assess and evaluate job announcements and write a targeted federal-style résumé using the guidance and sample résumé formats provided.

CHAPTER OBJECTIVES

✎ Required federal résumé information and format

✎ How to write a headline-style résumé

✎ Understanding federal job announcements

✎ Review sample résumés and formatting techniques

✎ Understanding narratives, occupational questionnaires, and KSAs

✎ How to apply for Senior Executive Service (SES) positions

I personally reviewed and rated hundreds of federal applications during my 35-plus years of federal service and participated in many interview and selection panels. I was also a rating official for select occupations for our organization and can tell you from first-hand experience that many highly qualified applicants never made the cut because they didn't devote the time or effort to properly complete their application packages. The old saying still stands, especially in government:

> The job isn't completed until the
> paperwork is done — and
> **DONE RIGHT**

I asked Barbara Adams to assist with this new edition to provide the most up-to-date application information available. Hiring reform dramatically changed the federal recruitment process in 2010. The hiring reform initiatives are presented in Chapter Three and outline the many changes that you must be aware of to achieve a "Best Qualified" rating.

Barbara is the President and CEO of CareerPro Global, Inc. (CPG), founded in 1986, one of the fastest-growing civilian, military, and federal career management services worldwide. Barbara and the CPG staff contributed the resume samples for this new edition and describe hiring reform in a logical and easy-to-understand fashion.

> Tailor your application to the job
> vacancy to which you are applying
> to improve your chances of earning
> the "Best Qualified" ranking.

To gain federal employment, candidates must be aware of two very specific strategies:

First, they must read the entire vacancy announcement and the position description if available. All too often, applicants transitioning from the military or private sector to the federal government do not read the entire announcement. Rather, they look at only the salary and the job description; if they like what they read, they decide to apply.

*R*ead the entire vacancy announcement or position description.

Many of those same people end up disappointed when, during an initial consultation, they realize that other mandatory elements were overlooked in their haste to find federal employment — elements they're unable to fulfill.

We'll discuss these elements in more detail later in this chapter to help you avoid those pitfalls.

Further, in reading the entire announcement, you will gain an up-front understanding of what supporting documents are required for the announcement. In many cases, we have seen candidates — who were perfectly qualified for a job — end up being rejected by the government because they failed to include a document requested as part of the *How to Apply* section of the announcement.

REMEMBER: READ, REREAD, AND READ AGAIN THE ENTIRE VACANCY ANNOUNCEMENT

Second, candidates must tailor their résumé to the position description or the vacancy announcement. The federal government does not want to hear that an applicant thinks he/she can do the job; rather, the government is looking for **specific examples that demonstrate that he/she can do the job**. For example, being self-taught in setting up a home com-puter network and having successfully set up one in a home is not the same as setting up a Local Area Network (LAN) for a multi-location agency spread over a 500-mile radius.

When tailoring your résumé to a specific job description or vacancy announcement, it is important to mirror what the announcement is looking for, as best as possible. There is no such thing as "too much information" — the more examples of your success in fulfilling the job description you can provide in accomplishment-focused statements, the higher your application package will be rated.

A federal style résumé is completely different from the simple one-page private sector résumé. There are over 40 specific informational data elements required and much of it repeats for each work experience. Before attempting to complete your résumé online, review the samples in this chapter and use the next section to complete your résumé. You must include all requested information and forms, and answer occupational questionnaires if required in the job announcement.

When you complete your résumé online read the instructions carefully.

I suggest writing your federal résumé using a word processor program prior to attempting to post it online. Some agencies still require hard copy submissions, and this way you can produce both a paper hard copy and electronic format. You will be able to spell check your résumé and you will have time to compose coherent work histories tailored to the job announcement or position description without time limits. To submit your application online simply copy and paste each section from your draft into the online résumé builder.

This process can dramatically improve your résumé, resulting in higher ratings, and you will be able to keep your résumé updated on your desktop. When you bid on other jobs in the same or similar occupational group you may be able to simply change the job announcement number and title and send it in. However, review each job announcement carefully. Even occupations in the same job series within the same agency can have significantly different requirements, and you must tailor your résumé to those criteria to improve your chances.

ASSISTANCE

You can write a professional federal style résumé using the guidance presented in this Chapter if you have the time and inclination to do so. It may not be easy, but it is the key to federal employment. Those who don't have the time or inclination to write their own application can get professional assistance. CareerPro Global (CPG) combines several decades of industry-writing experience with the most advanced technology to produce job-winning presentations for their clients, from entry-level to Senior Executive Service (SES), within or aspiring to work within the federal government. CPG has assisted more than 50,000 clients to apply for federal jobs.

If you decide that you need additional assistance writing your application you can request a free initial consultation by mentioning that you heard about CPG *in The Book of U.S. Government Jobs*, call 1-800-471-9201 to talk with a consultant about having them write a professional federal style résumé for you. You can also submit an online request for assistance at www.federaljobs.net/resume.htm.

REQUIRED INFORMATION

It is misleading to assume that a standard private sector résumé will land you a job with Uncle Sam. Most résumés are loosely structured and simply introduce the applicant to the company. Follow the guidance in this chapter to write successful applications and résumés for the job you want in government. The application is your first introduction to your potential new employer and one of the keys to successfully landing a federal job. You must write a professional federal style résumé and develop job search strategies that work. This book will help you achieve those goals.

> If your application or résumé doesn't include all the information that is requested in the job vacancy announcement, your application may be rejected.

In addition to information requested in the job vacancy announcement, your application or résumé **MUST** contain the following information:[1]

JOB INFORMATION

❑   Announcement number, title and grade(s) of the job for which you are applying.

PERSONAL INFORMATION

❑   Full name, mailing address *(with Zip code)* and day and evening phone numbers.

❑   Social Security number — Some agencies ask applicants to only list the last four digits of their Social Security number on federal résumés. Read the job announcement to determine what is required for the job you are applying for.

❑   Country of citizenship *(most federal jobs require United States citizenship)*.

❑   Veterans' Preference

✓   If you served on active duty in the U.S. military and were separated under honorable conditions, you may be eligible for Veterans' Preference. To receive preference if your service began after October 15, 1976, you must have a Campaign Badge, Expeditionary Medal, or a service-connected disability.

✓   To claim Veterans' Preference, you must include proof of your eligibility, such as a DD-214, Certificate of Release, or discharge from active duty or other proof.

❑   Reinstatement eligibility *(former federal employees must attach a SF-50 proof of their career or career-conditional status)*.

✔   Highest federal civilian grade held *(also give job series and dates held)*.

---

[1] Reprinted from OPM brochure OF 510

EDUCATION

❏   High school

✔   Name, city, and state *(Zip code if known)*

✔   Date of diploma or GED

❏   Colleges and universities

✔   Name, city, and state *(Zip code if known)*

✔   Majors

✔   Type and year of any degrees received *(if no degree, show total credits earned and indicate whether semester or quarter hours).*

❏   Send a copy of your college transcript only if the job vacancy announcement requests it.

WORK EXPERIENCE

❏   Give the following information for your paid and non-paid work experience related to the job for which you are applying. *(Do not send job descriptions.)*

✔   Job title *(include series and grade if federal job)*

✔   Duties and accomplishments

✔   Employer's name and address

✔   Supervisor's name and phone number

✔   Starting and ending dates (month and year)

✔   Average hours worked per week

✔   Base salary (do not include bonuses, etc.); indicate if salary is annual, monthly, weekly, or hourly.

❏   Indicate whether the agency may contact your current supervisor. If you are granting permission for an agency to contact a current or former supervisor, please include a valid telephone number. If you don't have a phone number or if the company is no longer in business, leave this area blank.

OTHER QUALIFICATIONS

❑   **Job-related** training courses *(title and year)*.

❑   **Job-related** skills; for example, other languages, computer software/hardware, tools, machinery, typing speed.

❑   **Job-related** certificates and licenses *(current only)*.

❑   **Job-related** honors, awards, and special accomplishments; for example, publications; memberships in professional or honor societies; leadership activities; public speaking; and performance awards. *(Give dates, but do not send documents unless requested.)*

AGENCY FORMS

In the past you had the option of using the *federal style résumé* or the *"Optional Application for Federal Employment"* OF-612 form. Most jobs now require at least partial online résumé submission using agency résumé builder software.

If you use the OF-612 form to apply for a job you will discover that it only includes space to enter work history from your current and previous employer. **Don't stop there**. To earn a rating as high as possible, include all related work experience as far back as 10 years or longer if necessary, including your military time. Many applicants do not add supplemental sheets to include related work experience that can earn them a "Best Qualified" rating for the job.

The government also uses the *"Declaration for Federal Employment,"* OF-306 form to collect information on conduct and suitability and also on other matters. Agencies have the option of asking applicants to complete this form at any time during the hiring process, and once selected for a position it is required. Generally, only the final few applicants, who have a good chance of receiving a job offer, would complete this form. The OF-306 warns applicants of the consequences of submitting fraudulent information, and by signing it you are certifying the accuracy of your application. Fraudulent applications are a basis for immediate dismissal.

You can download copies of the OF-612 form at http://federaljobs.net. All the information listed on the OF-612 is recommended for inclusion on federal style résumés.

Agency-specific Forms

When using an electronic application system, or for unique occupations with highly specialized requirements, agency-specific forms may be required. They are needed to address special qualifications necessary for the position. In addition, agency-specific questions are permitted to cover areas unique to certain agencies

*M*ost agencies collect this same data through online questionnaires.

or positions and therefore are not included on the optional forms or résumé. Read the job announcement section titled *"How to Apply"* to determine exactly what forms are required — typically a *résumé* or standard forms — and answer mandatory screening questions, KSAs or Occupational Questionnaires.

Computer Generated Applications

USAJOBs sponsored by OPM at www.usajobs.gov offers a comprehensive online résumé builder with online registration. Many agencies direct applicants to OPM's site to register and submit required application material. Other agencies use their own online résumé builder programs such as the National Science Foundation's *eRecruit* site or the Department of Homeland Security's *COAST* system used by the U.S. Coast Guard. In most cases you don't have an option except for reasonable accommodation that must be coordinated through the hiring agency for certain disabilities.

Take advantage of these services. However, it is best to know their limitations. They don't help you compose your work histories or answer occupational questionnaires. They will take the input you provide but the content is up to you. The more time and effort that you put into composing your résumé and tailoring it to the job announcement's required duties and specialized experience, the better chance you have of landing the job. Draft your résumé offline as suggested earlier in this chapter to produce a professional, complete, and well written application tailored to the job announcement.

The Federal Résumé and Format Types

As previously mentioned, the "constant" in applying for any federal vacancy announcement is the federal résumé. A federal résumé requires more than 40 specific blocks of data, whereas a civilian résumé covers the bare basics, such as employment and education history. Here are some other basic differences between a civilian and basic federal résumé.

Differences Between Civilian and Federal Résumés		
Criteria	**Civilian Résumé**	**Federal Résumé**
Length	1-3 pages	3-5+ pages, not including supplemental data
Compliance Information	Not applicable	Required, such as employer address, phone number, supervisor, salary, etc.
Social Security Number	Not required	Required
Education and Dates	Dates not required	Required
Employment Objective	Yes	No

Federal Résumé Formats

CPG observed that one of the biggest mistakes they see clients make is that they try to use a "one-size-fits-all" approach with their federal résumé. By this, we mean that we'll prepare a federal résumé that meets the Army's CPOL system character count requirements, only to receive a communication from the client in distress because he/she is having trouble loading his/her data into the USAJobs.gov system due to the different formatting required.

While all federal résumés typically require the same information, here are some common formats you might encounter, along with the significant character count requirements in order to file your application successfully online:

USAJobs

www.USAJobs.gov

- Overall Length: 30,000 characters

- Work Experience: 3,000 characters per work experience

- Education (includes relevant course work, licensures, and certifications): 2,000 characters to describe course work

- Job-Related Training: 2,000 characters

- Professional Publications: 2,000 characters

- Additional Information: 22,000 characters; enter job-related honors, awards, leadership activities, skills, and professional profile. KSAs may be copied and pasted into this field, depending on the announcement's instructions.

> Candidates may store up to five separate résumés for use on the USAJobs.gov site.

Application Manager

www.applicationmanager.gov

Application Manager was introduced on January 28, 2007 and is a separate system from USAJobs. Application Manager provides federal job seekers with a one-stop place for them to file all of their application materials, track their application status, and get instant access to communications from the hiring agency.

> While most every government job can technically be accessed in the Application Manager via its unique control number (found at the bottom of every vacancy announcement), it is important to follow the instructions in the *"How to Apply"* section of the vacancy announcement and to use the corresponding application system specified by the agency.

U.S. Navy and Marine Corps Civilian Jobs: CHART

chart.donhr.navy.mil

- Overall Length: Five pages, excluding the Additional Data Sheet; no maximum character length

- Work Summary: Six different work experiences; up to 7,500 characters for each (five-page maximum if applying with a hard copy)

- Professional Training and Education: 5,000 characters

- Professional Licenses and Certificates: 1,500 characters

- Performance Ratings, Awards, Honors, and Recognitions: 1,500 characters

- Other Information: List any information relevant to your career goal(s). Include publications, language proficiencies, memberships in professional organizations or honor societies, memberships in Acquisition Professional Community (APC), leadership activities, etc.: 7,000 characters

- Campaign badges and/or expeditionary medals received: 300 characters

The **CHART RESUMIX** format is in the process of being phased out and is expected to be obsolete by the end of 2011 in favor of the USAJobs résumé builder.

U.S. Army Civilian Jobs: Civilian Personnel Online (CPOL)

acpol.army.mil/employment/

- Overall Length: 20,000 characters or 6 pages, excluding the Supplemental Data information.

- Work Experience: 12,000 characters

- Education: 2,000 characters

- Additional Information (training, licenses, certifications, awards, etc.): 6,000 characters

- Cover letter: 1500 characters

- Users only get ONE version of their résumé to submit to all vacancies. You must wait 24 hours for the system to update to include recent changes.

> **Important:** Do not use quotation marks, ellipses (…), or dashes (--). If you enter a single dash, it must not have any spaces following or proceeding it and it must have a preceding and following character (e.g. "self-starter").

Below is an example of an error message you might receive from the CPOL system when you attempt to preview your résumé:

You entered the character "-" located in the phrase

"MM/DD/YYYY - MM/DD/YYYY"

List of allowable characters:

[A-Z],[a-z],[0-9],[comma],~!@#$%^&*()-_+={[}]|\<>?/.`

These errors will need to be corrected before you can finalize posting your CPOL résumé.

AVUE Digital Services

www.avuedigitalservices.com

- Overall Length: N/A

- Work History: 4,000 characters; as many jobs as necessary

- Additional Information: unlimited characters; enter performance appraisals, leadership activities, and special skills not covered elsewhere

Other Federal Résumé Formats

- *Federal Bureau of Investigation* **(FBI)**. The FBI Jobs character limitation for résumés is 16,000 characters and spaces total, or approximately eight, single-spaced pages of text. The candidate should include the following information, in order:

  ▸ Contact Data

  ▸ Education (chronologically arranged, starting with high school)

  ▸ Employment History (job title and grade level, if it was a federal job; duties and accomplishments; employer's name and address;

supervisor's name and telephone number; starting and ending dates, month and year; hours worked per week; and salary)

- ▸ Other Qualifications: Include such items as job-related training courses, job-related skills (e.g., typing speed), computer software/hardware skills, foreign language proficiency, job-related honors, awards, special accomplishments, publications, memberships in professional or honor societies, leadership activities, and performance awards

- ■ *Federal Aviation Administration* **(FAA)**. The FAA uses the Automated Staffing Application Program (ASAP) for the majority of its vacancy announcements.

  - ▸ The ASAP system is very similar to an online questionnaire, in which users will select the answers to each question and also copy and paste employment and education information from their résumé into the available blocks.

  - ▸ Work descriptions and KSAs should not exceed 4,000 characters per block.

- ■ *Central Intelligence Agency* **(CIA)**

www.cia.gov/careers/jobs/submit-résumé/index.html

  - ▸ Overall Length: N/A

  - ▸ Skills/Professional Licenses and Certifications: 1,000-character limit

  - ▸ Work Description: 1,000-character limit per position (three positions)

  - ▸ Overseas Experience: 1,000-character limit per position (two regions)

  - ▸ Military Experience: 1,000-character limit; include any special qualifications or certifications

- ■ *Defensive Information Systems Agency* **(DISA)**

www.disa.mil/careers/index.html

  - ▸ Work Experience: List five to eight years of relevant experience

  - ▸ Total Length: Five pages, plus one Supplemental Data page

Sample USAJobs.gov Résumé Format

WORK EXPERIENCE

Employer Name
Employer City/Town, State/Province
United States
Job Title
Pay Plan-Series-Grade (if federal civilian)

MM/YYYY to MM/YYYY or Present
$XX,000 per year
Average hours per week: XX
Supervisor: Name (if contact is Yes)
Phone: (only if contact answer is Yes)

→ DUTIES: Brief description of company, duties, and responsibilities.
→ ACCOMPLISHMENTS: List any significant accomplishments made.

EDUCATION

School Name
School City/Town, State/Province
United States
Degree/Level Attained
Earned (include if no degree completed)
Completion Date: MM/YYYY

Major:
Minor:
GPA: (Only list if 3.0 or higher)
XX Semester [or Quarter] Credits
Honors (if applicable)

RELEVANT COURSEWORK, LICENSURES, AND CERTIFICATIONS:

(List courses relevant to this school/program and that might correspond with your potential job duties. For example, if you are applying for a GS-2210 Network Administrator, be sure to include courses such as Introduction to Networking, Networking Basics, etc. Only list licenses obtained from this program, e.g., a nursing license. If you went to an individual program to obtain a license, e.g. a CPA, list that in Additional Information.)

JOB-RELATED TRAINING:

(List any programs you took that are job-related. These can include military training programs, one-day seminars, conferences, etc. that did not carry any course credit or count toward a degree or certificate program.)

RELATED INFORMATION

→ REFERENCES: (One reference required; we suggest that it be a professional reference. Include reference name and title, employer, phone and/or e-mail, and reference type.)
→ AFFILIATIONS: (Job-related only and only current affiliations.)
→ PROFESSIONAL PUBLICATIONS: (Articles, books, etc.)

ADDITIONAL INFORMATION

→ Professional Summary
→ Career Highlights
→ Awards
→ Military Experience

→ Professional Licenses
→ Professional Training
→ Affiliations

Sample Army CPOL Résumé Format:

WORK EXPERIENCE:

Company Name, MM/DD/YYYY to MM/DD/YYYY, Job Title
City, ST, United States
Supervisor: Supervisor Name, XXX-XXX-XXXX, Contact: Yes
XX-XXXX-XX [Federal Pay Plan if applicable], $XX,000 per year, XX hrs per week

→ DUTIES: Brief description of company, duties, and responsibilities.
→ ACCOMPLISHMENTS: List any significant accomplishments made.

EDUCATION:

College/University [OR use one of these other headings: High School, GED, Vocational, Technical]
College Name, MM/DD/YYYY to MM/DD/YYYY
City, State, United States
Degree, Major: Name; Minor: Name
GPA: X.XX, Sem Hrs: XXX [OR use Qtr Hrs, or briefly explain other system]
Courses completed and number of credit hours per course

ADDITIONAL INFORMATION:

→ Professional Summary
→ Career Highlights
→ Awards
→ Military Experience
→ Professional Licenses
→ Professional Training
→ Affiliations

Writing a Headline-Style Résumé Format

CareerPro Global, Inc. developed the Headline-Style Résumé Format in 1990 to assist veterans returning from Operations Desert Shield and Desert Storm. By utilizing the Headline-Style Résumé Format, CPG's writing team was able to best describe an area of expertise held by a veteran in terms that civilian employers could understand through the use of KEYWORDS and EXPERIENCE.

CPG then adapted the Headline-Style Résumé Format for all federal résumé applications in 1995 when the SF-171 was eliminated, and regular paper federal résumés and RESUMIX systems were launched. Today, we use the Headline-Style Résumé Format on all federal job applications to draw attention to specific areas of expertise a client holds and to assist federal hiring managers when analyzing applications for specific expertise and keywords. Federal Human Resources (HR) professionals have welcomed CPG's Headline-Style Résumé Format for years, and our federal applications have earned thousands of job candidate interviews leading to job offers.

Why Use the Headline-Style Résumé Format?

Human Resource (HR) professionals, who are generally the first people to screen all incoming résumés and applications use technology to their advantage today. In the past, they would have to read every application to identify the best job candidates.

CPOL and CHARTS Resumix systems optically scan résumés searching for keywords and phrases listed in the vacancy announcement. The headline format is an easy and effective way to ensure keywords and phrases are identified in Resumix systems. In other résumé building systems such as USAJobs and Application Manager the headline format assists HR representatives identify relevant keywords and phrases in your application. In most cases today, applications are reviewed by HR specialists not scanned by a computer; the headline method helps HR specialist quickly find relevant keywords and phrases in your résumé.

In the early stages of evaluation, even the most qualified applicants can be summarily rejected based upon the words they used to describe their experience.

For example, put yourself in the shoes of the HR/Hiring Manager. What will they look for in your résumé? What specific keywords are in the announcement? What keywords best exemplify your strengths and experience?

If your goal is to be an aircraft mechanic, important keywords might be hydraulics, airframe and power plant, structural repair, operational testing, inspections, or the names of specific tools and equipment used in that profession. Less-relevant keywords might be budget preparation, office automation equipment, or strategic planning.

Keep the announcement and your goals in sight at all times, and resist the temptation to highlight non-relevant skills, even if they sound important within the résumé. Only skills, knowledge, and abilities that are relevant to the specific position will be given credit and help qualify you for the job.

A résumé is only as good as the words and phrases used to describe a person's duties, accomplishments, and contributions to the employers they serve. Keep it action-oriented and interesting. Show results, especially the individual value of what you bring to a prospective job or organization, again, in the context of the announcement.

Before: The "BIG BLOCK"

The following represents the first style of federal résumé. All of the text flows together and it is difficult making heads or tails of the compilation. The transition to the headline style made it easier to differentiate critical résumé content, duties and responsibilities.

05/2002 to Present; 40-60 hrs/week; Brigade SR Electronic Systems Maintenance Technician, CW5/W05; $6,311.10/MO; Promoted to W5 Nov 99; U.S. Army, 1st Signal Brigade, Yongsan, South Korea, APO AP 96205-5271; MAJ Edwin Nall, 011-822-7913-4979 and/or GS-13 Gerald Zentner, 011-822-6352-3120; May Contact. Maintenance Branch Chief, Brigade S4 Senior Maintenance Technical Advisor/Subject Matter Expert with HQ, NETCOM/9th ASC, 8th U.S. Army (EUSA), AMC CECOM, and DoA staff, Team Chief of S4 Command Logistics Review Team, and Commander's SR Warrant Officer Advisor for the Army's largest Signal Brigade and Combat Service Support (CSS) section. Directly supervise SR Warrant Officer, two SR Non-Commissioned Officers (NCOs), one Korean national, and one DoA civilian. Manage maintenance support for two signal battalions, two strategic signal battalions, and five separate reporting units. Develop and implement policies and procedures to improve maintenance capabilities. Train and develop electronics maintenance supervisors of all levels in achieving equipment operational readiness objectives. Credited with flawless transfer of 87 signal systems (valued at $12.5M) during the 307th Signal Battalion's transformation to an Integrated Theatre Signal Battalion (ITSB). Successfully lobbied for transfer of $428 of critical repair parts from Bosun Industrial to C-E Division of Materiel Support Center, Korea (MSC-K), reducing turnaround of Tactical Satellite (TACSAT) systems submitted to General Support Repair Program (GSRP) by 35%. Procured necessary equipment gratis; "scrounged" ten 18K BTU Environmental Control Units (ECUs) valued at $50,000 as spares for critical communication assemblages as well as automation assets from NETCOM exceeding $200K. Requested and received 43 items from MSRA to fill shortages, saving $284,000. Persuaded EUSA G4 to add 1st Signal Brigade to GUIL HMMWV Services Contract with Labor Cost Sharing Funds. Driving force behind 92% operational readiness rate for brigade's ground maintenance fleet consisting of 1,100+ vehicles, trailers, and generators. Improved maintenance procedures by conducting on-site visits for brigade units, resulting in the selection of three 1st Signal Brigade units as finalists of the NETCOM FY04 Army Award for Maintenance Excellence competition. Coordinated a gratis lateral transfer of two $63,000 60KW generators from AMC to NETCOM to fill critical shortages in units deploying to Afghanistan. Arranged CECOM AND TBAD's provision of $1.3+ of gratis depot-level maintenance support assets. Pursued restoration of $216,000 of missing credits from CECOM/AMC. Initiated brigade's first-ever Logistics Conference attended by 200+ logisticians. Commended by NETCOM G4 for strong brigade maintenance program. Negotiated $100,000 annual Support Agreement between CECOM and 1st Signal Brigade for in-country support of 100 Environmental Control Units for key communication systems. Obtained 160+ items of test, measurement, and diagnostic equipment valued at $1.8M+. Driving force behind EUSA's receipt of Special Repair Authority for the AN.TSC-85/93 Satellite System. Revamped the Command Logistics Inspection (CLI) program to improve overall logistical posture. Reduced non-mission-capable communications systems through the sub-system management technique. Applied extensive knowledge in TMDE to facilitate the repair of six out of seven communication sets declared non-repairable; efforts resulted in a savings of $130,000+.

    This is a lot of material to read through; it's very difficult to read and is not very organized. Now, let's see how the Headline Format pulls it all together into a nice, neat little package:

After: The "HEADLINE-STYLE"Résumé Format

WORK EXPERIENCE: U.S. Army, 1st Signal Brigade (05/30/2002 - Present); Senior Electronic Systems Maintenance Technician, Supervisor: MAJ Dane Tynes, (315) 723-8992/4979; Contact: Yes, Grade: CW5/W05; Hours per week: 40

LEADERSHIP AND MANAGEMENT: Senior Maintenance Technical Advisor/Subject Matter Expert (SME) to Headquarters (HQ), Eighth U.S. Army, and Department of the Army (DoA) staff, Team Chief of the Command Logistics Review Team, and the Senior Advisor for the Army's largest forward-deployed Signal Organization. Significantly affect Korea Peninsula-wide logistical functions for the organization. Conduct staff-level liaison and coordination with the Defense Logistics Agency (DLA) and Air Materiel Command (AMC).

COALITION-BUILDING/COMMUNICATION: Establish rapport with executive-level officials and U.S. Army advisors. Lend expertise on logistics doctrine, training, leader development, organization, and manning. Initiated first-ever Logistics Conference, attended by 200+ logisticians.

QUALITY ASSURANCE (QA): Inspect subordinate organizations to render technical advice and support on supply, maintenance, and logistics management activities. Improve maintenance procedures, resulting in selection of three subordinate commands as finalists in the Fiscal Year (FY) 04 Army Award for Maintenance Excellence Competition. Stay current on signal systems such as fiber optics, electronic switching equipment, state-of-the art cable and relay systems, and Department of the Army (DA)logistical policies and procedures.

LOGISTICS MANAGEMENT: Develop, recommend, and implement policies and procedures that improve the readiness posture of the organization. Plan and direct logistical and contracting functions (e.g., supply, maintenance, facility engineering, contract /acquisition, food services, and transportation) to support nine separate organizations.

LOGISTICS POLICY, METHODS, AND PROCEDURES: Set short- and long-range plans and coordinate/direct all logistical functions. Interpret and implement existing policies, directives, and regulations pertaining to logistics support actions. Establish policy and operating guidelines to include planning, development, organization, management, direction, execution, and administration of maintenance missions.

LOGISTICAL FUNCTION INTEGRATION: Coordinate Korea-wide projects and programs, involving administrative, technical, and professional work in logistics. Integrate work of assigned teams. Transfer 87 communications systems valued at $12.5M during transformation to an Integrated Theater Signal Battalion.

Continued on the next page

RESOURCE MANAGEMENT: Commit resources to projects and program segments. Determine and justify manpower needs and funding requirements, continuity, and operational stability. Administer operating budget, covering training and transfer of excess items from U.S. military equipment inventory. Recommend future material requirements, ensuring proper integration through the acquisition process. Procure critical equipment at no additional cost; obtain ten 18K Environmental Control Units valued at $50K and more than $200K of automation assets to fill shortages. Restore $216K in missing credits for excess and/or unserviceable repair parts.

HUMAN RESOURCES (HR) MANAGEMENT: Manage diverse multiethnic international staff of military officers, mid-level managers, one Korean national, and one DoA civilian. Execute HR management programs and functions in performing supervisory work. Develop and assign goals, objectives, and policies. Train and develop technicians and supervisors to achieve equipment operational readiness objectives. Evaluate supervisory and non-supervisory work performance. Recommend subordinate organizational structure and personnel requirements to ensure proper management and assigned mission. Solve production problems, promote teambuilding, improve work practices, and arrange for employee developmental training.

By breaking up the "big block" and organizing it into different keyword sections (the keywords having been derived from the vacancy announcement itself), a candidate can give the hiring official a much clearer picture of what he/she has to offer within a much shorter amount of time.

Identifying and Using the Right Keywords

So where do you find these magic "keywords"— words that correspond to what the announcement is calling for and that will stimulate a hiring agent's interest in your skills?

The Vacancy Announcement. A great starting point in helping you identify the right keywords is to look at the target vacancy announcement. Besides the job description and duties, this should also include a comprehensive review of any specialized experience requirements, Selective Placement Factors (SPFs), KSAs, or qualifying factors included in the announcement as well as any occupational questionnaires, the latter of which typically place an emphasis on precisely the skills most important to a hiring manager.

Below is a sample qualification statement from an actual announcement, with the keywords highlighted.

QUALIFICATIONS REQUIRED (Sample)

Have one year of specialized experience, equivalent to the GS-12 level in the Federal Service, managing, directing, or supervising work to include duties such as development of strategic plans, budget formation and administration, fiscal management, human resources administration, project planning and execution, program evaluation, etc.

- The General Series Description. If you don't have a specific vacancy announcement to use as a reference, you can do one of two things. First, you can conduct a job search on USAJobs for titles matching your career objective and use those announcements to gain an idea of what the "hot" keywords are. Alternatively, you can visit the OPM website to review the position descriptions for each of the primary General Series; the sub-series are usually contained within these master documents. A list of the job descriptions can be found at http://federaljobs.net/quals2.htm.

- Outside the Box. Sometimes, we do things in the course of our work that we simply take for granted. For instance, a training manager's responsibilities might be to "train professionals on Microsoft Word" but that description can apply to millions of training managers. However, if, for example, you've conducted this training with a curriculum you developed via an interactive online interface, now you suddenly have several hidden keywords to work with that pack more of a punch: **curriculum development** and **online training.**

How and Where Do You Use Keywords?

It's good form to use keywords in all parts of the application process, including résumés, interview follow-up letters, essay statements, occupational questionnaires, and more. Carefully integrate them into the text, when and where appropriate, to be sure you are communicating a complete message of how you meet the qualifications of the position.

The Professional Summary

This section should be included in all résumé presentations, regardless of the agency or system. The location may vary, but it is a very important part of the résumé. In the federal résumé (paper presentation), this section is found after the Contact Information and Compliance Information. In an online application (which constitutes the vast majority of all federal applications), it will be placed at the end of the résumé in the Additional or Other Information section. Wherever the summary is placed, it should never be left off a résumé.

To be effective, the Summary of Qualifications (a.k.a. Career Highlights, Profile, Executive Qualifications, etc.) should include:

- Presidential Statement: A statement displaying your highest level of qualifications in the language of the specific announcement or target job.

- Number of years of work experience: Be specific; for example, "Twenty-seven years of progressive experience in office administration and executive support."

- Record of improvement/accomplishment: Whenever describing accomplishments, be precise. If possible, quantify results. For example, you could write, "Reorganized order-processing procedures to reduce time required by 30%."

- Specific skills and training applicable to the job objective.

- Areas of specialized proficiency (include Security Clearances and languages).

- Work ethic traits demonstrating desirable behaviors or competencies (keep this to one sentence; don't go overboard on the soft skills if you can't prove them with numbers).

Here is an example of a Presidential Statement with the keywords highlighted:

MANAGEMENT
Specializing in Information Technology • Human Resources • Project Management
Current Top Secret (SCI) Clearance

Offering more than 20 years of leadership experience with expertise in managing enterprise-wide Information Technology (IT) solutions.

- **Human Resources Management and Leadership:** Hire and manage high-performance teams, providing the leadership, mentoring, training, and guidance for excellence. Align corporate goals with individual goals, ensuring win-win solutions. Develop Human Resources (HR) technology solutions for education, governmental, and corporate clients. Currently completing Executive Master's Program (MBA) at Georgia Institute of Technology.
- **Information Technology/Software Development:** Manage successful multimillion-dollar IT initiatives and oversee software development, database development, and administration. Earned BS in IT, demonstrating ability to quickly learn state-of-the-art applications.
- **Project Management:** Visionary; lead enterprise-scale projects, applying effective project management skills to plan, develop, implement, and improve projects for educational, commercial, and Department of Defense (DoD) clients.
- **Additional Expertise:** Managed budgets worth more than $30M, ensuring accountability. Directed maintenance of jet engines for the President, based on technical and quality control management excellence.

Sample Headline-Style Format Résumé

Here is an example of how you can use keywords to create headlines within the employment section of a résumé. Note how the "headline" is followed by a brief description that captures the key points or accomplishments within the headline and avoids restating job descriptions.

HQ U.S. Special Operations Command (USSOCOM), 06/22/2007 to Present, Future Operations Officer, MacDill Air Force Base (AFB), Tampa, FL, United States, 40+ hours/week, $60,000 per year, Supervisor: John Jones, 222-222-2222, may contact.

Served as Strategist, planning future operations and coordinating with overall Department of Defense (DOD) initiatives of the Global War on Terrorism (GWOT).

PROGRAM PLANNING/EXECUTION: Conducted security-sensitive planning. Coordinated and execute biweekly Joint Synchronization Board comprised of up to 20 executive-level leaders ranging from colonels to three-star generals. Orchestrated the coordination and synchronization of Combatant Command, Joint Staff, and Office of the Secretary of Defense (OSD) actions; provided consultation and analysis-based options, recommendations, and solutions.

FINANCE OVERSIGHT/CONTRACT ADMINISTRATION: Developed and managed large-scale contracts such as Global Analysis Cell production initiative and Battle Staff Support Cell, totaling $1M+.

REPRESENTATION: Led concept development for a future GWOT prioritization tool, a strategic innovation designed to provide links between GWOT assessments and program prioritization.

IMPROVEMENT MANAGEMENT: Standardized National Implementation Plan (NIP) language across 56 sub-objectives; enabled reliable, uniform, results-based assessment for the GWOT. Provided development and implementation contributions to create Special Operations Staff Officer Courses to prepare inbound officers for duty. Provided authorial and editorial contributions during revisions of policy, such as for Special Operations Command Directive 71-4: refined its instructiveness and applicability.

ACCOMPLISHMENTS:
*Developed model for evaluating input provided for the National Defense Authorization Act 2006, Section 1206 report; influenced resourcing for emerging counterterrorism projects.

Notice also how the text is left-justified with no formatting; this is the recommended format for federal electronic applications. The information at the beginning of the section-including position title, employer, hours per week, salary, supervisor name, and contact information-is required for federal résumés.

Tips Checklist for Preparing an Electronic Résumé

As you have seen in the previous section in which we discuss the different types of online application systems (USAJobs, CPOL, CHARTS, etc.), there is no such concept as "one size fits all" when preparing a federal résumé. However, below are a few tips to help you bridge the compatibility differences in most of the common application systems.

☐   Use white space and line breaks to separate topics and sections

☐   Use 10- or 12-point type size

☐   Use a margin of at least one inch on all sides

☐   Use CAPITAL LETTERS to highlight sections

☐   No graphics of any kind, including bullets

☐   Use date format mm-yyyy (example: "May1988" would be "05-1988")

☐   No bold, italic, or underlined text

☐   Keep each employment block (duties and accomplishments) to about 3,000 characters and spaces each. (Note: If you must exceed this count, you can break up a job into two separate entries when you file your application online.)

Understanding the Federal Vacancy Announcement

A federal vacancy announcement comprises several parts, all of which must be read carefully. As a rule, all announcements posted on USAJobs.gov are uniform, meaning they have the same sections (just different information).

The elements of a vacancy announcement are:

1.   **Vacancy Announcement Number** –This is the identification number issued to each vacancy announcement. You must reference this number wherever it is required on all the materials you submit.

2.   **Opening Date** – This is the date when the vacancy announcement was initially opened for submission of applications.

3.   **Closing Date** –This is the final date that applications may be submitted for consideration for an available position. All applications must be received by midnight (Eastern Standard Time) on the closing date.

4.   **Position** – This is the title of the vacancy being announced.

5.   **Series and Grade** – This information indicates the pay plan, series, and grade for the available position.

6.   **Promotion Potential** – This information indicates if the position has the potential for promotion as well as describe the full performance level.

7.   **Salary** – This is the salary range for the available position.

8.   **Duty Location** – This is the geographic location where the position will be filled or located. The duty location determines which locality pay chart will be used to set your pay.

9.   **Who May Apply** – This area describes who is eligible to apply for the available position, such as "Federal Civil Service Employees" or "Public."

   a.   When a vacancy announcement includes Merit Promotion (MP), this means that applications will be accepted from current federal employees or employees who are reinstatement eligible. Working for a federal contractor does not constitute "federal employment status."

   b.   When the vacancy number includes the suffix Delegating Examining Unit (DEU), this means that applications will be accepted from all U.S. citizens. There may be reasons why a current or former federal employee may want to apply on a DEU (sometimes called Public or External vacancy), but typically, a current or former federal employee has more advantage if he/she applies on a Merit Promotion (MP) vacancy. Some reasons include:

      i.   On DEU referrals (candidate lists), "Best Qualified" names are provided (per position/per grade) to the selecting official.

      ii.   If an employee is a veteran, the employee may feel that the additional points for Veterans' Preference will be beneficial if he/she applies on the DEU vacancy announcement.

      iii.   If an employee is at a certain grade and/or series and feels that he has higher-level experience, the employee may want to apply on the DEU vacancy in order to reenter the government service at a higher grade and/or in a different series.

10.   **Major Duties** – This section details the duties and responsibilities of the available position.

11.   **Qualifications Required** – These are the basic knowledge, skills, and abilities that are required in order for applicants to qualify for the position, such as similar experience or a related educational background.

   a.   Time-in-grade requirements:

      i.   One year at the next lower grade is required to qualify for a promotional opportunity above the GS-5 level.

      ii.   An applicant must be within 60 days of meeting this requirement in order to apply for the promotional opportunity and be considered "qualified."

           iii.   If you have never worked for the government time-in-grade does not apply.

     b.   **Specialized experience requirements:**

           i.   For example, if an employee is a GS-07 clerk, he/she is not automatically eligible for a GS-07 budget analyst position.

           ii.   Applicants are required to have one year of specialized experience in order to meet the eligibility requirements of the GS-07 budget analyst to be ranked as eligible.

           iii.   If you have any questions about the job announcement including qualifying specialized experience call the Point of Contact (POC) listed in the job announcement. They will be able to anser you specific questions.

           iv.   Make sure your résumé provides information that clearly demonstrates that you meet the specialized experience requirements.

12.   **How You Will Be Evaluated** – This section describes how applicants will be evaluated for the position — whether they will be ranked on their knowledge, skills, and abilities or other characteristics required to perform the duties of the position.

13.   **How to Apply** – This section describes all of the materials that are required to complete the application. When applying, you must answer all of the questions contained in the vacancy announcement. Applicants must also submit a résumé. When you have an announcement from which to work, you must ensure the résumé is position-specific and covers all experience related to the announcement.

14.   **A résumé must substantiate the answers to the self-assessment questions.** Federal résumés cannot have "too much" information. Unlike in the private sector, applications for government jobs are like mini auto-biographies. The answers provided to the questions, substantiated by the résumé, are what federal HR specialists use to confirm minimum qualifications. HR specialists cannot assume anything; the number of years of experience is not enough information to demonstrate qualifications. Your résumé must fully explain what work you have done, for whom, for how long, and your specific role(s)/contributions.

     a.   When a vacancy announcement states that documentation is required, applicants must follow the announcement's instructions to submit required documents. Failure to submit required documentation may result in disqualification.

     b.   It is extremely important that applicants read the vacancy announcement in its entirety to ensure all requirements are met.

c.   If you have questions or require clarification, locate the Point of Contact (POC) HR representative listed on the vacancy announcement prior to the closing date. The HR representative can provide guidance and assistance, as needed.

d.   It is not recommended that applicants apply for a position on the day the vacancy announcement closes. It should be noted that all vacancies close at 8:59 p.m. PST and 11:59 p.m. EST. If you wait until the last minute to apply, you run the risk of experiencing technical issues that might prohibit you from completing your application process.

e.   Federal regulations require the person performing the submission, rather than a third party, to be the applicant.

While in the past, many vacancy announcements had a separate requirement for Knowledge, Skills, and Abilities (KSA) statements, recent developments in federal hiring mandate that KSAs are no longer required for initial applications for Competitive Service positions as of November 1, 2010. Although written statements about the competencies/KSAs are no longer required at the initial application, agencies will be reviewing the résumés to determine if evidence of the job competencies are described in the application.

However, many agencies still require candidates to complete occupational questionnaires, some of which call for a candidate to answer essay questions similar to the traditional KSAs. Again, be certain to read and reread every announcement, as candidates often miss the occupational questionnaire and end up submitting a partial application.

Let's look at an actual sample vacancy announcement. The example found on the next page has a mandatory occupational questionnaire, which we've highlighted within the announcement and which will be discussed in the next section. To keep you thinking about keywords, we've highlighted potential keywords and phrases, as well.

Job Title: SUPVY IT SPECIALIST (SYSANA/CUSTSUPT), GS-2210-13

Department: Department of Homeland Security
Agency: U.S. Coast Guard
Sub Agency: United States Coast Guard
Job Announcement Number: 10-2332-SE-TS-D

Salary Range:	$81,823.00 – $106,369.00/year
Series & Grade:	GS-2210-13/13
Promotion Potential:	13
Open Period:	October 04, 2010 to October 18, 2010
Position Information:	This is a full-time, permanent appointment.
Duty Locations:	1 vacancy – Portsmouth, VA
Who May Be Considered:	Open to all U.S. citizens

Job Summary: For 200 years, the United States Coast Guard (USCG) has answered the call to serve. Every day, our family of 7,000 civilians helps us save lives, protect the environment, safeguard the nation, and stop drug traffickers. In the nation's ports and waterways, along the coast, and on international waters, we are there, always ready.

The vacancy is being concurrently advertised under merit promotion procedures. You MUST apply to the concurrently advertised merit promotion announcement ending in 10-2332-SE-TS-M in order to receive consideration as a status applicant or consideration under non-competitive authorities such as military spouses eligible under Executive Order 13473; family members eligible under Executive Order 12721; veterans who are preference eligibles or who have been separated from the Armed Forces under honorable conditions after three years or more of continuous active service; applicants who qualify under special appointing authorities for veterans, such as 30% compensable disabled veterans; other special appointing authorities for persons with disabilities; and current and former federal civilian employees covered by an OPM interchange agreement.

NOTE: YOUR APPLICATION TO THIS PUBLIC VACANCY ANNOUNCE-MENT WILL ALLOW CONSIDERATION FOR ONLY THIS ANNOUNCE-MENT. WE CANNOT ELECTRONICALLY OR MANUALLY MOVE YOUR APPLICATION TO THE CONCURRENTLY ADVERTISED MERIT PROMO-TION ANNOUNCEMENT. PLEASE ENSURE YOU ARE APPLYING UN-DER THE CORRECT ANNOUNCEMENT.

This position is located at the U.S. Coast Guard, Command & Control Engineering Center, C4IT Service Center, Portsmouth, VA.

Key Requirements:

> ▸ U.S. citizenship is required.
>
> ▸ This position requires a SECRET clearance.
>
> ▸ This position requires travel.

Major Duties:

The incumbent of this position serves as the Requirements Section Chief and is responsible for developing and implementing section work processes and work schedules, establishing priorities, and assigning work based on capabilities of subordinates. Develops performance standards and evaluates the performance of subordinates. Interviews candidates, makes selections, effects disciplinary measures, and identifies developmental and training needs. Communicates and carries out Equal Employment Opportunity (EEO) policies to subordinates.

* Directs the proper preparation of command-generated and supported technical manuals and other documentation in support of various projects.

* Serves as Contracting Officer's Technical Representative (COTR) for major contracts and prepares specifications, Statements of Work (SOWs), and task orders, recommending acceptance or non-acceptance of product/services delivered by contractors.

* Establishes and implements CM procedures for all system software/hardware and subsystems managed by C2CEN and conducts configuration impact analyses of engineering change proposals.

* Directs the development and maintenance of an automated CM tracking system that tracks all hardware and software configurations and planned changes.

* Develops, revises, and maintains the Configuration Management Plan for C2CEN that controls modifications/enhancements to current and future systems.

* Directs the control process that provides baseline information, both hardware and software used for systems testing of prototype, or approved modification/enhancements to current and future systems.

* Maintains technical expertise in government and commercial standards affecting configuration management and assesses the impact of these standards upon supported systems.

* Maintains communication with private industry and other government agencies for the exchange of information on latest techniques in the areas of configuration management and change control.

Qualifications:

APPLICANTS MUST HAVE INFORMATION TECHNOLOGY (IT)-RELATED EXPERIENCE DEMONSTRATING EACH OF THE FOUR COMPETENCIES LISTED BELOW.

ATTENTION TO DETAIL – Is thorough when performing work and conscientious about attending to detail.

CUSTOMER SERVICE – Works with clients and customers (that is, any individuals who use or receive the services or products that your work unit produces, including the general public, individuals who work in the agency, other agencies, or organizations outside the government) to assess their needs, provide information or assistance, resolve their problems, or satisfy their expectations; knows about available products and services; is committed to providing quality products and services.

ORAL COMMUNICATION – Expresses information (for example, ideas or facts) to individuals or groups effectively, taking into account the audience and nature of the information (for example, technical, sensitive, controversial); makes clear and convincing oral presentations; listens to others, attends to non-verbal cues, and responds appropriately.

PROBLEM SOLVING – Identifies problems; determines accuracy and relevance of information; uses sound judgment to generate and evaluate alternatives and to make recommendations.

IN ADDITION, APPLICANTS MUST MEET THE SPECIALIZED EXPERIENCE OUTLINED BELOW:

For GS-13: One full year of experience (equivalent to at least the

GS-12 level in the Federal Service) related to applying IT concepts, principles, methods, and practices; missions and programs of customer organizations; organization IT infrastructure; performance management/measurement methods, tools, and techniques; systems testing and evaluation principles, methods, and tools; IT security principles and methods; requirement analysis principles and methods; new and emerging information technologies and/or industry trends; project management principles and methods; difficult and complex assignments and developing new methods, approaches, and procedures; providing advice and guidance on a wide range and variety of IT issues; command, control, and communications procedures and processes and command and control systems design; computer equipment configurations, system software, utility programs, and programming aids; application software design and development techniques; procurement process, representative responsibilities, and cost estimating to plan and oversee projects. This position does not have a positive education requirement.

If you are including education on your résumé, report only attendance and/or degrees from schools accredited by accrediting institutions recognized by the U.S. Department of Education.

All qualification requirements must be met by the closing date of the announcement.

How You Will Be Evaluated:

The U.S. Coast Guard system simplifies the federal application process by replacing the former KSA/JOB ELEMENT statements with online self-assessment questions. Your résumé and responses to the self-assessment questions are an integral part of the process for determining your qualifications for the position. Therefore, it is important to support your responses to the self-assessment questions by providing examples of past and present experience when requested.

When registering with USAJobs, you may also elect to receive notices for job openings that meet your areas of interest.

To preview questions, please <u>click here</u>. (Online link to questions)

Benefits:

The Coast Guard offers excellent benefits. For information pertaining to our benefits, visit <u>Coast Guard Civilian Careers</u>.

In addition, a newly appointed federal civilian employee, or federal civilian employee appointed after a break in service of 90 days or more, may receive service credit for prior non-federal civilian work experience, or experience in a uniformed service that otherwise would not be creditable for the purpose of determining his/her annual leave accrual rate. For more information, visit Providing Credit for Annual Leave.

You should also visit <u>Working for the Federal Government</u>.

Other Information:

Please be aware that applicants will be required to complete questions contained on the <u>Declaration for Federal Employment</u> (OF-306) at the time a tentative job offer is made. If selected, at the time of appointment, selectees will be required to update the OF-306. Certain responses on the form could pose a problem with suitability for employment determinations; e.g., an affirmative answer to a conviction of a felony.

Recruitment incentives may be authorized.

Males born after 12/31/59 and at least 18 years of age must be registered with the Selective Service System. Visit <u>Selective Service Registration</u>.

Moving expenses will not be paid.

This is a supervisory position, under provisions of the Civil Service Reform Act; first-time supervisors and/or managers will be required to serve a one-year probationary period.

All federal employees are required to have federal salary payments made by direct deposit to a financial institution of their choosing.

All selectees are subject to an appropriate investigation.

For Veterans' Preference eligibility, visit <u>Veterans' Employment Resources</u>.

More than one selection may be made from this announcement if additional identical vacancies in the same title, series, grade, and unit occur within 90 days from the date the certificate was issued.

If you are selected for this position, you will be subject to a determination of your suitability for federal employment.

The United States Coast Guard (USCG) is an Equal Opportunity Employer.

All qualified applicants will be considered, regardless of political affiliation, race, color, religion, national origin, sex, sexual orientation, marital status, age, disability, or other non-merit factors.

USCG provides reasonable accommodations to applicants with disabilities. If you need a reasonable accommodation for any part of the application and hiring process, please contact 703-235-1862. Decisions on granting reasonable accommodation will be made on a case-by-case basis. Visit Reasonable Accommodation.

How to Apply:

Applications (résumé and job-specific questions) for this vacancy must be received online by 12 midnight EST on the closing date of the announcement.

There are several parts of the application process that affect the overall evaluation of your application:

*Resume

*Responses to online core questions

*Responses to online self-assessment

*Supporting documents, if requested

High self-assessment in the vacancy questions that is not supported by information in your résumé, essay response, and/or supporting documents may eliminate you from consideration.

If applying online poses a hardship to you, the Help Desk listed on the announcement will provide assistance to ensure applications are submitted online by the closing date. You must contact the Help Desk prior to the closing date of this announcement to receive assistance. Hours of operation: Monday through Friday, 7:00 a.m. to 7:00 p.m. EST, excluding federal holidays.

Required Documents:

If you are claiming 10-point Veterans' Preference, you must submit a copy of your DD-214, "Certificate of Release or Discharge from Active Duty," which indicates the type of discharge you received, or other proof of eligibility, as well as an SF-15, "Application for 10-point Veterans' Preference," plus the proof required by that form.

Individuals who have special priority selection rights under CTAP or ICTAP provisions must be well qualified for the position to receive consideration for special priority selection. CTAP and ICTAP eligibles will be considered well qualified if they attain a cut-off score of 85. We require documentation to support CTAP or ICTAP eligibility at the time of application.

All documentation must be received by the closing date of the announcement and must indicate the vacancy announcement number on the documents. A fax coversheet will be provided to you from the system, with number and instructions to transmit the requested documents. (Jobs) U.S. Coast Guard, Ofc of Civ Pers, CG-1211SE, 2300 Wilson Blvd, Suite 500, Arlington, VA 22201.

Contact Information:

USCG Applicant Support
Phone: 866-656-6830
Fax: 703-235-1892
E-mail: mgshelp@monster.com
Agency Information:
United States Coast Guard
2300 Wilson Blvd
Suite 500
Arlington, VA 22201
Fax: 703-235-1892

What to Expect Next:

Once your complete application is received, we will conduct an evaluation of your qualifications and determine your ranking. The most highly qualified candidates will be referred to the hiring manager for further consideration and possible interview. We expect to make a selection within 30 to 90 days of the closing date of this announcement. To check your application status for this job, please go to My USAJOBS, input your user ID and password, and select "Track your online job applications."

EEO Policy Statement: **www.usajobs.gov/eeo**

Reasonable Accommodation Policy Statement: www.usajobs.gov/raps

Veterans Information: www.usajobs.gov/vi

Legal and Regulatory Guidance: www.usajobs.gov/lrg

End of Sample Job Announcement

Understanding Narratives, Occupational Questionnaires, and KSAs

Occupational questionnaires can be extremely important in the applicant evaluation process, since they may be scored. Poor responses may prevent you from being considered among the "Best Qualified" group.

The federal résumé or application is the information that tells Human Resources (HR) if you are qualified for the job and your responses to the essay questions further describe your skills using concrete examples.

A key point to remember about all qualification requirements and question-naires is that they must be job-related. An agency cannot ask for anything that is not in the job's position description.

What Is an Occupational Questionnaire?

An occupational questionnaire primarily measures a candidate's proficiency in various skills required for the job. Typically, the questions consist of multiple-choice or Yes/No responses to gauge the experience level a candidate has. A narrative may be required to help substantiate the candidate's experience.

Here is the corresponding occupational questionnaire to our previous vacancy example, which we've shortened to include just a sampling of the questions. Note that for the essay questions, the agency provides specific character-count limits.

SAMPLE OCCUPATIONAL QUESTIONNAIRE

---

* 1. Which of the following best describes your experience analyzing and resolving problems ranging from administrative issues to changing requirements to hardware/software problems?

1. I have not had experience, education, or training in performing this task.

2. I have had education or training in performing this task but have not yet performed this task on the job.

3. I have performed this task on the job with close supervision from a supervisor or senior employee.

4. I have performed this task as a regular part of the job, independently and usually without review by a supervisor or senior employee.

5. I have supervised performance of this task and/or I have trained others in performance and/or am normally consulted as an expert for assistance in performing this task.

* 2. Please describe your experience implementing and monitoring the progress of system enhancements and modifications.

1. I have not had experience, education, or training in performing this task.

2. I have had education or training in performing this task but have not yet performed this task on the job.

3. I have performed this task on the job with close supervision from a supervisor or senior employee.

4. I have performed this task as a regular part of the job, independently and usually without review by a supervisor or senior employee.

5. I have supervised performance of this task and/or I have trained others in performance and/or am normally consulted as an expert for assistance in performing this task.

* 3. Please provide a narrative supporting your answer to the above question, including information on the circumstances, the complexity of the work, the length of time, and the organization where the work was performed.

Maximum length of 8,000 characters.

* 4. Which of the following statements best describes your experience as the lead in business matters that includes serving as the Contracting Officer's Technical Representative (COTR)?

1. I have not had experience, education, or training in performing this task.

2. I have had education or training in performing this task but have not yet performed this task on the job.

3. I have performed this task on the job with close supervision from a supervisor or senior employee.

4. I have performed this task as a regular part of the job, independently and usually without review by a supervisor or senior employee.

5. I have supervised performance of this task and/or I have trained others in performance and/or am normally consulted as an expert for assistance in performing this task.

* 5. Which of the following statements best describes your experience in reviewing, evaluating, and recommending changes and additions to the baseline standard image and architecture, as needed, to meet planned organizational needs and requirements?

1. I have not had experience, education, or training in performing this task.

2. I have had education or training in performing this task but have not yet performed this task on the job.

3. I have performed this task on the job with close supervision from a supervisor or senior employee.

4. I have performed this task as a regular part of the job, independently and usually without review by a supervisor or senior employee.

5. I have supervised performance of this task and/or I have trained others in performance and/or am normally consulted as an expert for assistance in performing this task.

* 6. Please provide a narrative supporting your answer to the above question, including information on the circumstances, the complexity of the work, the length of time, and the organization where the work was performed.

Maximum length of 8,000 characters.

KNOWLEDGE, SKILLS AND ABILITIES (KSAs)

Most applicants look at writing KSAs as drudgery; however, it is a necessary part of your employment application, if requested on the job announcement. To qualify for a position you must meet two types of factors: *Selective Factors* and *Quality Ranking Factors*.

KSAs are attributes needed to perform a specific job function that is demonstrated through qualifying training, education and experience. The following definitions will help you understand what the selecting official is looking for when reviewing your application and résumé:

Knowledge – An organized body of information, usually of a factual or proce-dural nature, which if applied, makes adequate performance on the job possible.

- Examples include knowledge of:

> Federal regulations and directives
> Operational systems and procedures
> Budget and accounting principals
> Engineering practices
> Environmental compliance law
> Administrative practices

When addressing "knowledge" questions, you need to do more than simply write that you know how to do something. You'll want to demonstrate your knowledge with a concrete example.

Example: Knowledge of research and writing.
Poor: I have researched and written various training materials for past employers.

Better: In 2010, as a Career Development Specialist for CareerPro Global, I exhibited my knowledge of writing and research by undertaking the complete development of the Certified Military Résumé Writer program, a ten-module, self-paced professional certification approved for offering and accreditation by Career Directors International. I consulted numerous resources to include the Office of Personnel Management, the structure of military performance appraisals, etc. After identifying the key elements necessary to effectively transition military candidates to federal and civilian programs, I developed the program outline and began completing the interactive training modules to include lecture material and exercises.

Skill — The manipulation of data, things, or people through manual, mental or verbal means. Skills are measurable through testing, can be observed, and are quantifiable. Often refers to expertise that comes from training, practice, etc.

- Examples include skill in:

> Keyboard data entry
> Motor vehicle operation
> Computer software proficiency
> Electronic or computer repair
> Carpentry, plumbing and/or HVAC repair
> Second language proficiency

Example: Skill in fact-finding, problem analysis, problem resolutions, and development of concrete action plans to solve problems.

Poor: As an administrative support provider with more than 25 years of experience, I have often faced challenges or tasks that required fact-finding, problem analysis, problem resolutions, and development of concrete action plans to solve problems. These problems include logistics, resource planning and allocation, and optimization.

Better: As an administrative support provider with more than 25 years of experience, I have often faced challenges or tasks that required fact-finding, problem analysis, problem resolutions, and development of concrete action plans to solve problems. When I began my current position with the Health and Development Center (SHDC) on the Minot State University campus, I arrived to find the records system was in complete disarray.

I created a system based on the filing system I had learned and used extensively during my years in the United States Air Force (USAF). My system included a single repository and required extensive file purging and maintenance. I designed a computerized database to record all entries.

Older files were purged or scanned into the electronic system, as necessary, duplicate records were removed, and all personal records and files that were not to be maintained were shredded to properly maintain privacy and confidentiality. I trained other employees and documented the system. As a result, the records were in order, easily maintained, and easily retrieved.

Ability — The capacity to perform a physical or mental activity at the present time. Typically, abilities are apparent through functions completed on the job. Abilities and skills are often interchangeable in KSAOs. The main difference is that ability is the capacity to perform, where a skill is the actual manipulation of data, things or people. You may have the ability, but unless observed through actions, that ability may not transfer to a skill set.

●   Examples include the ability to:

> Organize and plan work (observed at work)
> Analyze situations, programs and problems
> Communicate orally and in writing
> Coach and mentor others

Example: Ability to gather, analyze, and present facts; communicate effectively, using tact and courtesy; and plan, organize work, and meet deadlines.

Poor: I have learned, throughout my 25 years of experience, that effective communication using tact and courtesy is crucial to enlisting the cooperation of people to work together and meet deadlines. Using this ability, I have consistently ensured projects are completed on time and ahead of schedule.

Better: I have learned, throughout my 25 years of experience, that effective communication using tact and courtesy is crucial to enlisting the cooperation of people to work together to put plans into action and meet deadlines. My commitment to and skill in gathering, analyzing, and presenting facts in a tactful, sensitive manner has led to my selection for various protocol positions.

My position with the North Atlantic Treaty Organization (NATO) in Turkey as part of the United States Air Force (USAF) required a great deal of sensitivity and awareness. In addition to rank and military service, members were ranked according to the date their nation was admitted to NATO, and they were very sensitive to perceived offenses regarding their position. Nowhere was this more readily apparent than the assignment of on-base parking. Extreme tact and courtesy was required for dealing with parking spot assignments and the daily complaints that made their way to my desk. Everyone wanted a better parking space; such requests normally could not be accomplished without depriving a higher-ranking person of their space. If a higher-ranking individual moved onto the base, a lower-grade person would lose his/her parking space. If someone was scheduled to depart the base for another assignment, the phone lines lit up and e-mail boxes filled with requests from a variety of people who wanted the parking space that would become available.

KSA CHECKLIST

Use this list to ensure that you have included key information. It's important to consider these areas when drafting your KSA statements. When you first start to draft your KSAs, don't worry about the specifics such as exact dates, contact information, etc. You can add that later. It is best to simply write down anything and everything, even the least significant events. After you get it all down then add specifics and put them in logical sequence. Review and rewrite your KSAs several times. Let your draft sit overnight and review it again the next day. You will be surprised at what you left out on the first draft.

❑ **Experience** — Include experience for all offices, departments or agencies that you worked for to show depth and range of experience. For example, include that you tracked interoffice correspondence at multiple locations, or that you tracked budgets for headquarters. Also show expertise in what you do well such as having A++ certification, maintain LANS/WANS for several locations, thoroughly familiar with Peachtree accounting software, proficient at office organization, etc.

❑ **Supervision** — If you don't have a supervisory background, did you work independently with minimal supervision and make decisions for your program areas? If so, state that in your KSAs. Were you assigned to be an acting supervisor on several occasions? Do you draft memorandums and letters for your supervisor's signature? Do you manage/supervise programs or projects?

❑ **Complexity Factors** — Did you write reports or work on large projects coordinating activities for various groups? Does your job impact the safety of others, and what standards do you follow and utilize in your present and past jobs? Do you have certifications, licenses, specific training, or accreditation that would help you land this job?

❑ **Achievements and Impact** — How did you show initiative and creativity in your office while working under adverse conditions? Were you responsible for major programs, product, or activities? If so list them. What did you do to save time, money, and resources or to improve the work environment?

❑ **Awards/Recognition** — Include all awards — monetary awards, letters of achievement, time-off awards, or write-ups in your office newsletter. Include scholastic nominations as well, and any service awards or recognition received from volunteer work.

❑ **Contacts** — If you dealt with headquarters staff, the general public, EPA or OSHA inspectors, local authorities, or government officials, list them in your KSAs.

❑ **Fashionable Trends** — Mention current trends such as "BPE" Business Process Engineering, Model Work Environment initiatives, MBO — Management by Objectives, Partnership, Quality Work Groups, etc. If you have exposure to these and other initiatives, list them in your write-up.

What Are Short Narratives?

Short narratives are typically included as part of the online assessment questionnaire that agencies are now including as part of the application process.

Because of the federal hiring reform initiative, agencies are switching to a format in which they ask an applicant to complete multiple sections of an online assessment consisting of multiple-choice questions and then ending with a short narrative to demonstrate the multiple-choice response.

Simply mentioning that you have a specific knowledge, skill, ability, or characteristic is not enough. You'll want to <u>focus on demonstrating exactly how you applied your knowledge, skill, ability, or other characteristic</u> to solve a work-related challenge.

How Long Should a Narrative Response Be?

When preparing any short narrative responses, pay close attention to any character/space limitations. This information will generally be included below the text box field on the online assessment or may be included in the vacancy announcement itself. If no such guideline is provided, a good rule of thumb is to limit your narrative to about 4,000 characters and spaces.

A good rule of thumb is to limit your narrative to about 4,000 characters and spaces.

Preparing Narrative Responses

Job applicants often wonder why the government asks for questionnaires and narrative responses when these are already addressed in the announcement and résumé.

The difference between the information contained in your résumé versus what you'll include in the narrative response is that narrative responses need to be specific and derive from your experiences, not duties. (Major duties that are relevant to the job being sought can—and should—be listed on the federal résumé.)

Narratives need to demonstrate and complement the experience that is listed on a résumé. They tell a value-added story; the more comprehensive the examples are in relation to the statement asked, the higher the applicant will score on his/her narratives and the more qualified he/she will be in the initial selection process.

You'll want to include at least two solid examples; however, one very detailed example will usually suffice.

What Information Can Be Included in a Narrative Response?

No matter what the narrative is called, it is important to remember that the response must be factual and from your experience. Candidates who are chosen to be interviewed will have to defend their statements in an interview and possibly provide even more detail during the interview as it pertains to a specific narrative response; therefore, it is vital that you ensure you are accurate and thorough in the information you provide in any written statements.

The government will accept both paid and unpaid experiences; education (degrees, courses, and research projects); awards and recognitions; and quotes from endorsement letters or letters of recommendation.

Addressing KSAs within the Résumé

As we've discussed, even though KSAs are supposed to be eliminated in job announcements because of hiring reform, many agencies still require you to submit essay-style narrative responses later in the hiring process, or as part of an online assessment or occupational questionnaire.

Further, you may be required to address KSAs within the body of the résumé itself. In these cases, it is best to call the contact on the job announcement to clarify what he/she wants. The big difference between writing full essay responses and integrating KSAs into a résumé is use of the word "I." A résumé should be written in "implied first person;" for example, you would write, "Developed comprehensive plans for standardizing office procedures for a staff of 20" instead of "I developed comprehensive plans for …."

Because of hiring reform, agencies continue to use new ways to address KSAs, but you may come upon one of the following scenarios:

#1– You might be asked to address the KSAs with short first-person narratives in the bottom "Additional Information" section of your résumé. In this case, remember everything we've discussed about writing strong KSA statements.

#2 – You might be asked to include a section in your résumé with brief descriptions of your competency in each KSA, but not in full essay format. For example:

KSA: Ability to write persuasively and effectively in English.

Summary example:

Excellent writer with a comprehensive command of English language and grammar. By using summarization techniques as much as possible, established a reputation for brevity, clarity, congruency, and logical format. As a Mortgage Service Representative with Redstone Federal Credit Union, responded in writing to customer inquiries and concerns pertaining to their monthly payments and payoff amounts, as well as requests for corrections to be made to their files. As a result, customers were better informed and made positive remarks about clear and consistent customer service.

Another example of this KSA:

Excellent writer with a comprehensive command of English language and grammar. By using summarization techniques as much as possible, established a reputation for brevity, clarity, congruency, and logical format. As an Assistant Manager at a Target store, realized that internal communications were non-existent. Developed a newsletter containing useful information for employees, including interviews and case studies with the sales associates who had generated the most credit card sales for the month. Created a bulletin board in the employee break room to share pertinent information. The new written communications channels greatly enhanced employee morale and productivity.

#3 - You might also be asked to "represent" the KSAs within the overall résumé without addressing them directly. This means that you can simply use the keywords from the KSAs as headlines in your accomplishments. For example:

KSA: Knowledge of research and analysis techniques to perform management-related studies.

Headline paragraph using the KSA as keywords:

DEEP KNOWLEDGE OF RESEARCH AND ANALYSIS TECHNIQUES TO PERFORM MANAGEMENT-RELATED DUTIES; as Budget Officer, selected to assist the Human Resource Office in developing a workforce plan. Researched and analyzed planning documents; reviewed current and projected financial information and budgets to determine staffing trends and anticipated budgetary changes. Discovered a need for enhanced training to better align skill sets with job duties. Implemented a concerted cross-training program; within one year, all personnel had received the recommended levels of remedial or additional training.

Sample Résumés

Sample Vacancy Announcement Sections and Corresponding Résumé for an Entry-Level Position with key words highlighted.

OPEN PERIOD: August 31 - September 3, 2010

POSITION: Program Specialist, GS-0301-5/7

HIRING AGENCY: Department of Homeland Security (DHS)
                            Federal Emergency Management Agency (FEMA)

DUTY LOCATIONS: Boston, MA; New York, NY; Philadelphia, PA; Chicago, IL; Denton, TX; Kansas City, MO; Oakland, CA; Bothell, WA

Requirements

- The incumbent will perform tasks related to special projects involving administrative and program issues

- U.S. citizenship

- May work at locations other than official duty station

Duties

- Participates in the orientation sessions, training conferences, and regularly scheduled meetings.

- Participates and successfully completes all rotational and special assignments, work assignments, and training, as assigned.

- Works with supervisor to develop an Individual Development Plan (IDP).

- Conducts individual and collective research for special studies, projects, and surveys, as assigned.

Qualifications

GS-05: At least three years of progressively responsible experience, one year of which demonstrated your ability to analyze problems to identify significant factors, gather pertinent data, and recognize solutions; plan and organize work; and communicate effectively orally and in writing; OR four-year course of study leading to a Bachelor's degree; OR a combination of the required experience and education for this grade level.

GS-07: At least one year of specialized experience, equivalent to at least the GS-05 level of the federal government, that included applying knowledge of project management techniques and skills in performing a wide variety of progressively responsible work assignments involving program and project planning. Examples of such work include: assisting in coordinating projects among different groups of individuals; participating in developing tentative plans for small project of study; assisting in making recommendations for program changes to improve quality of work; preparing summaries, narrative statements, and analyses of facts; communicating orally with a variety of individuals and/or groups to gather or provide project and/or program information; and drafting documents and reports involving a variety of programs and/or projects; OR one year of graduate-level education or meet the requirements under the superior academic achievement provision; OR a combination of the required experience and education for this grade level.

This sample résumé was compiled by CPG for the Program Specialist, GS-0301-5/7 position (with keywords from the job announcement highlighted):

Barbara Adams
173 Pierce Avenue
Macon, Georgia 31204

Contact Phone: (478) 742-2442
Contact E-mail: badams@careerprocenter.net

U.S. Citizen
Social Security Number: 000-00-0000
Veterans' Preference: N/A
Highest Previous Grade: GS-301-4, 07/2010 to Present

Vacancy Identification Number: AN377862, PROGRAM SPECIALIST, GS-301-5/7

PROFESSIONAL SUMMARY:

High-performance professional with a broad range of experience analyzing, planning, and improving programs for government and private-sector agencies. As Program Support Specialist with the Federal Emergency Management Agency (FEMA), coordinated Emergency Operations Center information for Response Division personnel, improving overall efficiency by 30%. Specific expertise in emergency response; member of Certified Community Emergency Response Team (CERT).

QUALIFICATIONS SUMMARY

+ Demonstrated ability to analyze problems related to emergency management, identify significant factors, gather pertinent data, and recognize solutions.

+ Proven ability to independently plan and organize work; strong project management skills.

+ Excellent oral and written communication skills; able to clearly articulate issues, recommend program improvements and potential courses of action, and communicate effectively, both individually and in groups as well as orally and in writing with a variety of internal and external customers.

+ Recognized for ability to coordinate projects related to emergency management among individuals and groups with varying agendas and interests.

+ Specific experience in emergency management through internships and course work; undergraduate degree with emergency management major and Superior Academic Achievement.

RELEVANT WORK EXPERIENCE

07/2010 to Present, PROGRAM SUPPORT SPECIALIST, GS-301-4, Response Division, Federal Emergency Management Agency (FEMA), 536 S. Main Street, Atlanta, GA, 40 hours per week, Lisa Becker, 478-742-2882, may contact.

PARTICIPATE IN PLANNING, DEVELOPING, AND IMPLEMENTING VARIOUS EMERGENCY MANAGEMENT PROJECTS AND PROGRAMS for FEMA Region V. Analyze and evaluate needs, existing resources, various data, and information to create, build, and improve quality emergency management programs. Work with management, colleagues, and external stakeholders individually and in groups to obtain and assess information and develop plans and projects. Research resource requirements, identify actions needed, and assist in the development of program plans. Identify necessary resources to implement programs. Communicate plans to community, governmental, and other stakeholders. Monitor progress of project and program implementation, adjusting to meet changing priorities, conditions, and feedback. Work on projects, both individually and in groups.

PREPARE AND DRAFT A RANGE OF WRITTEN COMMUNICATIONS, includ-ing documents, reports, summaries, narrative statements, and analyses of facts. Ensure all written communications are clear, concise, and complete; demonstrate understanding of subject matter, as well as relevant FEMA policies and procedures. Use Microsoft (MS) Word, Excel, PowerPoint, and Access to prepare narrative, graphic, and numeric written communications. All communications display proper grammar, sentence structure, and vocabulary.

USE OUTSTANDING INTERPERSONAL, COLLABORATIVE, AND ORAL COMMUNICATIONS SKILLS; INTERACT DAILY WITH A WIDE range of people from various backgrounds; interactions include senior management; colleagues; representatives of federal, state, and local governments; and industry and community groups. Communicate program progress, logistical issues, concerns, and issues and potential solutions. Share information among various stakeholders and respond to routine questions and concerns. Work successfully to establish commonality of purpose among sometimes-contentious and competing stakeholders with varying agendas and interests. Consistently demonstrate courtesy, professionalism, and tact, even under stressful and emergency conditions.

INDEPENDENTLY PLAN AND ORGANIZE DAILY ACTIVITIES; DEMON-STRATE ATTENTION TO DETAIL; ensure all projects adhere to deadlines and comply with all laws, regulations, policies, and procedures. Work to foster effective, collaborative relationships across various constituencies with some-times-competing agendas; troubleshoot areas of disagreement to promote mission accomplishment.

USE KNOWLEDGE OF THE THEORIES, PRINCIPLES, AND PRACTICES OF EMERGENCY MANAGEMENT and related disciplines to inform analyses and recommendations. Research Stafford Act and other relevant laws, regula-tions, policies, and procedures to ensure understanding and compliance. Monitor pending legislative and other changes; prepare and present information on potential changes and their impact to personnel.

ACTIVELY PARTICIPATE IN AND SUCCESSFULLY COMPLETE VARI-OUS TRAINING ACTIVITIES related to emergency management. Ensure all assignments are completed in a timely manner. Share learning with colleagues; prepare and present information from self and formal study to colleagues, both orally and in writing.

KEY ACCOMPLISHMENTS:

+ Established Point of Contact (POC) information for all electric utilities throughout FEMA Region V for use by Watch Center for outage and emergency information.

+ Coordinated Emergency Operations Center information for Response Division personnel, improving overall efficiency by 30%.

+ Established media contact information for FEMA Region V Watch Center for critical news information.

+ Created Emergency Warden Notification System for Response Division, improving response time from ten minutes down to three.

+ Coordinated and received training from Watch Center personnel to handle emergency calls and notifications.

+ Updated Emergency Support Function information for use by personnel in the Regional Response Coordination Center.

+ Reviewed changes to upcoming legislation and presented to FEMA Region V personnel.

09/2009 to 12/2009, INTERN, Training and Exercise Division, Federal Emer-gency Management Agency (FEMA), 536 S. Main Street, Atlanta, GA, 40 hours per week, Lisa Becker, 478-742-2882, may contact.

ANALYZED AND EVALUATED NEEDS OF FEMA'S REGIONAL TRAIN-ING AND EXERCISE DIVISION to identify and recommend program improvements. Planned and implemented several vital projects related to training. Worked collaboratively with other divisions as well as partner local, state, and federal agency personnel to identify needs and coordinate training requirements and programs, including the National Level Exercise planning. Monitored and maintained records regarding logistics, participation, and evaluations. Made recommendations to improve effectiveness of training; prepared multiple reports and analyses on training event evaluations to provide better information on their effectiveness as well as more easily identify opportunities for improvement.

DEMONSTRATED OUTSTANDING ORAL COMMUNICATION SKILLS in interacting with federal, state, and local personnel as well as senior management and colleagues. Ensured all communications were appropriate for the audience intended and demonstrated knowledge of emergency management theories, principles, and practices as well as political realities. Displayed professionalism, courtesy, and tact in all communications.

USED MS WORD, EXCEL, POWERPOINT, AND ACCESS to prepare a wide range of narrative, graphic, and numeric reports, analyses, summaries, and other documents. Documents were clear, concise, complete, and appropriate for the audience intended.

KEY ACCOMPLISHMENTS:

+ Created several well-received new databases using MS Access, Word, and Excel to track and maintain employee-training records to ensure regulatory compliance and readiness.

+ Successfully participated in the planning and preparation of the high-profile National Level Exercise.

+ Created discussion-based evaluations and checklists for use in FEMA training conferences and interagency training.

+ Analyzed and graphed data from various FEMA training conferences for review and summation.

+ Recipient of letter of commendation from FEMA National Preparedness organization for contributions to National Level Preparedness Exercise 2011.

Summers 2000 to 2006, LIFEGUARD, Chicago Park District, Grove Avenue, Alpharetta, GA, 40 hours per week, $11.50 per hour, James McKinnon, 478-555-0001, may contact.

PROVIDED CROWD CONTROL AND EMERGENCY MANAGEMENT SERVICES for as many as 20,000 beach-goers a day. Continually assessed and evaluated crowds, incidents, and activities to identify and address emergencies as part of a 15-person team. Responded appropriately to promote safety and recreation for families and individuals of varying backgrounds, cultures, and languages.

INTERACTED WITH A WIDE RANGE OF FEDERAL AND LOCAL AGEN-CY EMERGENCY PERSONNEL, including the U.S. Coast Guard (USCG), Chicago Fire Department, and Chicago Police Department, as well as diverse citizens of all ages, cultures, and levels of understanding, including those who were not English-speaking or those whose English skills were limited. Communicated vital emergency and routine information clearly, concisely, and calmly, despite the highly stressful nature of some communications. Answered questions from visitors and other stakeholders, some of whom were passionate in their views, to inquiries about laws, regulations, and policies. Consistently demonstrated courtesy, tact, and professionalism in all interactions.

RESEARCHED, INTERPRETED, AND APPLIED SAFETY RULES AND REGULATIONS for beach patrons. Determined violations and ensured compliance. Prepared written reports, as required, in response to various incidents.

OTHER WORK EXPERIENCE

Summer 2008, TEACHER'S AIDE, Ritten School, 141 Turner Avenue, Atlanta, GA, 20 hours per week, $8.50 per hour, Scott Kirk, 478-555-0002, may contact.

PLANNED AND PRESENTED curricula and lesson plans to engage as many as 20 students with learning and developmental disabilities in learning. Developed and implemented individualized motivational strategies to reach students with varied learning styles, skills, and abilities. Participated in the selection of learning aids; utilized a wide variety of tools to encourage learning.

INTERACTED ONE-ON-ONE WITH STUDENTS, PARENTS, AIDES, and others on a wide variety of issues to encourage effective learning and social interactions of students. Collaborated with others to promote effective practices. REGULARLY COMMUNICATED PROGRESS AND CONCERNS to school administrators, teachers, other staff, and parents. Made recommendations for improvements. Demonstrated courtesy, tact, and professionalism in all interactions.

04/2000 to 09/2008, MANAGER, Milas, 10918 S. Watershed Avenue, Atlanta, GA, up to 30 hours per week, $12 per hour, Ted Telega, 478-555-0003, may contact.

COORDINATED, MANAGED, AND OVERSAW equipment, maintenance, and logistics phases of business projects during season. Developed detailed completion schedules for projects, including tasks, assignment of responsibility, and timelines; modified and rescheduled, as needed, to adjust to changing conditions. Coordinated the work of deliveries and equipment maintenance for complex projects. Analyzed projects to determine the effectiveness as well as goals and objectives. Monitored and tracked projects' progress; ensured complex, multifaceted projects operated at maximum levels of efficiency and cost-effectiveness. Recommended solutions to reduce costs and increase operational efficiency and effectiveness.

OVERSAW CUSTOMER ACCOUNT ADMINISTRATION and processes for a variety of services. Scheduled and coordinated meetings to discuss proposals. Conducted market research to identify available vendors, costs of services, and other information. Solicited potential vendors. Received bids and conducted cost-price analyses of bids to determine reasonableness and compliance with established requirements and regulations. Prepared contract documents. Contracts administered ranged up to $1,000,000.

DEMONSTRATED STRONG ORAL COMMUNICATION AND INTERPERSONAL SKILLS; interacted with a wide range of both internal and external customers with varying levels of understanding and education on a daily basis. Frequently communicated with vendors, clients, and management to report progress and notify them of any change in plans. Exercised professionalism, tact, and discretion in all interactions. Worked to establish immediate trust, credibility, and effective working relationships with co-workers, customers, vendors, and management. Utilized oral communications not only in one-on-one interactions but also to give reports and presentations. Collaborated effectively.

PREPARED WRITTEN DOCUMENTS, including contracts, purchase and sales agreements, bids, correspondence, and project plans. Ensured all written materials demonstrated subject matter knowledge and strong analytical skills and are appropriate for the audience intended. Used MS Word, Excel, and PowerPoint for written products. All written work demonstrated knowledge of grammar, sentence structure, and vocabulary.

DIRECTED AND MONITORED LOGISTICS; surveyed worksites; planned, organized, and monitored deliveries and set up accordingly. Communicated expectations, time frames, and corporate policies. Monitored work performance to ensure schedules and deadlines were met. Provided feedback; handled problems, complaints, and issues.

INDEPENDENTLY PLANNED AND ORGANIZED WORK; set priorities to ensure optimal performance and results. Identified opportunities for cost reductions in terms of time and resource usage and recommended solutions for procedural inefficiencies.

EDUCATION

2010, Bachelor of Science, University of Georgia, Atlanta, GA, Major: Emergency Management; Minor: Law Enforcement and Justice Administration. 122 semester hours, GPA: 3.2

Relevant Course work:

+ Terrorism and Criminal Justice: Traced the development of terrorism through groups involved in domestic, religious, international, and state-sponsored terrorism

+ Principles of Emergency Management: Presented theories, principles, and approaches to emergency management.

+ Hazards and Disasters in Emergency Management: Overview of the relationships between natural and technological hazards and disasters and associated requirements for mitigation, preparation, response, and recovery.

+ Dimensions of Disaster: Examined empirical versus theoretical approaches to disasters, human behavior in disasters, and contemporary research.

+ Weapons of Mass Destruction in Health Science: Examined various forms of Weapons of Mass Destruction (WMD) and discussion of primary, secondary, and tertiary practices. Developed press releases and other documents to communicate with public officials and citizens.

Awards: Dean's List: Fall 2008, Spring 2009

2004, Diploma, St. Mary's High School, Chicago, Illinois

Awards: Dean's List

PROFESSIONAL CERTIFICATIONS

Certified Community Emergency Response Team (CERT) member, 2009

Professional Development Series Certified, 2009

Professional CPR/First Aid/Preventing Disease Transmission/Oxygen Administration/Automated External Defibrillator, 2008

PROFESSIONAL EMERGENCY MANAGEMENT INSTITUTE (EMI) TRAINING

Orientation to Disaster Response Operations; IS-00003, Radiological Emergency Management; IS-00005.a, An Introduction to Hazardous Materials; IS-00100.a, Introduction to Incident Command System; IS-00120.a, Introduction to Exercises; IS-00139, Exercise Design; IS-00197.em, Special Needs Planning Considerations for Emergency Management; IS-00200.a, ICS for Single Resources and Initial Action Incidents; IS-00230.a, Fundamentals of Emergency Management; IS-00235, Emergency Planning; IS-00241, Decision Making and Problem Solving; IS-0244, Developing and Managing Volunteers; IS-00292, Disaster Basics; IS-00520, Introduction to Continuity of Operations Planning for Pandemic Influenzas; IS-00546.a, Continuity of Operations Awareness Course; IS-00700, National Incident Management System: An Introduction; IS-00800.b, National Response Framework: An Introduction

COMPUTER SKILLS

Microsoft (MS) Office (Word, Excel, PowerPoint, Access, Outlook)
MS InfoPath
Internet Research
Adobe Acrobat
Google Earth

End of Sample résumé

This sample résumé was compiled by CPG for a mid-level Human Resources (HR) Specialist (with main keywords capitalized):

Barbara Adams
173 Pierce Avenue
Macon, Georgia 31204

Phone: 478-742-2442
E-mail: badams@careerprocenter.net

U.S. Citizen
Social Security Number: xxx-xx-xxxx
Veterans' Preference: N/A
Highest Previous Grade: N/A

PROFESSIONAL PROFILE

Award-winning HUMAN RESOURCES (HR) AND PROGRAM MANAGE-MENT PROFESSIONAL with demonstrated skills in processing HR actions; planning, formulating, and directing HR programs; and communicating effectively with management and employees. Certified Professional in Human Resources Professional (PHR). Outstanding analytical skills; demonstrated ability to analyze complex information and provide effective assistance and guidance to management and staff on a wide variety of HR-related issues. Trained in emergency management; firsthand knowledge of programs related to emergency management workforce programs through frontline experience during Hurricanes Ivan, Dennis, and Katrina. Recognized for exceptional oral and written communication skills; proven ability to write HR policies and procedures using the full range of Microsoft (MS) Office Suite.

RELEVANT PROFESSIONAL HISTORY

03/2008 to Present, HUMAN RESOURCES COORDINATOR/BENEFITS FINANCIAL ANALYST, Ole Industries, 54 Cumberland Ave., Atlanta, GA, 40+ hours per week, $57,968 per year, Lisa Becker, 478-555-0001, please contact me first.

Skillfully manage and implement benefits and related HUMAN RESOURCES (HR) PROGRAMS AND PROCESSING for 3,800+ employees and 200 retirees. HR programs include health insurance, life insurance, retirement, leave [especially Family Medical Leave Act (FMLA)], 401(k) plans, and Workers' Compensation, among others. Analyze and assess employee and retiree needs, benefits contracts, budgets, and use trends in order to plan, formulate, and monitor programs, identify issues, and resolve. Provide written and oral recommendations to senior management for enhancing programs, maximizing their effectiveness and minimizing costs.

PROCESS ACTIONS, including benefits enrollment, benefits termination, benefits changes, and vendor invoices. Processed on-boarding documents for new employees. Review all documents for completeness prior to processing. Provide advice and guidance to new and existing employees on proper completion of enrollment and on-boarding documents. Monitor and track to ensure timely and accurate processing. Identify and resolve any processing, coverage, or payment problems.

DEVELOP A WIDE RANGE OF WRITTEN PRODUCTS, including human resources and benefits policies and procedures, analyses, recommendations, correspondence, orientation presentations, and reports. Examples of reports and analyses prepared include trend analyses, budget reports, benefits tax returns, and documents in support of wire transfers to the benefits vendors for premium payments and annual negotiation and plan design process. Also prepare well-received on-boarding packet for new hires. Prepare written responses to inquiries from employees and vendors. Ensure all documents demonstrate subject-matter expertise and are appropriate for the audience intended. Written documents are clear, concise, and complete; demonstrate knowledge of grammar, sentence structure, and vocabulary. Use the full range of MS Office Suite, including Word, Excel, PowerPoint, and Outlook, on a daily basis to prepare written narrative, numeric, and graphic products.

REVIEW, ANALYZE, INTERPRET, APPLY, DEVELOP, AND PROVIDE TECHNICAL INSTRUCTIONS AND GUIDANCE regarding HR and benefits programs. Determine the need for and assist in the development of written policies and procedures for various HR and benefits programs; review and recommend approval upon completion. Write Standard Operating Procedures (SOPs) for local HR and benefits functions, as needed.

USE OUTSTANDING ORAL COMMUNICATION SKILLS in the performance of duties, including one-on-one, in meetings, and during presentations. Effectively interact with diverse individuals of all organizational levels, from senior management to employees, as well as vendors and contractors, to share information, provide training, respond to questions and concerns, provide guidance and assistance, create policies and procedures, and resolve problems. Serve as Point of Contact (POC) on complex benefits and related HR issues. Ensure all oral communications are timely; demonstrate the highest levels of professionalism, courtesy, and tact on all occasions, including those that are controversial and/or sensitive. Authorized to represent the Company with benefits vendors.

USE KNOWLEDGE OF MANAGEMENT AND PROGRAM ANALYSIS THEORY AND TECHNIQUES TO PLAN AND CONDUCT REVIEW, ANALYSIS, AND EVALUATION OF VARIOUS HR AND BENEFITS PROGRAMS to assess effectiveness and efficiency in supporting organizational objectives and goals. Participate in design and development of analytical and assessment tools, including spreadsheets, turnover, budget, and other information. Identify, analyze, and evaluate problems and issues of a complex nature in HR and benefits work procedures and operations; analyze on-boarding and background investigation programs, among others; make recommendations for improving methods to collect and process timely and accurate data. Use skill in applying analytical and evaluative methods and techniques to review and assess complex benefits discrepancies; work with vendor and budget office to correct misapplied charges for several employees and managers. Conduct a review of vendor transactions; research, analyze, and ensure accuracy of expenditures and report findings. Conduct pension program audits; identify, research, and correct discrepancies. Analyze and evaluate office policies and procedures on a continual basis, recommending improvements to increase effectiveness, efficiency, and productivity in the office.

RESEARCH, ANALYZE, INTERPRET, AND APPLY federal, state, and company laws, regulations, policies, procedures, and guidance related to HR and benefits, including the Fair Labor Standards Act (FLSA), Family Medical Leave Act (FMLA), ERISA, COBRA, Workers' Compensation, Health Insurance Portability and Accountability Act (HIPAA), Occupational Safety & Health Administration (OSHA), Americans with Disabilities Act (ADA), Older Workers Benefit Protection Act, and others. Provide authoritative guidance to management and employees on interpretation and application of relevant laws and regulations; monitor and track pending legislation and regulatory requirements and guidelines; develop recommendations regarding impact of pending legislation on company practices. Develop guidance, as needed.

PROVIDE OUTSTANDING CUSTOMER SERVICE; BUILD AND MAINTAIN EFFECTIVE RELATIONSHIPS with senior management, vendors and contractors, employees, colleagues, and subordinates. Work collaboratively to develop, collect, and analyze complex benefits and HR information, advocate for recommendations, and establish and implement cost-effective projects. Approach interactions with a clear perception of organizational and political reality; use contacts and relationships to gain support and understanding for programs and recommendations.

PLAN AND CONDUCT ORIENTATION PROGRAMS for new hires. Research and develop materials, including MS PowerPoint slides and handouts, on the full range of benefits programs, including health insurance, life insurance, flexible spending accounts, leave, and other benefits. Present detailed information about benefits programs; respond to questions, help new hires complete forms, and provide authoritative advice about eligibility, benefits entitlements, claims, and similar information. Orientation programs are conducted weekly for as many as seven new hires at each session. Review completed forms to ensure accuracy and completeness for timely processing and enrollment.

CONDUCT EXIT INTERVIEWS with departing employees; analyze information from interview process in order to make detailed written recommendations on areas for improvement. Identify negative trends with an eye toward continual improvement and/or corrective action.

PREPARE AND PROCESS A VARIETY OF HR FORMS AND ACTIONS for automated system; ensure accuracy on completed forms. Interpret actions and determine appropriate coding; verify service dates, benefits entitlements, promotions, and related HR issues. Provide advice and assistance to less-experienced HR personnel on proper coding.

KEY ROLE IN IMPLEMENTATION OF WORKFORCE RECRUITMENT, an automated applicant-tracking program. Recognized Subject Matter Expert (SME) on system; liaison between company and vendor. Provided input on project implementation plan, provided technical requirements to meet company needs, delivered status updates and briefings to senior-level personnel, and oversaw the establishment of user controls and smooth flow of information between system and employee system. Developed and conducted training session for recruiters, system administrators, and managers. New system nearly halved recruitment process time.

PROJECT LEAD FOR ON-BOARDING PROJECT; coordinated across business units located nationwide to ensure project met business needs. Analyzed and evaluated existing policies, procedures, and processes related to new hires and made detailed recommendations for streamlining policies and procedures, consistent with best practices. Resulting new hire package was automated, streamlined, and uniform throughout the country as well as increased productivity, reduced low-tenure terminations, and enhanced management and new employee satisfaction.

USE KNOWLEDGE OF HR PRINCIPLES, CONCEPTS, AND PRACTICES; SME on employee benefits and other HR programs. Ensure all recommendations, guidance, and advice support business requirements.

PROMOTE TEAM APPROACH to problem-solving and mission accomplishment. Lead and/or participate on project teams of employees; set and adjust short-term priorities; prepare schedules for completion of work; selectively consider difficulty and requirements of work, skills, and capabilities. Review work requirements and quality standards. Ensure productivity measures are met. Encourage creativity and innovative thinking on projects and assignments; emphasize teamwork and customer focus. Develop and mentor employees; recommend training to enhance technical skills; promote positive and constructive conflict resolution. Implement Equal Employment Opportunity (EEO) and diversity; develop and maintain respectful work climate.

MAINTAIN CURRENCY IN HR field through attendance at professional conferences and training, active membership in professional organizations, training, research, and review of professional journals and best practices. Share knowledge with colleagues through formal and informal presentations, discussions, and written materials, as appropriate. Professional Human Resources (PHR) certification.

KEY ACCOMPLISHMENTS: Record of achievement; nominated by VP of Human Resources and received quarterly employee recognition award for providing technical knowledge and expertise for company-wide reimplementation of applicant-tracking system. Designated as technical liaison for iRecruiter, an integrated, automated recruitment and workforce planning system; system was implemented on time and greatly enhanced operational efficiency. Led team to create and implement new-hire packet used by all business units. Selected to train employees on regulatory requirements of HIPAA.

06/2000 to 12/2007, BUSINESS MANAGER/PERSONNEL SERVICES SPECIALIST, Florida Department of Law Enforcement, Tampa Regional Operations Center, FL, 40+ hours per week, $49,100 per year, June Cleaver, 478-555-0002, may contact.

USED KNOWLEDGE OF HUMAN RESOURCES (HR) THEORIES, PRINCI-PLES, CONCEPTS, AND PRACTICES TO PROVIDE A WIDE RANGE OF HR SUPPORT to managers and employees for a state agency of more than 1,000 employees; analyzed complex HR information and organizational requirements; conducted workforce analyses; and developed and implemented complex HR programs, including staffing and recruitment, pay and benefits, employee rela-tions, performance management, emergency response, Continuation of Opera-tions (COOP), classification, and related programs. Participated in strategic planning as well as the development and implementation of HR goals and objectives; ensured programs aligned with the organization's strategic goals and strengthened mission accomplishment. Processed personnel actions, ensuring timely and accurate entry into automated personnel system. Actions processed included new hires, reassignments, promotions, terminations, and retirements; also processed pay and benefits matters.

CONDUCTED WORKFORCE NEEDS ASSESSMENTS AND ANALYSES to ensure ongoing capabilities on both a daily basis as well as following emergen-cies. Identified the numbers and kinds of employees, as well as supporting facilities and services needed to meet organizational goals and objectives. Served as Project Lead of high-profile team to rebuild Pensacola Regional Operations Center, which supported ten counties in the Florida Panhandle, following devas-tation from Hurricane Ivan across the area. Developed and implemented a project plan, including tasks, due dates, responsibilities, and a $1 million budget. Coordi-nated with internal and external stakeholders, including the Agency's administra-tor, budget director, contractors, and senior leadership to seek input and provide weekly status reports. Monitored project execution, adjusting to changing conditions and feedback, as needed. Oversaw procurements and contractors, ensuring all products and work met expectations and specifications. Ensured all procurement and other activities were consistent with Florida State regulations. Completed rebuild under budget and in less than the expected time frame. Designated Emergency Support Function (ESF) Planner following Hurricanes Ivan, Dennis, and Katrina; timekeeper for all deployed staff; coordinated activi-ties with a wide range of agency and external personnel.

ANALYZED WORKFORCE AND RECRUITMENT TRENDS and developed effective approaches to meet anticipated agency needs. Consulted with managers to determine hiring needs and provided strategic and technical assistance. Col-lected and analyzed candidate data, turnover, and related information to pinpoint positive and negative trends. Identified and recommended cost-effective strategies to increase applicant pool and target appropriate recruitment sources while ensuring quality candidates.

PROVIDED EXPERT HR ADVICE, GUIDANCE, AND ASSISTANCE to managers and employees on the full range of complex HR issues, including confidential and sensitive issues. Interpreted and implemented federal and state personnel laws, regulations, and policies used in processing personnel actions and resolving problems for recruitment and placement, benefits, and other issues. Ensured appropriate application of State of Florida merit competition regulations. Developed and administered hiring assessments consistent with the Uniform Guidelines for Employee Selection Procedures. Authoritative source of information on HR regulations, policies, and procedures.

ENGAGED IN PROACTIVE ORAL COMMUNICATIONS with a wide variety of personnel, including agency leadership, senior management, colleagues, potential job applicants, and others in order to provide information, advocate for new approaches, respond to a wide range of questions, and solve problems. Sponsored and conducted conference calls with internal and external stakeholders to discuss policy changes, proposals, and other administrative topics. Prepared and presented briefings, training, and reports on HR and other matters to a wide variety of audiences; ensured all presentations were appropriate for target audience. Provided expert and timely advice and counsel on sensitive employee-relations matters. Updated managers on status of any ongoing personnel issues. Demonstrated professionalism, tact, and courtesy on all occasions.

RESEARCHED, ANALYZED, INTERPRETED, AND APPLIED TECHNICAL LAWS AND REGULATIONS, including Equal Employment Opportunity (EEO), Fair Labor Standards Act, FMLA, OSHA, merit hiring, and other relevant federal and agency HR regulations, policies, and procedures. Researched best practices to provide information for consideration. Ensured programs complied with relevant regulations. Source of information on these regulations for both internal and external stakeholders.

ESTABLISHED AND MAINTAINED EFFECTIVE COLLABORATIVE RELATIONSHIPS with a diverse range of personnel, including senior agency personnel, managers, employees, and colleagues. Worked to identify mutual goals; exploited commonalities of purpose to further organizational objectives and mission accomplishment. Demonstrated customer service, professionalism, courtesy, and tact on all occasions, even when delivering negative information or when under stress. Maintained confidentiality.

CONTINUALLY ASSESSED WORK PROCESSES AND PROCEDURES with a goal of process improvement. Used Quality Assurance (QA) and program management principles to conduct evaluations, identify areas needing improvement, and recommend cost-effective alternatives to better meet mission. Surveyed customers as part of program and process evaluation; incorporated stakeholder feedback into recommendations.

PURCHASE CARDHOLDER for State of Florida; authorized to make purchases for supplies and equipment. Ensured all purchases were consistent with state regulations. Held other fiscal responsibilities, including executed and/or monitored regional budget(s) to include general revenue, trust funds, and grants and donation trust funds, overtime, petty cash, and Operating Capital Outlay (OCO). Verified, certified, and processed receipts for purchases; identified variances and resolved.

PROVIDED LEADERSHIP AND DIRECT SUPERVISION AND GUIDANCE to as many as five direct reports; mentored staff to embody customer service. Planned and assigned work based on priorities and according to each employee's capabilities; prepared schedules for completion of work. Provided advice, counsel, and instruction to employees on work and administrative matters; mentored them to exceed organizational goals and objectives. Monitored work, ensuring all quality and timeline requirements were met; conducted performance evaluations. Recommended appropriate actions regarding hiring, firing, promotion, and reassignment. Identified and assessed developmental needs and provided training. Provided disciplinary actions when warranted and handled rare employee complaints. Modeled EEO principles and diversity objectives in all actions. Planned and conducted group and individual training sessions for staff, as well as program managers throughout the ten-county area. Interviewed prospective candidates and made selections.

ANALYZED DATA AND PREPARED A VARIETY OF WRITTEN REPORTS, ANALYSES, PRESENTATIONS, PROGRAM POLICIES, AND PROCEDURES related to HR, budget, emergency response, and other administrative matters; prepared in-depth Human Resources Operating Manual. Ensured all written information demonstrated cogent analysis and subject-matter expertise. Written products were targeted toward various audiences, from potential recruits to senior management; all were appropriate for the audience intended. Used the full range of MS Office Suite automation products, including Outlook, Word, Excel, and PowerPoint as well as other proprietary systems to prepare narrative, numeric, and graphic reports, presentations, and analyses.

KEY ACCOMPLISHMENTS: Developed first-ever Human Resources Operating Manual to detail and standardize processes and functions; manual adopted and used throughout the State of Florida. Key participant in developing and implementing successful emergency workforce planning and response after Hurricane Ivan. Selected for high-profile, five-week Leadership Training Program. Participated in domestic emergency and security exercises. Nominated by Regional Director as SME for statewide strategic planning process panel.

CERTIFICATION

Certified Professional in Human Resources (PHR), 2009

RELEVANT PROFESSIONAL TRAINING

Emergency Management:

Basic Incident Command Systems
Introduction to National Incident Management System (NIMS)
Introduction to National Response Plan (NRP)
Introduction to Incident Command System for Law Enforcement
Intermediate Incident Command System
Advanced Incident Command System
Domestic Preparedness Training

Human Resources and Supervision:

Strategic Planning Process Panel, 12/2006
Foundational Leadership Program, 07/2006
Human Diversity, 06/2006
High-Impact Project Management, 11/2005
Basic Supervisory Training, 01/2000

AWARDS AND RECOGNITION

Cash award and certificate for outstanding work on recruitment system, 2008

Davis Productivity Award, 2005

EDUCATION

1996, Bachelor of Science Degree, Business Administration, University of Miami, Miami, FL, 64 semester hours

1994, Associate of Arts Degree, Business Administration, Hillsborough Community College, Tampa, FL, 109 semester hours

1992, Diploma, Hillsborough High School, Tampa, FL

End of Sample Résumé

This sample résumé was compiled by the author, Dennis V. Damp, for a mid-level Human Resources (HR) Specialist with an IT background (with main keywords highlighted):

JOHN Q. ADAMS
SSN: xxx-xx-xxxx

3401 Main Street
Hyattsville, MD 20782
Work telephone: 222-222-2222
Home telephone: 333-333-3333

E-mail address: jqadams79@gonext.com

Citizenship: United States
Federal Status: N/A
Veterans' Preference: Yes, 5 points / DD-214 form available

OBJECTIVE

Management Analyst, GS-0343-07/09
National Archives and Records Administration
Announcement Number: 0916 LV, Closing Date 10/09/2010

PROFILE

Lead automation analyst for a large organization consisting of 797 workers located at seven offices in Maryland, Virginia, Pennsylvania, and Delaware. Novell, A+, Net+, and Microsoft Applications certified.

Results-oriented analyst and computer specialist with sound analytical, automation applications, and technical expertise. Provides a full range of continuing automation technical and advisory services to operating offices, system users, company officials, and warehouse managers.

Collateral duties included researching potential Local Area Network (LAN) deployment at branch and field offices, automation security administrator for the organization, and provided new system integration training. Attended numerous strategy sessions with vendors, managers, and staff to explore feasibility of expanding automation system capabilities.

PROFESSIONAL AND PERSONAL STRENGTHS

LEADERSHIP CHARACTERISTICS: Highly motivated, proven, and proactive leader recognized for sound judgement and entrusted with highly confidential and sensitive information.

PROFESSIONAL RESPONSIBILITIES: Conscientious and flexible when delegating and executing professional responsibilities and known for the ability to work effective with work groups and teams to get the job done, and done right.

MISSION ORIENTED: Committed to the organization's mission and yet tactful and willing to work complex issues collaboratively to reach the desired outcome. Multi-task oriented and makes sound decisions due to technical expertise under pressure

EXPERIENCE

COMPUTER ANALYST, 04-1999 to Present; 40 hours/week, annual salary $47,956

Hendricks Inc, 435 Smithfield Drive, Smithfield, MD 20782

Supervisor: Gene Porter, 202-123-2456, Extension 410. You may contact my present and all previous supervisors.

Proficient in most Microsoft applications including Word, Excel, Powerpoint, Scheduler, Project, Frontpage 2003 and Access. Trained over 127 users in software applications over the past two years. Designed Hendricks' corporate Web site that was awarded several Internet design awards. Three of my articles were published in major national magazines concerning NOVELL upgrades and system integration issues. Copies available upon request.

DUTIES & RESPONSIBILITIES

AUTOMATION EXPERT: Technical automation expert for Leesburg, Virginia, headquarters, Novell LAN operations.

LAN SYSTEM MANAGEMENT: Analyze and advise management on all aspects of system integration and LAN applications. Recommended file system upgrade and LAN integration through Wynnframe deployment. Initiate daily LAN backups.

FEASIBILITY STUDIES: Perform feasibility studies and analysis of staff and field office automation needs. Recommend automation system improvements and upgrade.

COMPUTER MAINTENANCE: Maintain DELL NT computer work stations at headquarters for 127 employees. Debug, repair and service operating systems and software/hardware throughout the organization.

E-MAIL SYSTEM ADMINISTRATOR: Maintain company Lotus Notes e-mail for the organization. Updated address databases and worked with vendors concerning major problems and software failures.

COST-BENEFIT ANALYSIS: Perform cost/benefit evaluation for work station upgrades and LAN automation expansion at field facilities.

COMPUTER TRAINING: Train 127 users on new system functions and software applications.

WEBMASTER: Company Web site Webmaster, proficient in html and htmls.

BUDGET ANALYSIS: Develops company's annual Information Resource Management (IRM) budget.

AUTOMATION SECURITY ADMINISTRATOR: Site automation administrator, maintaining all user data, access levels, and system security passwords and documentation.

TECHNICAL DOCUMENTATION: Maintain a comprehensive technical and software applications user library.

ACCOMPLISHMENTS

AUTOMATION CONFIGURATION: Developed written automation configuration reports for upper management to consolidate three field offices into a central hub facility at Baltimore, Maryland.

AUTOMATION NETWORK MANAGEMENT: Management accepted my Wynnframe LAN field integration recommendation after I completed a comprehensive cost/benefit analysis and feasibility study for the upgrade. I developed gant and milestone charts using Microsoft Project to schedule, coordinate, and complete the upgrade using internal resources. Trained users after field installation was complete.

WEBMASTER: Designed the company's Internet Web site. Management accepted my proposal after viewing an interactive Powerpoint presentation that I developed and viewing a live online demonstration that featured the Web site functionality. I received a substantial cash bonus for developing the site.

STRATEGIC PLANNING TEAM MEMBER: Member of the company's strategic planning committee. The committee presented the CEO with plans for major Internet security improvements and a cost/benefit analysis for our automation needs through 2008. The study included a major expansion to two additional states scheduled for 2007.

COMPUTER SPECIALIST, 06-1994 to 04-1999, 40 hours/week, annual salary $32,545

National Rental Corporation, 101 Fifth St., Silver Spring, MD 20901

Supervisor: Charles Massie, 202-234-2345.

Responsible for system administration, maintenance, and new software training for 47 specialists and five managers. Designed, updated, and modified office automation applications for the organization and serviced over 67 desktop and laptop computers and office Local Area network — LAN. Worked closely with department managers and vendors to create and maintain appropriate technical documentation for all system users. Collateral responsibilities included researching potential LAN deployment at branch offices and new system integration training. Attended numerous strategy sessions with vendors and mangers to explore the feasibility of expanding office automation system capabilities.

DUTIES & RESPONSIBILITIES

SYSTEM ADMINISTRATOR: System administrator for the organization's information processing systems. Coordinated all upgrades, scheduled maintenance, and assigned user names and passwords.

LAN MAINTENANCE: Performed daily LAN backups of critical office databases and assisted specialists with local computer backup as needed.

SPECIAL PROJECTS: Initiated and monitored special projects including automation software deployment for the entire organization. Team lead for LAN/WAN configuration and maintenance.

WEB SITE MANAGEMENT: Set up Internet accounts for all company vendors and trained staff on data collection applications.

ACCOMPLISHMENTS

TEAM LEAD: Recommended improvements, evaluated, coordinated, and implementation of NOVELL server upgrades. Upgrades were accomplished with minimal system downtime and negligible impact to clients and staff.

WRITTEN REPORTS AND ORAL PRESENTATIONS: Developed numerous written reports and gave oral presentations to managers on various IRM and ADP issues including NOVELL deployment, user system upgrades, and automation security threats and system enhancements.

IRM SECURITY: Developed organizations IRM security directives/regulations. Trained managers and staff on security concerns and provided methods to improve online security at all levels of the organization.

FEASIBILITY STUDIES: Performed a feasibility study to implement a paperless office. Researched options, developed plans, performed a cost/benefit analysis, and presented a proposal to the Chief Executive Officer. The plan was successfully implemented throughout the organization.

COMMUNICATIONS SYSTEM REPAIRMAN, 05-1992 to 06-1994, 40 hours/week,

Annual Salary $17,789

U.S. Army, National Training Center, 11th Armored Regiment, Operations Group

Fort Irwin, CA 92310-5067

Supervisor: Msgt Don Riley, 760-999-9999

Attained the active duty rank of Sergeant. Responsible for maintaining and servicing the training center's field communications systems including Frequency Modulated-FM handsets, telephone equipment, and Very High Frequency-VHF and Ultra High Frequency-UHF transmitters and receivers used to communicate with air support and armored cavalry command units. Assigned collateral duties to maintain field computers used to direct and coordinate troop movements with headquarters command. Responsible for analyzing and advising training command staff of communication problems and concerns.

DUTIES AND RESPONSIBILITIES

ELECTRONICS MAINTENANCE: Provided field and shop level maintenance for FM hand held transceivers and VHF/UHF transceivers.

COMPUTER MAINTENANCE: Programed field computers used for troop movement and developed user technical documentation for critical field deployments. Assisted computer specialists with field computer repair.

LOGISTICS SUPPORT: Logistical support including ordering of spare parts and supplies and storage of line replaceable units.

TELEPHONE SYSTEM MAINTENANCE: Troubleshoot telephone and switching equipment problems.

ACCOMPLISHMENTS

COMMUNICATIONS SYSTEMS MANAGEMENT: Coordinated the utilization of limited communication resources for field deployment at the training center for over 2,000 active duty and reserve troops. Prioritized order of delivery communication needs for all deployments.

TOP SECRETE CRYPTO CLEARANCE: Crypto trained for Top Secret scrambled communications between command centers and senior field command officers. Responsible for safeguarding equipment and destroying it at all costs if enemy infiltration discovered.

COST-BENEFIT ANALYSIS: Developed, evaluated, and performed a cost/benefit analysis for a communications deployment scheme at the training centers that was implemented at all Department of Defense training facilities.

EDUCATION

Community College of Baltimore, Baltimore, MD 21201, associates degree in computer technology, graduated with high honors, 05-1990

ADDITIONAL TRAINING

Communications Electronics School, US Army, 1992 (6 months)

Microsoft Office, April (40 hours), 1993

Work Station Integration & LAN Connectivity (160 hours), 1994

NOVEL Certification Course (80 hours), 1995

Microsoft Office Professional (40 hours), 1996

Quality of Worklife and Team Work (40 hours), employer sponsored

LAN/WAN Office Configuration Management Course (240 hours), 1999

A+ / Net + Software/Hardware Certification Course (200 hours), 2003

OTHER QUALIFICATIONS

AWARDS

US ARMY Dickens Award for Outstanding Achievement. Awarded for developing a communications deployment strategy that was accepted by the DOD for all ARMY training centers, 1991.

Designed, developed and published Hendricks' web site. Received a substantial cash bonus for developing the site, 2002.

LICENSES/CERTIFICATIONS

FCC Radio Telephone License with Ship Radar endorsement (Current)

NOVEL Certified 1999

A+ / NET + Certified 06-2003

Competent Toastmaster status 05-1997. In addition to the courses I have taken to acquire further knowledge for the positions I have held, I also have experience and expertise in the following areas:

INTERPERSONAL RELATIONS

Deal effectively and professionally with people. A team player as evidenced by my military background and success at Hendricks Corp. to integrate and consolidate branch offices. I enjoy working in groups and have been trained in Quality Worklife (QWL) and Partnership initiatives.

COMMUNICATIONS AND WRITING SKILLS

Joined Toastmasters International in 1995 and achieved Competent Toastmaster status in May 1997. Several of my networking integration studies were published in national journals in 2002. In 2004 I completed oral communications and report writing courses at a local community college. Maintain an excellent grasp of the English language and have experience in a variety of different writing styles including reports, grant requests, informational material, speeches, brochures, and promotional material.

TRAINING SKILLS

Conducted classes for office automation and software applications to over 200 employees. I also provide on-the-job training to individual users on an as needed basis and frequently train managers on new applications and Internet security options and procedures.

OFFICE SKILLS

Knowledgeable in all aspects of office operations and proficient in operating a wide variety of office machinery including word processors, copiers, postage meters, telephone systems, including PBX, fax machines, electronic mail, computer modems as well as all types of audiovisual equipment. Able to set up, calibrate, and configure all types of electronic equipment from printers, and telephone systems, to recorders, cameras and other ancillary equipment. Knowledgeable with Powerpoint.

End of Sample Résumé

How to Apply for Senior Executive Service (SES) Positions

The SES, which was founded as part of the Civil Service Reform Act of 1978, is composed of the men and women charged with leading the continuing transformation of government. These leaders possess well-honed executive skills and share a broad perspective of government and a public service commitment.

Members of the SES serve in the key positions just below the top Presidential appointees (e.g., the Presidential Cabinet); some SES personnel can be appointed by the President.

SES members are the major link between these appointees and the rest of the federal workforce. They operate and oversee nearly every government activity in approximately 75 federal agencies and are expected to have executive qualifications in five key Executive Core Qualifications (ECQs): leading change, leading people, results driven, business acumen, and building coalitions.

Structure of the SES Pay System	Minimum	Maximum
Agencies with a Certified SES Performance Appraisal System	$119,544	$179,700
Agencies without a Certified SES Performance Appraisal System	$119,544	$165,300

Scientific and Professional (ST) and Senior Level (SL)

SES positions are classified as positions at or above the GS-15 or equivalent. These positions involve one or more of the criteria set forth in 5 United States Code (USC) 3132 (e.g., directing the work of an organization, monitoring progress toward organizational goals, etc.).

Within the SES, there are two subcategories, as follows:

ST (Scientific and Professional) positions are classified above the GS-15 level and involve high-level research and development. ST positions are established under 5 USC 3104 and are always in the Competitive Service.

SL (Senior Level) positions are classified above GS-15. The work of the position does not involve the fundamental research and development responsibilities that are characteristic of ST positions. SL positions may be in either the Competitive or the Excepted Service. The vast majority of SES positions are SL.

Who Is Eligible for SES?

People who are looking to transition to the federal government are often attracted to the high level of responsibility and compensation offered at the SES level. However, just because someone has run his/her own small business and held the title of Chief Executive Officer (CEO) or Chief Information Officer (CIO) doesn't necessarily mean that he/she is automatically eligible for SES status.

To determine your eligibility for an SES position, you must go through a Qualification Review Board (QRB) process, which considers your executive qualifications. The QRB consists of three unique cases, as follows:

■   Criterion A cases are based on demonstrated executive experience. Candidates must show that they have demonstrated experience/competence in all five ECQs as part of their application for SES positions.

■   Criterion B cases are based on successful participation in an Office of Personnel Management (OPM)-approved SES Candidate Development Program (CDP). Candidates who compete government-wide and successfully complete a CDP are eligible for non-competitive appointment to the SES. (However, successful completion does not guarantee placement in the SES.)

■   Criterion C cases are based on candidates having special or unique qualities that indicate a likelihood of success in the SES. Candidates must demonstrate that they have the qualifications for the position and the potential to quickly acquire full competence in the five ECQs. The package submitted for QRB approval must contain the agency's assessment of why the selectee uniquely qualifies for the position and an Individual Development Plan (IDP) that focuses on the specific ECQs that need to be enhanced.

Executive Core Qualifications (ECQs)

There are five ECQs in which all SES candidates must be able to demonstrate a high level of proficiency. As you evaluate whether you would be a fit for the SES, use this list of ECQs as a good starting point to ascertain the strength of your professional background.

The five ECQs are as follows:

1.   **Leading Change.** The ability to bring about strategic change, both within and outside the organization, to meet organizational goals. Inherent to this ECQ is the ability to establish an organizational vision and to implement it in a continually changing environment. Characteristics that should be demonstrated in this ECQ include Creativity and Innovation, External Awareness, Flexibility, Resilience, Strategic Thinking, and Vision.

2. **Leading People**. The ability to lead people toward meeting the organization's vision, mission, and goals. Inherent to this ECQ is the ability to provide an inclusive workplace that fosters the development of others, facilitates cooperation and teamwork, and supports constructive resolution of conflicts. Characteristics that should be demonstrated in this ECQ include Conflict Management, Leveraging Diversity, Developing Others, and Team-building.

3. **Results Driven**. The ability to meet organizational goals and customer expectations. Inherent to this ECQ is the ability to make decisions that produce high-quality results by applying technical knowledge, analyzing problems, and calculating risks. Characteristics that should be demonstrated in this ECQ include Accountability, Customer Service, Decisiveness, Entrepreneurship, Problem Solving, and Technical Credibility.

4. **Business Acumen**. The ability to manage human, financial, and information resources strategically. Characteristics that should be demonstrated in this ECQ include Financial Management, Human Capital Management, and Technology Management.

5. **Building Coalitions**. The ability to build coalitions internally and with other federal agencies, state and local governments, non-profit and private-sector organizations, foreign governments, or international organizations to achieve common goals. Characteristics that should be demonstrated in this ECQ include Partnering, Political Savvy, and Influencing/Negotiating.

The Federal Candidate Development Program (CDP)

For those who are determined to gain employment in the SES but who might not have the necessary qualifications, the SES Federal Candidate Development Program (CDP) offered by the government helps give candidates a competitive edge for SES consideration.

Participating agencies that offer an SES CDP program have collaborated with trainers to ensure candidates receive the most comprehensive training to prepare them for a challenging career at the SES level. While the class size, application process, and topics vary according to the agency, the program must typically be completed within 12-18 months of enrollment and concurrently with a candidate fulfilling his/her other job responsibilities. The goal of the CDP is to:

- Prepare participants for SES certification by OPM

- Establish a pool of qualified candidates for SES positions

- Prepare future executives for collaborative leadership

Candidates who complete the program and obtain certification by an SES QRB may be selected for an SES position anywhere in the federal government without further competition.

For more information on the SES and CDP, visit http://federaljobs.net/ses.htm.

How Does SES Differ from Other Position Classifications?

The SES is the highest competitive level a candidate can reach in the federal government, short of being a Presidential appointee or an elected official. As such, it's a very competitive program because there are only a few positions within each agency.

Some primary differences between SES and the other positions include:

- Veterans do not receive hiring preference for SES positions; this is because 5 USC 2108(3), which defines the term "preference eligible," explains that this term does not include applicants for, or members of, the Senior Executive Service.

- SES members have their own association: the Senior Executive Association (SEA). The SEA is a professional association representing the interests of the members of the career Senior Executive Service. SEA maintains a website on which members may access valuable resources, including legal help and member forums.

- SES members do not necessarily have to be status candidates. In an effort to recruit the best and brightest leaders, more and more agencies are opening up their SES candidate pool to private-industry personnel who are able to exhibit the ECQs within a context that would fit the open SES position.

The SES Application Process

SES positions are posted on USAJobs.gov; however, the application process varies between agencies. Some agencies require the submission of an SES, detailed narratives outlining each of the Executive Core Competencies (generally ten pages), and essays describing a candidate's possession of Technical Qualifications (TQs), which are an additional one to two pages each; others will accept only a five-page federal résumé that includes the ECQs and any required TQs.

SES applicants are sometimes required to address their experience, accomplishments, and Executive Core Qualifications (ECQs) within a five-page résumé. CPG has developed a five-page, all-inclusive SES and ECQ résumé format that continues to be well received by many agencies and by OPM. However, if you are selected for an SES position, you may still have to develop a full set of ECQs within a very short timeframe — usually one week.

You will want to read the SES announcement carefully for specific instructions. Links to additional information about the SES application process can be found online at www.federaljobs.net/ses.htm.

Assistance with Applying for Federal Jobs

In this chapter, we provided current information about the federal job landscape and the many changes occurring from hiring reform. However, in our opinion, the federal application process will continue to be a challenge. Information is being shuffled around and the federal hiring process is still very confusing. The federal hiring reform is evolving and there will always be special circumstances to address in applications.

CareerPro Global (CPG) has been assisting private-sector, former military, and federal employees with qualifying for interviews within the federal government for more than two decades. We have a staff of highly trained, certified, and experienced writers for all series, grades, and careers in government.

As the only career management service to have earned ISO 9001:2008 international quality certification, CPG has raised the bar in application development, quality, customer service, document security, and many other aspects of business strategy. We encourage you to reach out to us when you find a vacancy announcement in which you are interested. We can help you develop your application materials and earn the highest ranking possible.

For assistance submit your current résumé and vacancy announcement to www.careerproplus.com and request a consultation, or call 800-471-9201 to speak to a Master Federal Career Coach (MFCC). Mention that you learned about our service from *The Book of U.S. Government Jobs* and receive a free consultation.

Chapter 6 Contributors

Barbara A. Adams: Barbara is the President and CEO of CareerPro Global, Inc. (CPG), founded in 1986 and recognized as one of the leading pioneers in the careers services industry. Barbara has built CPG into one of the largest, most respected, and fastest-growing career services organizations industry-wide. Barbara is committed to CPG's core factors that include quality product, exceptional customer service, honesty, integrity, and a passion for helping others achieve their career goals. She believes so strongly in these core factors that she positioned CPG to raise the bar by developing an ISO 9001:2008 guided process (the first in the careers industry), through which all of our processes are reviewed for quality. CPG proudly earned full ISO 9001:2008 Certification in July 2010. Barbara is the co-author of the Master Federal Career Coach (MFCC) and Certified Military Résumé Writer (CMRW) certifications credentialed by Career Directors International, a recognized career industry-credentialing authority. She holds five career industry credentials, remains on the pulse of all hiring trends, and is very active within the careers community. For application assistance development, contact Barbara at badams@careerprocenter.net.

Lee Kelley: Lee is a former Army Captain, Iraq War vet, and senior writer and trainer with CPG. He is also the newly appointed Director of Veteran Transitions, and runs our new blog, (www.veteranstransitionhq.wordpress.com) Veteran Transition Headquarters.

Lee is a highly versatile and award-winning author who has been asked to write for the New York Times on several occasions. His books include Fire in the Night: Creative Essays from an Iraq War Vet, and A Life Well-Built: The Authorized Biography of Brigadier General Richard Fisher. Lee was a 2009 TORI™ nominee for best military résumé, and is a CMRW and a certified MFCC with trainer designation (T). Also an MFCC co-author and an empowering coach, Lee has assisted hundreds of clients in developing their federal application materials and in achieving their own career goals. Lee may be contacted at lee.kelley@careerprocenter.net.

Patricia Duckers: Patricia has more than ten years of experience as an accomplished Career Coach, Senior Résumé Writer, and personal branding strategist. She is also a co-author of the MFCC and CMRW credentials. Patricia is a sought-after writer specializing in military and federal résumé development, consistently earning her clients the "Best Qualified" rating. Patricia holds eight career industry credentials, including the distinguished Master Career Director (MCD) distinction awarded to industry professionals who have demonstrated a continual commitment in providing the vision, tools, motivation, strategies, and expertise to guide clients to success. Patricia is a 2010 TORI™ (Toast of the Résumé Industry) nominee and first-place winner for "Best Cover Letter." Pat holds multiple industry certifications, including MFCC (T). For application assistance development, contact Patricia at patriciad@careerprocenter.net.

Nancy H. Segal: Nancy has more than 30 years' experience in federal Human Resources (HR) management, having worked extensively with both managers and employees to help them understand and navigate the federal hiring process. Nancy is a sought-after speaker and trainer on federal HR issues, and is the co-author of a book on the Department of Defense's former performance management system, and is a senior résumé writer at CPG specializing in SES packages. Nancy is also a certified MFCC- T, and can be contacted at nancy.segal@careerprocenter.net.

CHAPTER SEVEN
Veterans and Military Dependent Hiring

Veterans can take advantage of special-emphasis civil service hiring programs including, *Veterans Preference*, the *Veterans Recruitment Act (VRA)*, and the *Veterans Employment Opportunities Act (VEOA)*. In certain circumstances mothers of veterans and military spouses may be eligible for special appointing authorities or derived veterans' preference.

I took advantage of a special-emphasis hiring program when I was discharged from the U.S. Air Force under the ***Palace Chase*** program in 1973. I was hired full time as an avionics technician for the Air National Guard. The Palace Chase program helped reduce the size of the military as the Vietnam war was ending.

The federal government has an outstanding record of employing veterans. Veterans hold a far higher percentage of jobs in the government than they do in private industry. In large part, this is due to laws providing Veterans' Preference and special appointing authorities for veterans, as well as the fact that agencies recognize that hiring veterans is just good business.

Over 30% of all federal employees are veterans.

CHAPTER OBJECTIVES

✎   Understand Veterans' Preference

✎   Explore Veterans Preference, VRA and VEOA Programs

✎   Opportunities for disabled veterans

✎   Military Transition Planning *(Working for Uncle Sam Again)*

✎   Special hiring programs for military dependents

SPECIAL HIRING INITIATIVES FOR VETERANS

On November 9, 2009, the President issued an Executive Order establishing a Council on Veterans Employment to enhance recruitment of and promote employment opportunities for veterans in the government with a goal of making the federal government a leader in promoting employment for veterans. In addition, 19 federal agencies, including all Presidential Cabinet-level agencies, plus a number of others, are required to establish a Veterans Employment Program Office responsible for enhancing employment opportunities for veterans within the agency.

VETERANS PREFERENCE

Veterans' Preference gives eligible veterans preference in appointment over many other applicants. Veterans' Preference applies to virtually all new appointments in the Competitive Service and many in the Excepted Service. Veterans' Preference does not guarantee veterans a job and it does not apply to internal agency actions such as promotions, transfers, reassignments, and reinstatements.

Not all veterans receive preference for federal civilian employment, and not all active duty service qualifies for Veterans' Preference. Only veterans discharged or released from active duty in the Armed Forces under honorable conditions are eligible for Veterans' Preference. This means preference eligibles must have been discharged under an honorable or general discharge. If you are a "retired member of the Armed Forces," you are not included in the definition of preference eligible unless you are a disabled veteran, or you retired below the rank of major or its equivalent.

There are two types of preference eligibles: those with a service-connected disability (formerly titled 10 point preference) and those without (formerly titled 5 point preference). Under hiring reform the point system is being replaced with a category rating system. Until hiring reform is fully implemented you may encounter the old terminology of 5 and 10 point preference. Preference eligibles are divided into four basic groups as follows:

- CPS – Disability rating of 30% or more (10 points)

- CP – Disability rating of at least 10% but less than 30% (10 points)

- XP – Disability rating less than 10% (10 points)

- TP   Preference eligibles with no disability rating (5 points)

When agencies used a numerical rating and ranking system to determine the best qualified applicants for a position, an additional 5 or 10 points were added to the numerical score of qualified preference eligible veterans.

The category rating system places preference eligibles who have a compensable service-connected disability of 10 percent or more (CPS, CP) at the top of the highest category on the referral list (except for scientific or professional positions at the GS-9 level or higher). XP and TP preference eligibles are placed above non-preference eligibles within their assigned category.

Vets Without a Service Connected Disability — *(Five Point Preference)*

If your active duty service meets any of the following, and you do not have a disability rating from the Department of Veterans Affairs (VA) of 10% or more, you have preference. This preference entitles you to be hired before a non-veteran whose application is rated in your same category. To meet this criterion, your service must meet one of the following conditions:

- 180 or more consecutive days, any part of which occurred during the period beginning September 11, 2001 and ending on a future date prescribed by Presidential proclamation or law as the last date of Operation Iraqi Freedom, OR

- Between August 2, 1990 and January 2, 1992, OR

- 180 or more consecutive days, any part of which occurred after January 31, 1955 and before October 15, 1976.

- In a war, campaign or expedition for which a campaign badge has been authorized or between April 28, 1952 and July 1, 1955.

Vets with a Service Connected Disability — *(Ten-Point Preference)*

You are a 10 point preference eligible if you served at any time, and you:

- have a service connected disability

- received a Purple Heart

- are the spouse, widow, widower, or mother of a deceased or disabled veteran (derived preference)[1]

> Purple Heart recipients are awarded the same preference category as those with a service-connected disability.

When applying for federal jobs, eligible veterans should claim preference on their application or résumé. Applicants claiming disability, 10-point preference, must complete form SF-15, Application for 10-Point Veteran Preference. Veterans who are still in the service may be granted five points tentative preference on the basis of information contained in their applications, but they must produce a DD Form 214 prior to appointment to document their entitlement to preference.

---

[1] Derived preference, www.fedshirevets.gov/job/familypref/index.aspx

Note: Reservist who are separated from the reserves but don't currently receive retired pay aren't considered "retired military" for purposes of veterans' preference.

If you are not sure of your preference eligibility, visit the OPM's website, Feds Hire Vets at **www.fedshirevets.gov/Index.aspx** and/or the Veterans Guide at www.fedshirevets.gov/hire/hrp/vetguide/index.aspx. You can also contact the designated veterans' hiring program coordinator for your agency of interest; agency coordinator contact information can be found at the end of this chapter.

A preference eligible who is passed over on a list of eligibles is entitled, upon request, to a copy of the agency's reasons for the pass-over and the examining office's response.

If the preference eligible is a 30 percent or more disabled veteran, the agency must notify the veteran and OPM of the proposed pass-over. The veteran has 15 days from the date of notification to respond to OPM. OPM then decides whether to approve the pass-over based on all the facts available and notifies the agency and the veteran.

> Entitlement to veterans' preference does not guarantee a job. There are many ways an agency can fill a vacancy other than by appointment from a list of eligibles.

Filing Applications After Examinations Close

A 10-point preference eligible may file an application at any time for any position for which a nontemporary appointment has been made in the preceding three years; for which a list of eligibles currently exists that is closed to new applications; or for which a list is about to be established. Veterans wishing to file after the closing date should contact the agency that announced the position for further information.

SPECIAL APPOINTING AUTHORITIES

The following special authorities permit the noncompetitive appointment of eligible veterans. Use of these special authorities is entirely discretionary with the agency; no one is **entitled** to a special appointment.

VETERANS' RECRUITMENT APPOINTMENT (VRA)

The VRA is a special authority by which agencies can appoint an eligible veteran without competition at any grade level through General Schedule (GS) 11 or equivalent. The VRA is an excepted appointment to a position that is otherwise in the competitive service. After two years of satisfactory service, the veteran is converted to a career-conditional appointment in the competitive service.

When two or more VRA applicants are preference eligibles, the agency must apply veterans' preference as required by law. (While all VRA eligibles have served in the armed forces, they do not necessarily meet the eligibility requirements for veterans' preference under section 2108 of title 5, United States Code.)

Veterans' Recruitment Appointment (VRA) is an excepted authority that allows agencies, to appoint eligible veterans without competition. If you:

- are in receipt of a campaign badge for service during a war or in a campaign or expedition; OR

- are a disabled veteran, OR

- are in receipt of an Armed forces Service Medal for participation in a military operation, OR

- are a recently separated veteran (within the last 3 years), AND

- separated under honorable conditions (this means an honorable or general discharge), you are VRA eligible.

You can be appointed under this authority at any grade level up to and including a GS-11 or equivalent. This is an excepted service appointment. After successfully completing 2 years, you will be converted to the competitive service. Veterans' preference applies when using the VRA authority.

Agencies can also use VRA to fill temporary (not to exceed 1 year) or term (more than 1 year but not to exceed 4 years) positions. If you are employed in a temporary or term position under VRA, you will not be converted to the competitive service after 2 years. There is no limit to the number of times you can apply under VRA.

Eligibility Requirements

In addition to meeting the criteria above, eligible veterans must have been separated under honorable conditions (i.e., the individual must have received either an honorable or general discharge under honorable conditions).

Clarifications

Under the eligibility criteria, not all five-point preference eligible veterans may be eligible for a VRA appointment. For example, a veteran who served during the Vietnam era (i.e., for more than 180 consecutive days, after January 31, 1955, and before October 15, 1976) but did not receive a service-connected disability or an Armed Forces Service Medal or campaign or expeditionary medal would be entitled to five-point veterans' preference. This veteran, however, would not be eligible for a VRA appointment under the above criteria.

As another example, a veteran who served during the Gulf War from August 2, 1990, through January 2, 1992, would be eligible for veterans' preference solely on the basis of that service. However, service during that time period, in and of itself, does not confer VRA eligibility on the veteran unless one of the above VRA eligibility criteria is met.

Lastly, if an agency has two or more VRA candidates and one or more is a preference eligible, the agency must apply veterans' preference. For example, one applicant is VRA eligible on the basis of receiving an Armed Forces Service Medal (this medal does not confer veterans' preference eligibility). The second applicant is VRA eligible on the basis of being a disabled veteran (which does confer veterans' preference eligibility). In this example, both individuals are VRA eligible but only one of them is eligible for veterans' preference. As a result, agencies must apply the procedures of 5 CFR 302 when considering VRA candidates for appointment.

How to Apply

Veterans should contact the federal agency personnel office directly where they are interested in working to find out about VRA opportunities. Complete a résumé or an Optional Application for Federal Employment OF-612 and forward it with a cover letter to selected agencies. Refer to the Veterans Employment Program Offices in this Chapter and the resources listed in Chapter Three and the Appendices for specific agency addresses and telephone numbers. Also, visit www.federaljobs.net for direct links to more than 140 federal agency recruiting sites. Chapter Six will help you draft your federal style résumé.

Send a cover letter with your application explaining that you are a VRA candidate and would like to be considered for an appointment. Send a copy of your DD-214 form, number 4 copy with your cover letter and application.

Follow up each submission with a phone call. It helps to call an agency first and obtain a name and address to which you can send an application. Send applications to every office and department that interests you.

Agencies **do not have to hire through the VRA program**. Only if your education and work experience meets their requirements, they have openings, and like what they see will they make you an offer. Be tactful and don't be demanding.

30% OR MORE DISABLED VETERANS

These veterans may be given a temporary or term appointment (not limited to 60 days or less) to any position for which qualified (there is no grade limitation). After demonstrating satisfactory performance, the veteran may be converted at any time to a career-conditional appointment.

Eligibility

- retired from active military service with a service-connected disability rating of 30% or more; or

- you have a rating by the Department of VA showing a compensable service-connected disability of 30% or more.

Terms and conditions of employment

Initially, the disabled veteran is given a temporary appointment with an expiration date in excess of 60 days. This appointment may be converted at any time to a career conditional appointment. Unlike the VRA, there is no grade limitation.

How to Apply

Veterans should contact the federal agency personnel office where they are interested in working to find out about opportunities. Veterans must submit a copy of a letter dated within the last 12 months from the Department of Veterans Affairs or the Department of Defense certifying receipt of compensation for a service-connected disability of 30 percent or more.

Disabled Veterans Enrolled in VA Training Programs

Disabled veterans eligible for training under the Department of Veterans Affairs' (VA) vocational rehabilitation program may enroll for training or work experience at an agency under the terms of an agreement between the agency and VA. The veteran is not a federal employee for most purposes while enrolled in the program, but is a beneficiary of the VA.

The training is tailored to individual needs and goals, so there is no set length. If the training is intended to prepare the individual for eventual appointment in the agency (rather than just work experience), OPM must approve the training plan. Upon successful completion, the veteran will be given a Certificate of Training showing the occupational series and grade level of the position for which trained. This allows any agency to appoint the veteran noncompetitively for a period of one year. Upon appointment, the veteran is given a Special Tenure Appointment which is then converted to career-conditional with OPM approval.

In all cases, you must provide acceptable documentation of your preference or appointment eligibility. The number 4 copy of your DD-214, "Certificate of Release or Discharge from Active Duty," is necessary to document the character of service. If claiming 10-point preference, you will need to submit a Standard Form 15, "Application for 10-point Veterans' Preference."

VETERANS EMPLOYMENT OPPORTUNITIES ACT (VEOA)

The Veterans Employment Opportunities Act (VEOA) gives veterans access to federal job opportunities that might otherwise be closed to them. The law requires that:

- Agencies allow eligible veterans to compete for vacancies advertised under the agency's merit promotion procedures when the agency is seeking applications from individuals outside its own workforce.

- All merit promotion announcements open to applicants outside an agency's workforce include a statement that these eligible veterans may apply.

The law also establishes a new redress system for preference eligibles and makes it a prohibited personnel practice for an agency to knowingly take or fail to take a personnel action if that action or failure to act would violate a statutory or regulatory veterans' preference requirement.

This authority permits an agency to appoint an eligible veteran who has applied under an agency merit promotion announcement that is open to candidates outside the agency.

To be eligible a candidate must be a preference eligible or a veteran separated after three years or more of continuous active service performed under honorable conditions.

Those with derived preference are also eligible for VEOA. There is not a requirement to select a VEOA applicant over another applicant as in a VRA appointment to an external announcement. Another difference is that there is no requirement for the positions applied for to be lower than a GS-11 as there is under VRA criteria.

Terms and conditions of employment

Veterans receiving a VEOA appointment will be given a career or career conditional appointment in the competitive service. Veterans interested in applying under this authority should seek out agency merit promotion announcements open to candidates outside the agency. There is no advantage for veterans with career status or reinstatement eligibility to apply under VEOA, because they already have the eligibility to apply to merit promotion announcements and there is no preferential treatment for those applying under VEOA.

Positions Restricted to Preference Eligibles

Examinations for custodian, guard, elevator operator, and messenger are open only to preference eligibles as long as such applicants are available.

VETERANS DISCRIMINATION COMPLAINTS

The Uniformed Services Employment and Reemployment Rights Act of 1994 (**USERRA**) prohibits discrimination in employment, retention, promotion, or any benefit of employment based on your uniformed service. The Department of Labor, through the VETS, assists all persons having USERRA claims.

If you are a disabled veteran and you believe an agency discriminated against you in employment because of your disability, you may file a disability discrimination complaint with the offending agency under regulations administered by the Equal Employment Opportunity Commission (EEOC).

MILITARY TO FEDERAL TRANSITION
Working for Uncle Sam After the Military

Military personnel approaching discharge or retirement often explore federal sector employment options. Most military retirees are in their late thirties or early forties and have 20 or more high income producing years to work before they stop working. Approximately 22.4% percent of the federal workforce have veterans preference and an additional 6.2% are retired military. Veterans are accustomed to federal regulations and the bureaucratic environment that's inherent within the government and military.

Most military skills and training easily converts to federal occupations, and your military time may be creditable toward federal retirement. There are many other benefits for creditable military service, including a higher annual leave accrual rate which could allow you to earn four or more weeks of annual leave per year

I made the transition from military to federal after completing active duty in 1972. I was drafted during the Vietnam War in 1968, and when I reported for my physical I was given the opportunity to join the Air Force. Two weeks after discharge I was hired by the Department of Defense (DOD) to maintain avionics systems, the same job I had on active duty. The big difference was that my pay increased dramatically. I was earning $2,500 a year as a sergeant in the Air Force in 1972, and my starting DOD annual salary was just under $10,000. Don't expect those big increases today. Military pay is now far more competitive due to the all volunteer service. After working for the DOD for three years, I applied to the Federal Aviation Administration and was hired to maintain ground-based navigation and communication systems.

The federal government uses the same National Stock Number (NSN) ordering system that I used in the military. The regulations and manuals were similar as well, except you don't have the Uniform Code of Military Justice (UCMJ) to contend with or wear military uniforms. The FAA sent me to two years of formal training during my career. Most agencies provide comprehensive training so you don't have to have the specific equipment, systems, or software applications, just the basic qualifications that will help you succeed in your job.

Need Assistance

If you need assistance with your federal application, request a free initial consultation with CareerPro Global (CPG) by mentioning that you heard about their service in *The Book of U.S. Government Jobs*. Call 1-800-471-9201 to talk with a consultant about having them write a professional federal style résumé for you. CPG combines several decades of industry-writing experience with the most advanced technology to produce job-winning presentations for their clients (many of whom are veterans and retiring military personnel). You can also submit an online assistance request to CPG at www.federaljobs.net/resume.htm.

FAMILY MEMBER (DERIVED PREFERENCE)

Derived Preference is a method where you, as the spouse, widow/widower, or mother of a veteran may be eligible to claim veterans' preference when your veteran is unable to use it. You will be given XP Preference (10 points) in appointment if you meet the eligibility criteria.

Both a mother and a spouse (including widow or widower) may be entitled to preference on the basis of the same veteran's service if they both meet the requirements. However, neither may receive preference if the veteran is living and is qualified for Federal employment.

> The derived preference for spouses is different than the preference the Department of Defense is required by law to extend to spouses of active duty members in filling its civilian positions. For more information on that program, contact your local Department of Defense personnel office.

Spouses are eligible when your veteran has a service-connected disability and has been unable to qualify for any position in the civil service.

Widows/Widowers are eligible if you did not divorce your veteran spouse, have not remarried, or the remarriage was annulled, and the veteran:

- served during a war or during the period April 28, 1952, through July 1, 1955, or in a campaign or expedition for which a campaign medal has been authorized; OR

- died while on active duty that included service described immediately above under conditions that would not have been the basis for other than an honorable or general discharge.

Mothers of deceased veterans are eligible when your son or daughter died under honorable conditions while on active duty during a war or in a campaign or expedition for which a campaign medal has been authorized. Additionally, you must:

- be or have been married to the father of your veteran; AND

- live with a permanently disabled husband; OR

- be widowed, divorced, or separated from the veteran's father and have not remarried; OR

- if remarried, be widowed, divorced, or legally separated from your husband at the time you claim derived preference.

Mothers of disabled veterans are eligible if your son or daughter was separated with an honorable or general discharge from active duty, including training service in the Reserves or National Guard, and is permanently and totally disabled from a service-connected injury or illness. Additionally, you must:

- be or have been married to the father of your veteran; AND

- live with a permanently disabled husband; OR

- be widowed, divorced, or separated from the veteran's father and have not remarried; OR

- if remarried, be widowed, divorced, or legally separated from your husband at the time you claim derived preference.

NOTE: Preference is not given to widows or mothers of deceased veterans who qualify for preference under 5 U.S.C. 2108 (1) (B), (C) or (2). Thus, widows or mothers of deceased disabled veterans who served after 1955, but did not serve in a war, campaign, or expedition, would not be entitled to claim preference.

MILITARY SPOUSE PREFERENCE

Dependents of military and civilian sponsors and spouses of active duty military personnel receive hiring preference when applying for civilian employment with Department of Defense agencies. The Military Family Act expanded hiring preference to many jobs previously not available to this program and for jobs within the states, territories, and U. S. Possessions.[2]

Family member employment assistance programs are available at most large military bases. Visit your local Civilian Personnel Office (CPO) and Family Support Center for employment information, career assistance and counseling, job skills training, and personal development workshops.

---

[2] DOD Instruction (DODI) 1400.23 (Appendix 3)

MILITARY SPOUSE APPOINTING AUTHORITY

The Military Spouse Appointing Authority allows agencies to appoint a military spouse without competition. Agencies can choose to use this authority when filling competitive service positions on a temporary (not to exceed 1 year), term (more than 1 year but not more than 4 years), or permanent basis. The authority does not entitle spouses to an appointment over any other applicant.

As a military spouse you are eligible under this authority if your active duty military spouse receives a Permanent Change of Station (PCS) move, has a 100% disability rating; or died while on active duty. Each of these categories has different eligibility criteria that must be met.

Active Duty Spouse PCS

As a military spouse you must be authorized to relocate on the PCS orders and relocate to the new duty station. Military spouses can only be appointed within the reasonable daily commuting distance of the new duty station and the appointment must be made within 2 years of the PCS. You will be asked to provide a copy of the PCS orders.

Based on 100% Disability

You are eligible if your active duty spouse retired under Chapter 61 of title 10, United States Code with a 100% disability rating from the military department or retired or was released from active duty and has a disability rating of 100% from the Department of Veterans' Affairs or the military department. There is no geographic limitation under this category. You will be required to provide documentation of your spouse's disability.

Based on Service Member's Death

If your spouse was killed while on active duty and you are not remarried, you are eligible. There is no geographic limitation in this category. You will be required to provide documentation of the death and your marital status at the time of death.

Additional Information

A Veterans Employment Program Office list of individuals responsible for promoting veterans' recruitment, employment, training and development, and retention within their respective agencies is available online.

www.fedshirevets.gov/AgencyDirectory/index.asp

CHAPTER EIGHT
Overseas Employment Opportunities

There are over 89,204 federal employees working for the federal government in 140 foreign countries, in the United States territories, and in Alaska and Hawaii.[1] The positions that are most often available are administrative, technical and professional, accountants, auditors, foreign service officers, budget and program officers, management analysts, nurses, procurement officers, shorthand reporters, equipment specialists, engineers, social workers, housing officers, teachers, and alcohol and drug abuse specialists. Clerical (clerk-typist, stenographer) and secretary positions are normally filled locally overseas.

The Defense Department is the largest overseas employer, with 47,229 workers, and the State Department is number two, with 22,291 employees stationed abroad.

CHAPTER OBJECTIVES

✎ Learn how positions are filled overseas

✎ Understand the conditions of overseas employment

✎ Locate hiring agencies and job opportunities *(includes a hiring agency directory and contact information)*

✎ Review overseas job resources *(periodicals with job ads, job hotlines, and Internet Web sites)*

---

[1] Employment & Trends, September 2009

Job recruitment practices vary. In the U.S. territories, Hawaii, and Alaska most positions are filled through competitive civil service announcements. Various positions overseas are filled through Excepted Service and Nonappropriated Fund Instrumentality (NAFI) hiring programs. Excepted Service positions are described in Chapter Three. Nonappropriated Fund positions are paid using money generated within the Department of the Army and other military branches through services and sales revenues. These positions are primarily governed by military regulations.

When positions are filled locally overseas, U.S. citizens living abroad, dependents of citizens employed or stationed overseas, or foreign nationals can be hired. Most countries have agreements with U.S. installations that require the hiring of local nationals whenever possible to bolster the local economy. All positions held by foreign nationals are in the Excepted Service. Excepted Service positions are not subject to OPM's competitive hiring requirements.

Of the 89,204 overseas civilian federal employees, 62,838 were U.S. citizens as of September 2009.[2] Since the last edition of this book, total overseas federal civilian employment increased slightly. The Department of Defense is the largest employer of civilians overseas. Consequently, the majority of jobs are located at military installations.

Most of the upper and mid-level positions are filled through internal placement. Internal placement allows government employees who desire to work overseas to apply for the positions in-house. If there are no in-house bidders, agencies then advertise through competitive announcements. Overseas applicants should contact individual Agency and OPM Web sites for job listings.

CONDITIONS OF EMPLOYMENT

Overseas workers must meet various requirements: physical, security, qualifications, tour of duty, etc. Announcements list specific restrictions, conditions, and special qualifications.

PHYSICAL EXAMINATIONS

Individuals wanting to work overseas must meet certain stringent requirements. Thorough physical exams for both the applicant and, in many cases, accompanying dependents require physicals. You must be able to physically adapt to the conditions at various locations that may not have adequate healthcare facilities. Individuals on medication or who require special care will not be considered for certain positions. Any physical impairment that would create a hazard to others or to the applicant, or would reduce performance level, will disqualify the applicant.

---

[2] Federal Civilian Workforce Statistics, Employment and Trends, September 2009.

SECURITY CLEARANCE CHECKS

All applicants considered for appointment must pass a comprehensive security clearance, character and suitability check. These investigations take from a few weeks to several months to complete. If you are selected for a position, you will be appointed conditionally, pending the results of the investigation.

TRANSPORTATION AGREEMENTS

Individuals selected for overseas assignment are generally required to sign a transportation agreement. Typically, overseas tours are usually 3 years initially and can be extended for an additional 2 for a total of 5 years.

FOREIGN LANGUAGE REQUIREMENTS

A foreign language that would not be a position requirement in the States may be required for certain overseas positions. The job announcement will specify if a language is required. Several agencies appoint candidates without the required language skill and give them a period of time to develop language proficiency.

DEPENDENTS

Most agencies permit professional employees to take dependents with them. Professional positions are generally considered to be mid-level positions and above. Other employees can often arrange for dependents to follow them at a later date.

PAY AND BENEFITS

Overseas employees in foreign areas receive the base pay on the GS pay charts with annual cost-of-living adjustments. Additional allowances such as a post differential are provided where conditions warrant. Military base privileges are authorized in many circumstances and Department of Defense schools are available for dependent children through grade 12.

Because the employee's base pay in foreign areas actually goes down due to no locality payments, overseas employment may not be a good place to work prior to retirement. Without locality pay, your retirement annuity will be less since it is based on the employee's three year average salary.

On September 30, 2010, OPM published an Interim Rule making Alaska and Hawaii separate whole State locality pay areas and including the other non-foreign areas in the Rest of U.S. locality pay area. The Non-Foreign Area Retirement Equity Assurance Act of 2009, phases-in locality pay for employees in the non-foreign areas. For 2011, employees in the non-foreign areas will receive 2/3 of the applicable locality pay percentage approved by the President for their location.

Basic benefits are the same for all civil service employees. Overseas employees also receive travel to their overseas duty station, transportation and storage of household goods, and extra vacation with paid transportation to return stateside between tours of duty. Review Chapter One for a list of available benefits.

COMPETITION

There are a limited number of overseas positions and competition is keen. However, if you are well qualified and available for most locations, there are opportunities available. The normal rotation of current employees back to the United States creates a large number of recurring vacancies.

CITIZENSHIP

Applications are accepted only from U.S. citizens and American Samoans. However, the hiring of locals at overseas military installations is authorized to bolster the local economy. All positions held by foreign nationals are in the Excepted Service.

APPLYING FOR OVERSEAS JOBS

Apply early. It pays to apply for federal jobs well in advance of the time you will be available for employment. Many overseas jobs, especially jobs with the Department of Defense, require submission of an online application. Refer to Chapter Six for detailed federal employment application guidance.

TEMPORARY EMPLOYMENT

Federal agencies often hire temporary employees. You may be considered for both temporary and permanent positions. If you accept a temporary appointment, your name may remain on the register for consideration for permanent positions. Temporary employment is usually for one year or less, but may be extended for one additional year.

NAFI JOBS

Department of Defense agencies employ over 140,000 *Non-Appropriated Fund Instrumentalities (NAFI)* workers in post exchanges, military clubs and recreation services. These positions are not in the competitive service and they are funded by the revenue generated by the exchanges and clubs. Applications for these jobs must be submitted to the individual agencies or personnel offices. The NAFI personnel office can assist you with locating NAFI jobs worldwide:

- NAFI Personnel Policy Office
  1400 Key Boulevard, Suite B200
  Arlington, VA 22209-5144
  (703) 696-3318 or (703) 696-3310
  www.cpms.osd.mil/ — E-mail: cpmsnote@cpms.osd.mil
  www.acpol.army.mil/employment/naf.htm

OVERSEAS FEDERAL JOB SOURCES

This section presents resources that can be used to locate federal job announcements for overseas jobs. Refer to Chapter Three's Common Job Source lists for additional resources. Appendix D provides a complete list of federal occupations. Also, refer to Appendix C for detailed descriptions of government agencies and departments.

Resource headings include job openings, *Hiring Agency Directory*, and general information. The Hiring Agency Directory lists addresses of many agencies that offer overseas employment. Job openings include publications with job ads, job hotlines, and Internet Web sites. The general information section lists related books, pamphlets, brochures, and computer software. All job sources are listed alphabetically. A number of the periodicals and books listed in this chapter are available at libraries.

JOB OPENINGS

Periodicals with job ads

Federal Career Opportunities — Federal Research Service, PO Box 1708, Annandale, VA 22002; 1-800-822-5027 or 703-914-JOBS. You can e-mail question to info@fedjobs.com. Federal job listings, $9.95 per month, $19.95 for a three month subscription. Includes federal and private sector job listings. The vacancy listings are available online at www.fedjobs.com. Other job hunting resources are available.

Federal Jobs Digest — P.O. Box 89, Edgemont, PA 19028; 610-725-1769, www.jobsfed.com; publishes online database job listings and bi-monthly subscription to Federal Jobs Digest. Visit site for details and pricing.

Job Hotlines

Department of Defense Education Activity (DODEA)

The Department of Defense Education Activity (DODEA), ATTN: Teacher Recruitment, 4040 N. Fairfax Drive, Webb Building, Arlington, VA 22203, phone: **(703) 588-3983.** Applications are processed online at www.dodea.edu. Select "Human Resource." On the Human Resources Page select "Employment" to locate job vacancy announcements with links to the online application. A description of the DODDS teacher program is featured later in this chapter.

USA JOBS by Phone – Federal government job hotline **1-703-724-1850** or TTY 978-461-8404. This service is operated by the Office of Personnel Management and the phone answers 24 hours a day. Callers can leave voice-mail messages with their name, address, and phone number. Easy-to-use voice prompts and voice commands allow access with any touchtone or rotary dial telephone. (Not all vacancies are listed on this service. Agencies with direct hire authority announce vacancies through their individual human resources departments.)

Peace Corps Recruiting Contacts (www.peacecorps.gov) The Peace Corps has numerous university programs. For specific information contact the Peace Corps, Paul D. Coverdell Peace Corps Headquarters,1111 20th Street, NW, Washington, D.C. 20526, phone **1-800-424-8580.**

U.S. Department of State jobs (www.state.gov). Direct Inquiries about Foreign Service to: HR/REE/REC, 2401 E Street NW, Suite 518H, Washington, DC 20522, phone: 202-261-8888. Employment 24 hour **hotline: 703-875-7490.** Call this number for current Foreign Service Specialist job openings. The State Department employs 37,968 persons, of whom 22,261 work overseas.

Internet Web Sites

Army Civilian Personnel Online (www.cpol.army.mil/) Very helpful with links to the Atlantic and Pacific employment Web sites. Includes application online forms, job listings, and much more.

Army CPO Links   (Www.acpol.army.mil/employment/) This page offers job listings worldwide with comprehensive searches for all occupations. Includes links to job vacancies in the Pacific, Atlantic, Korea, and all Army stateside regions.

Central Intelligence Agency (www.cia.gov/) Complete information on CIA employment opportunities, with job lists.

Federal Departments that deploy personnel overseas include:

Agriculture	www.usda.gov
Commerce	www.commerce.gov
Defense	www.defense.gov
Homeland Security	www.dhs.gov
Interior	www.doi.gov
Justice	www.justice.gov
State	www.state.gov
Transportation	www.dot.gov
Treasury	www.treasury.gov
Veterans Affairs	www.va.gov

FBI (www.fbijobs.gov/) Visit its site for complete information on job opportunities and vacancy announcements.

Federal Jobs Network (http://federaljobs.net)

This career center helps anyone who is actively seeking government employment and current federal employees looking for career progression. The overseas section includes many of the links in this chapter. Visit this site for the latest updates

National Security Agency (www.nsa.gov/careers) Visit their employment page for job announcements and for information on the agency and its mission.

USAJOBS — Sponsored by OPM (www.USAJOBS.gov)

This site provides a comprehensive listing with full search capability for many federal job vacancies, general employment information, with online applications for some jobs and a résumé builder.

HIRING AGENCY DIRECTORY

TABLE 8-1 OVERSEAS EMPLOYMENT BY DEPARTMENT		
Department	**Overseas Employment**	**Total Employment**
Agriculture	884	104,469
Commerce	398	80,167
Defense	47,229	736,592
Education	6	4,101
Energy	21	16,145
Health & Human Services	332	67,449
Homeland Security	3,700	179,905
Housing & Urban Development	80	9,585
Interior	366	75,381
Justice	2,059	113,495
Labor	39	16,902
State	22,261	37,464
Transportation	322	57,277
Treasury	679	109,189
Veterans Affairs	4,571	297,318

Data Obtained from Table 2 of OPM's September 2009 Employment Trends

The following list of agency personnel offices that hire overseas is not complete. Some agencies employ small numbers of workers for overseas assignments.

Foreign Agriculture Service (FAS) www.fsa.usda.gov/pas

Contact the Information Division, Mail Stop 0506, 1400 Independence Avenue SW, Washington, DC 20520. Phone, 202-720-5237.

Formed in 1953 by executive reorganization, FAS is one of the smaller USDA agencies, with about 900 employees. FAS operates worldwide with staff in more than 75 posts covering more than 130 countries. Washington-based marketing specialists, trade policy analysts, economists, and others back up the overseas staff.

In addition, FAS has four domestic outreach offices that provide a complete range of export services to new-to-export companies and trade organizations, to help expand their business knowledge of export opportunities and USDA export assistance programs.

Roughly 70 percent of the annual FAS budget is devoted to building markets overseas for U.S. farm products. This includes the funding for all FAS trade and attaché offices overseas, as well as the agency's work with U.S. commodity associations on cooperative promotion projects. The remaining funds cover other trade functions, including gathering and disseminating market information and trade policy efforts. Click on the careers tab at http://www.fas.usda.gov to locate FAS job vacancies.

Positions are generally filled from the Professional and Administrative Career Examination. Agricultural occupations that are assigned overseas include Agricultural Program Specialist GS-1145, Agricultural Marketing Series GS-1146, Agricultural Market Reporting GS-1147, and Agricultural Engineering GS-0890.

Economists start at the GS-9 pay grade and have promotion potential to the GS-12 grade. The Foreign Agriculture Service carries out its tasks through its network of agricultural counselors, attaches, and trade officers stationed overseas.

Department of Commerce — www.commerce.gov/

The United States & Foreign Commercial Service is one of four official Foreign Affairs Agencies under the Foreign Service Act of 1980. The Commercial Service is responsible for commercial affairs. Foreign service officers in the Commercial Service are assigned to foreign and domestic field offices, as well as Washington, D.C., to promote the export of United States goods and services and defend United States commercial interests abroad. The Commercial Service, through its customized business solutions, creates economic prosperity and more and better jobs for all Americans. Employment information and job vacancies are available online.

Department of Defense — www.whs.mil/HRD/

Human Resources Directorate, Washington Headquarters Services, 2521 Crystal Drive, Arlington, VA 22202, phone 703-604-6219. The DOD is the largest overseas employer and provides hiring support to other federal agencies, including the Departments of the Air Force and the Navy, through its Overseas Employment Program (OEP). The OEP gives first consideration to qualified employees currently working at federal installations overseas. Former employees with reinstatement rights, and current government employees, should contact DOD Civilian Personnel Offices (CPOs) at DOD installations. When positions can't be filled in-house, the human resources department opens a competitive register to fill the position.

Department of the Army — www.cpol.army.mil/

The Department of the Army consolidated all hiring, and you can search this site for jobs in any country. Generally locals are hired for trades, laborers, equipment operators, and crafts and clerical positions. Dependents of military and civilian U.S. citizens assigned abroad receive hiring preference for many of these positions. Contact Civilian Personnel Offices at local Army posts for vacancies.

This site links to the Atlantic and Pacific overseas employment Web sites. Includes application online submission, listings, and much more.

PACIFIC Opportunities

Most federal jobs in the Pacific overseas areas are with the Department of Defense. Many positions in DOD agencies are currently filled under a special appointment authority for hiring family members of U.S. military or civilian personnel stationed in foreign areas. Jobs not filled by the special appointment authority are frequently filled by federal employees who transfer overseas or U.S. citizens living in the local areas on a temporary or time-limited basis. Generally, the greatest demand is for experienced engineering, administrative, educational, technical, and scientific occupations. Federal employees in Hawaii and Guam receive cost-of-living allowances (COLAs) in addition to their basic pay.

ATLANTIC Opportunities

The majority of positions are in Germany, Belgium, Italy, and Africa. Germany is where the largest number of employees are stationed. The majority of these jobs are filled by residents of the host country or by family members of military and civilians officially stationed in Europe. Approximately 5 percent are U.S. citizens who were recruited outside of Europe. Local Army Civilian Personnel Offices (CPOs) have primary responsibility within Europe for most noncareer, technical and administrative positions.

If you seek employment with the Departments of the Army, Navy or Air Force, or any other federal agency in the Atlantic region, the U.S. Army, Europe, and the Seventh Army (USAREUR), located in Leiman, Germany, is the delegated examining authority by the Office of Personnel Management for certain positions above the GS-7 grade level.

Status and Nonstatus applicants who are seeking employment in the Atlantic Overseas Area for GS-7 and above positions should apply through the online system listed on the above listed Web sites.

A status applicant is one who previously worked for the federal government and obtained career status. Nonstatus applicants that have never worked for the federal government must establish eligibility with the Office of Personnel Management or with an agency that has been delegated examining authority, such as the USAREUR.

Department of Defense Dependent School System (DODDS)

The Department of Defense Education Activity (DODEA), ATTN: Teacher Recruitment, 4040 N. Fairfax Drive, Arlington, VA 22201-1634, phone: (703) 588-3983. Applications are processed online at www.dodea.edu.

Elementary and secondary schools have been operating on U.S. military bases overseas since 1946 for children of military and civilian personnel. The DODDS provides educational opportunities comparable to those offered in the better school systems in the United States. This segment of U.S. public education consists of 194 elementary, middle, and secondary schools. The schools are located in 14 districts located in 12 foreign countries, seven states, Guam, and Puerto Rico with enrollment of 86,000 students and 8,700 educators.

School Locations:

European Region — Belgium, England, The Netherlands, Germany, Bahrain, Italy, Portugal, and Spain

Pacific Region — Japan, Guam, and Korea

Americas Region — Alabama, Georgia, Kentucky, New York, North Carolina, South Carolina, Virginia, Puerto Rico, and Cuba

Salary:

Overseas salaries are comparable to the average of the range of rates for similar positions in urban school jurisdictions in the U.S. having a population of 100,000 or more.

The school year consists of 190 duty days, with a minimum of 175 days of classroom instruction. Teachers are currently paid on several different pay bands (bachelor's degree, bachelor's degree plus 15 semester hours, master's degree plus 30 semester hours, and doctor's degree).

Housing and Living Conditions

In some areas, living quarters are provided by the U.S. government. These quarters may be in dormitories, apartments, old hotels, converted office buildings, or new modern facilities. These U.S. government quarters are usually provided without charge.

Visit the Web site for the overseas location where you desire to teach.

DODEA Worldwide Web Sites:

- Pacific   www.pac.dodea.edu/
- Europe   www.eu.dodea.edu/
- Guam   www.pac.dodea.edu/
- Cuba   www.am.dodea.edu/

Department of Homeland Security — www.dhs.gov

This department has 188,983 employees, of whom 39,700 are stationed overseas. The Department of Homeland Security (DHS) was founded to increase communication, coordination and resources and has three primary missions:

- Prevent terrorist attacks within the United States,
- Reduce America's vulnerability to terrorism, and
- Minimize the damage from potential attacks and natural disasters.

DHS was created to provide one single government agency with the primary mission of homeland security. It consolidates security functions from 100 government organizations to provide a single, unified homeland security structure that improves protection against today's threats and is flexible enough to help meet the unknown threats of the future.

The Department of Homeland Security has unique and challenging career opportunities. Homeland Security employees help secure our borders, airports, seaports and waterways; research and develop the latest security technologies; respond to natural disasters or terrorist assaults; and analyze intelligence reports.

The Department of Homeland Security was the most significant transformation of the U.S. government in over a half-century and is transforming and realigning government security activities into a single department.

Department of Justice — www.justice.gov

DOJ, 950 Pennsylvania Avenue NW, Washington, DC 20530. Phone, 202-514-2000. Agency-wide employment job line for attorneys and law students is available at **202-514-3397.**

The DOJ's mission is to enforce the law and defend the interests of the United States according to the law; to ensure public safety against threats foreign and domestic; to provide federal leadership in preventing and controlling crime; to seek just punishment for those guilty of unlawful behavior; and to ensure fair and impartial administration of justice for all Americans.

Drug Enforcement Administration (DEA) — Drug Enforcement Administration, Office of Personnel, 8701 Morrissette Drive, Springfield, VA 22152. Phone 202-307-1000. Employs several hundred workers overseas. The DEA is an agency under the Department of Justice. Visit the Web site at www.dea.gov or Call **1-800-332-4288** for Special Agent employment opportunities.

Department of Transportation (DOT) - www.dot.gov

Transportation Administrative Service Center (TASC) DOT Connection, Room PL-402, 400 Seventh Street SW, Washington, DC 20590. Phone, 202-366-4000.

Employees work in hundreds of occupations including many professional and technical categories. Employs a large number of electronics technicians and engineers. The majority of overseas employment is with the Federal Aviation Administration (FAA).

I spent the majority of my 35 years with the federal government working for the FAA in Airways facilities, now called Technical Operations, working with Air Traffic Control.

Federal Aviation Administration (www.faa.gov). Visit the Web site for stateside and overseas employment listings.

Aviation safety inspectors, pilots, electronic system specialists.

Department of State — www.state.gov

The Foreign Service employs thousands of Foreign Service officers and specialists who serve in 180 countries and at more than 265 posts around the world. Application procedures for employment with the U.S. Department of State vary according to the direction in which you take your career. Foreign Service officers, for example, must pass the Foreign Service Officer Selection Process.

Of the 37,464 total employment, 22,261 employees work overseas. Visit the Web site and explore the many opportunities available in Foreign Service. Direct inquires to: Office of Recruitment, Examination and Employment, U.S. Department of State, 2201 C Street NW, Washington, DC 20520. Phone, 202-647-4000.

Foreign Service officers, enforcement specialists, technical specialists, medical care specialists, administrative specialists, advisors, building operations, and internships.

The Foreign Service of the United States is America's diplomatic, commercial, and overseas cultural and information service. This agency assists the president and secretary of state in planning and carrying out American foreign policy at home and abroad. Personnel spend an average of 60 percent of their careers abroad, moving at two- to four-year intervals. Many overseas posts are in small or remote countries where harsh climates, health hazards, and other discomforts exist, and where American-style amenities frequently are unavailable.

English Language Skills

The Foreign Service requires all employees to have a strong command of the English language. All Foreign Service officers must be able to speak and write clearly, concisely, and correctly. The Departments of State and Commerce and the United States Intelligence Agency give high priority to English-language skills in selecting officers and evaluating their performance.

Foreign Language Skills

Knowledge of a foreign language is not required for appointment. Candidates without such knowledge are appointed as language probationers and must acquire acceptable competency in at least one foreign language before tenure can be granted. Officers can attend classes at the *National Foreign Affairs Training Institute*, which offers training in over 40 languages. These agencies seek persons with knowledge of Arabic, Chinese, Japanese, or Russian.

Department of the Treasury — www.treasury.gov

1500 Pennsylvania Avenue NW, Washington, DC 20220. Phone, 202-622-2000. The Department of the Treasury is the primary federal agency responsible for the economic and financial prosperity and security of the United States, and as such is responsible for a wide range of activities including advising the president on economic and financial issues, promoting the president's growth agenda, and enhancing corporate governance in financial institutions.

In the international arena, the Department of the Treasury works with other federal agencies, the governments of other nations, and the International Financial Institutions (IFIs) to encourage economic growth, raise standards of living, and predict and prevent, to the extent possible, economic and financial crises.

Almost every major field of study has some application to the work of this service. A substantial number of positions are filled by persons whose major educational preparation was accounting, business administration, finance, economics, criminology, and law. There are, however, many positions that are filled by persons whose college major was political science, public administration, education, liberal arts, or other fields not directly related to business or law.

Department of Veterans Affairs — www.va.gov

The VA headquarters is located at 810 Vermont Avenue NW, Washington, DC 20420. Phone, 800-949-0002. The department operates programs to benefit veterans and members of their families. Benefits include compensation payments for disabilities or death related to military service; pensions; education and rehabilitation; home loan guaranty; burial; and a medical care program incorporating nursing homes, clinics, and medical centers. Most of the 4,571 overseas employees work in Hawaii, Alaska, and Puerto Rico.

> *Employs most medical specialties. This system does not require civil service eligibility.*

CHAPTER NINE
The U.S. Postal Service

The U.S. Postal Service's annual operating revenue was $67 billion in 2010 and it pays approximately $2 billion in salaries and benefits every two weeks. There are 671,687 workers in 300 job categories for positions at 38,000 post offices, branches, stations, and community post offices throughout the United States. The average pay and benefits for career bargaining unit employees increased dramatically from $62,348 per year in 2006 to $72,099 in 2010, a 14% increase while the private sector suffered through one of the most extensive recessions in modern history. [1]

Adding benefits, overtime, and premiums, the average bargaining unit annual compensation rate was $72,099.

Informative Sites:
www.usps.com/employment
www.postalwork.net

CHAPTER OBJECTIVES

- ✎ Learn about Postal Service opportunities
- ✎ Understand the employee pay and classification system
- ✎ Determine employee qualification requirements
- ✎ How to apply for exams
- ✎ Review postal clerk and mail carrier occupations *(nature of work, working conditions, training, job outlook, and earnings)*

---

[1] Comprehensive Statement on Postal Operations, 2010 — USPS

Vacancies are advertised internally by the USPS and not by the Office of Personnel Management. Visit their Web site at http://usps.com/employment for job vacancies.

The Postal Service has many challenges ahead. They lost $8.5 billion in 2010 and curtailed hiring due to a 20% mail volume reduction over the past 4 years and the continuing recession. Over 20,000 USPS employees accepted early retirement in 2010 and the Postal Service has eliminated over 200,000 positions through attrition or retirement in the past 10 years, half of those since 2007.

The good news is that the economy is recovering and revenues should increase as business returns to normal. Then when you factor in the 39,000 USPS employees that retired in 2010 and the nearly 300,000 Postal Service career employees that will become eligible for retirement over the next decade, opportunities should abound.

SALARY EXPECTATIONS

Starting pay in 2010 was $20.94 per hour, $43,555 per year, for part time flexible mail carriers in 2007. Mail handlers start at $15.65 per hour, $32,553 per year, and clerks start at $19.19 per hour, $39,915 per year. Workers are initially hired under the part-time flexible pay scale and typically work 40 hours or more per week, There are also Executive and Administrative Schedules for non-bargaining unit members, with pay ranging from $20,875 up to an authorized maximum of $108,166.

EMPLOYEE CLASSIFICATIONS

Initial appointments are either casual or transitional (temporary) or Part-Time Flexible (Career). Hourly rates for Part-Time Flexible employees vary depending upon the position's rate schedule. Some positions are filled full-time, such as the Maintenance (Custodial) classification.

- Full-Time and Part-Time Flexible (career) employees compose the *Regular Work Force*. This category includes security guards. Part-Time Flexible employees are scheduled to work fewer than 40 hours per week and they must be available for flexible work hours as assigned. Part-Time Flexible employees are paid by the hour. Hourly rates vary from $16.72 for PS Grade 3 Step BB to $31.62 for PS Grade 11 step P.

- A *Supplemental Work Force* is needed by the Postal Service for peak mail periods and offers casual (temporary) employees two 89-day employment terms in a calendar year. During Christmas an additional 21 days of employment can be offered to Supplemental Work Force employees. Transitional (temporary) employees can work up to 360 days in carrier positions.

Entrance exams are not required for supplemental work force jobs, and these positions cannot be converted to full-time positions. However, you will be able to apply for future job vacancies and take the 473 Postal Exam in your area when they are advertised. Many, if not the majority of, postal workers today start out in casual or transitional positions and eventually apply, pass the exam, and get hired.

College students may be considered for casual (temporary) employment with the Postal Service during the summer months. The rate of pay is from $6.55 to $22.50 per hour. Tests are not required and appointments cannot lead to a career position. Apply early for summer work. Contact post offices in your area no later than February for summer employment applications. Casual temporary positions are also advertised on the Postal Service's employment and job listing Web site at www.usps.com/employment. in your area by no later than February for summer employment applications.

EMPLOYMENT RESOURCES

There are several resources that provide valuable information for those interested in working for the Postal Service. Visit these sites or call the listed number for additional information:

www.usps.com/employment (Official Postal Service recruitment site)
www.postalwork.net (Job information and links)

www.postalemployeenetwork.com/index.htm (Resources for postal workers. Offers a free electronic newsletter subscription.)

www.PostalReporter.com (Postal service employment information)

QUALIFICATION REQUIREMENTS

Various standards from age restrictions to physical requirements must be met before you can take one of the Postal Service exams.

Age Limit

You must be 18 to apply. Certain conditions allow applicants as young as 16 to apply. Carrier positions requiring driving are limited to age 18 or older. High school graduates or individuals who terminated high school education for sufficient reason are permitted to apply at age 16.

Entrance Exams

Clerks, carriers, rural carriers and other mail-handling job applicants must pass an entrance exam. Specialties such as mechanic, electronic technician, machinist, and trades must also pass a written test. The overall rating is based on the test results and your qualifying work experience and education. Professionals and certain administrative positions don't require an entrance exam or written test. They are rated and hired strictly on their prior work experience and education. The clerk and carrier exams are the 473 and 473 C and 473 E Exams. The only difference among the three is the occupational title and the methods of taking the exams.

The **473 Major Entry Level Jobs Exam** covers the following positions:

✔ **City Carrier**
✔ **Rural Carrier**
✔ **Mail Processing Clerk**
✔ **Sales, Service, and Distribution Associate**
✔ **Mail Handler**

This exam, also referred to as the *473 Battery Examination,* covers the vast majority of entry-level hiring. Custodial positions are reserved for veteran preference eligibles by federal law. The USPS also requires *motor vehicle* and *tractor trailer operators,* and highly skilled maintenance positions such as *Building Equipment Mechanic, Engineman, Electronics Technician, and General Mechanic* to successfully pass an entrance exam. All of the skilled maintenance positions require examination 931. A separate announcement, examination 932, is required for Electronics Technician positions.

Eight sample exams and a study guide are included in the book *Post Office Jobs,* 5th edition, and includes a sample *473 Battery Examination* in Chapter Five to help you prepare for this test. This book is available at bookstores or you can order by phone, 1-800-782-7424.

The 473 examination and completion of forms will require approximately three hours and 15 minutes, with half of the exam taken online when you first apply and a second proctored exam at a local testing facility in your area. Jobs with the U.S. Postal Service are highly competitive due to the excellent salary and benefits offered. It's essential that you study for the exam and pass the test with the highest score possible to improve your chances. Applicants scoring between 90% and 100% will get called sooner than lower graded applicants and they have a better chance of being hired.

Citizenship

Applicants do not have to be U.S. citizens. If you have permanent alien resident status in the United States of America or owe allegiance to the United States you can apply for Postal Service jobs.

Physical Requirements

Physical requirements are determined by the job. Carriers must be able to lift a 70-pound mail sack and all applicants must be able to efficiently perform assigned duties. Eyesight and hearing tests are required. Applicants must have at least 20/40 vision in the good eye and no worse than 20/100 in the other eye. Eyeglasses are permitted.

State Driver's License

Applicants must have a valid state driver's license for positions that require motor vehicle operation. A safe driving record is required and a Postal Service road test is administered for the type of vehicle that you will operate.

Drug Testing (Substance Abuse)

The Postal Service maintains a comprehensive program to ensure a drug-free workplace. A qualification for postal employment is to be drug free, and this qualification is determined through the use of a urinalysis drug screen. When you are determined to be in the area of consideration for employment, you will be scheduled for a drug screening test.

APPLICATION PROCEDURES

The Postal Service significantly changed the application process in 2008, and you now apply for specific job vacancies. Previously, you had to sign up for a test that was administered every two to three years in your area. Applicants who passed the exam were placed on a hiring register in rank order by exam score. When vacancies occurred in an area, the Postal Service would contact the highest ranked candidates and call them in for an interview. You could be on the list for two years or more and never get called, and when the list was closed you had to reapply by retaking the same test.

Exam registers became outdated quickly as applicants found other employment, and they were difficult to maintain. The hiring process was decentralized, and many were excluded from the list because they missed the exam testing notification in their area. Now, when a vacancy exists the Postal Service advertises the job on its centralized Web site and you apply for a specific job that will be filled between four and six weeks of the job announcement's closing date.

To apply for postal positions, first visit www.postalwork.net/jobs.htm, this book's companion Web site, and review the step-by-step instructions with helpful hints on how to apply for post office jobs on the official Web site. This site shows screen shots of the official application pages with instructions to help you successfully navigate the new *eCareer* application system. Don't be sidetracked by major private-sector jobs board ads. The Postal Service seldom advertises on any of the large online jobs boards, and if it does you are linked directly to the official site at **http://usps.com/employment** to apply at no cost.

There are many postal job scams online and in newspaper classifieds that list toll-free numbers and charge fees ranging from $70 to over $200 for exam study guides. The application process is free to all who apply. Visit your local library to use the new 5th edition of the study guide titled *"Post Office Jobs"* to prepare for the exam, or you can purchase a copy at your local bookstore.

Apply online at www.usps.com/employment. Most libraries offer online access. Job opportunities are also advertised at local post offices, in national and local newspapers, journals and periodicals. Read the caution notice above prior to calling any toll-free number.

A passing score of 70 percent or better is required for your name to be added to the register. The highest-rated applicants will be called to complete additional paperwork, take a drug screening test, and an interview. Your score determines your placement on the list.

Apply for each job separately. However, after you initially register online, pass the test, and obtain an **Exam History Code,** you can enter this code at the beginning of the application process to avoid having to retest. To improve your chances, apply for all positions that you qualify for. Your exam results are valid through the exam date shown on your Notice of Rating.

VETERANS PREFERENCE

Veterans receive five or 10-point preference. Those with a 10 percent or greater compensable service-connected disability are placed at the top of the register in the order of their scores. All other eligibles are listed below the disabled veterans group in rank order. The Veterans Preference Act applies to all Postal Service positions. Refer to Chapter Seven for detailed information on veterans' preference.

Custodial exams for the position of cleaner, custodian, and custodial laborer are exclusively for veterans and present employees. This exam is open only to veterans' preference candidates.

POSTAL MAIL CARRIERS

Nature of the Work

Postal Service mail carriers deliver mail to residences and businesses in cities, towns, and rural areas. Although carriers are classified by their type of route—either city or rural—duties of city and rural carriers are similar. Most travel established routes, delivering and collecting mail. Mail carriers start work at the post office early in the morning, when they arrange the mail in delivery sequence. Automated equipment has reduced the time that carriers need to sort the mail, allowing them to spend more of their time delivering it.[2]

Mail carriers cover their routes on foot, by vehicle, or by a combination of both. On foot, they carry a heavy load of mail in a satchel or push it on a cart. In most urban and rural areas, they use a car or small truck. The Postal Service provides vehicles to city carriers; most rural carriers use their own vehicles and are reimbursed for that use. Deliveries are made to houses, to roadside mailboxes, and

---

[2] Excerpted from the 2010-2011 Occupational Outlook Handbook, Department of Labor

to large buildings such as offices or apartments, which generally have all of their tenants' mailboxes in one location.

Besides delivering and collecting mail, carriers collect money for postage-due and COD (cash-on-delivery) fees and obtain signed receipts for registered, certified, and insured mail. If a customer is not home, the carrier leaves a notice that tells where special mail is being held. After completing their routes, carriers return to the post office with mail gathered from homes, businesses, and sometimes street collection boxes, and turn in the mail, receipts, and money collected during the day.

Some city carriers may have specialized duties such as delivering only parcels or picking up mail only from mail collection boxes. In comparison with city carriers, rural carriers perform a wider range of postal services, in addition to delivering and picking up mail. For example, rural carriers may sell stamps and money orders and register, certify, and insure parcels and letters. All carriers, however, must be able to answer customers' questions about postal regulations and services and provide change-of-address cards and other postal forms when requested.

Work Environment

Most carriers begin work early in the morning—those with routes in a business district can start as early as 4 a.m. Overtime hours are frequently required for urban carriers. Carriers spend most of their time outdoors, delivering mail in all kinds of weather. Though carriers face many natural hazards, such as extreme temperatures and wet and icy roads and sidewalks, serious injuries are often due to the nature of the work, which requires repetitive arm and hand movements, as well as constant lifting and bending. These activities can lead to repetitive stress injuries in various joints and muscles.

Employment

The U.S. Postal Service employed 343,300 mail carriers in 2008. The majority of mail carriers work in cities and suburbs, while the rest work in rural areas.

Postal Service mail carriers are classified as casual, transitional, part-time flexible, part-time regular, or full time. Casuals are hired for 90 days at a time to help process and deliver mail during peak mailing or vacation periods in rural areas. Transitional carriers are hired on a temporary basis in cities for a period of one year. Part-time, flexible workers do not have a regular work schedule or weekly guarantee of hours but are called as the need arises. Part-time regulars have a set work schedule of fewer than 40 hours per week, often replacing regular full-time workers on their scheduled day off. Few carriers are classified as part-time employees, especially among rural carriers. Full-time postal employees work a 40-hour week over a 5-day period and made up 85 percent of mail carriers in 2008.

Training, Other Qualifications, and Advancement

All applicants for Postal Service mail carrier jobs are required to take an examination. After passing the exam, it may take 1 to 2 years or longer before being hired because the number of applicants generally exceeds the number of job openings.

There are no specific education requirements to become a Postal Service mail carrier; however, all applicants must have a good command of the English language. Upon being hired, new carriers are trained on the job by experienced workers. Many post offices offer classroom instruction on safety and defensive driving. Workers receive additional instruction when new equipment or procedures are introduced. In these cases, usually another postal employee or a training specialist trains the workers.

Other qualifications. Postal Service mail carriers must be at least 18 years old. They must be U.S. citizens or have been granted permanent resident-alien status in the United States, and males must have registered with the Selective Service upon reaching age 18.

All applicants must pass a written examination that measures speed and accuracy at checking names and numbers and the ability to memorize mail distribution procedures. Job seekers should contact the post office or mail processing center where they wish to work to determine when an exam will be given. Applicants' names are listed in order of their examination scores. Five points are added to the score of an honorably discharged veteran and 10 points are added to the score of a veteran who was wounded in combat or is disabled. When a vacancy occurs, the appointing officer chooses one of the top three applicants; the rest of the names remain on the list to be considered for future openings until their eligibility expires—usually 2 years after the examination date.

When accepted, applicants must undergo a criminal-history check and pass a physical examination and a drug test. Applicants also may be asked to show that they can lift and handle mail sacks weighing 70 pounds. A safe driving record is required for mail carriers who drive at work, and applicants must receive a passing grade on a road test.

Good interpersonal skills are important because mail carriers must be courteous and tactful when dealing with the public, especially when answering questions or receiving complaints. A good memory and the ability to read rapidly and accurately are also important.

Postal Service mail carriers may begin on a casual, transitional, part-time, or flexible basis and become regular or full-time employees in order of seniority, as vacancies occur. Carriers can look forward to obtaining preferred routes as their seniority increases. Postal Service mail carriers can advance to supervisory positions on a competitive basis.

Job Outlook

Employment of Postal Service mail carriers is expected experience little or no change through 2018. Keen competition is expected for mail carrier jobs because of the attractive wages and benefits and relatively low entry requirements.

Employment of mail carriers is expected to decline by about 1 percent through 2018. Employment will be adversely affected by several factors. The use of automated "delivery point sequencing" systems to sort letter mail and flat mail directly, according to the order of delivery, reduces the amount of time that carriers spend sorting their mail, allowing them to spend more time on the streets delivering mail. The amount of time carriers save on sorting letter mail and flat mail will allow them to increase the size of their routes, which will reduce the need to hire more carriers. Additionally, the Postal Service is moving toward more centralized mail delivery, such as the use of cluster mailboxes, to cut down on the number of door-to-door deliveries. However, as the population continues to rise and the number of addresses to which mail must be delivered increases the demand for mail carriers in some areas of the country will grow.

Employment and schedules in the Postal Service fluctuate with the demand for its services. When mail volume is high, such as during holidays, full-time employees work overtime, part-time workers get additional hours, and casual workers may be hired.

Those seeking jobs as Postal Service mail carriers can expect to encounter keen competition. The number of applicants usually exceeds the number of job openings because of the occupation's low entry requirements and attractive wages and benefits. The best employment opportunities for mail carriers are expected to be in areas of the country with significant population growth as the number of addresses to which mail must be delivered continues to grow.

Earnings

Median annual wages of Postal Service mail carriers were $49,800 in May 2008. The middle 50 percent earned between $41,270 and $51,250. The lowest 10 percent earned less than $37,400, while the top 10 percent earned more than $52,400. Rural mail carriers are reimbursed for mileage put on their own vehicles while delivering mail.

Postal Service mail carriers enjoy a variety of employer-provided benefits similar to those enjoyed by other Federal Government workers. The National Association of Letter Carriers and the National Rural Letter Carriers Association together represent most of these workers.

OCCUPATIONS LIST

(Partial Listing)

Craft & Wage per hour positions:

Administrative Clerk	General Mechanic
Auto Mechanic	Letter Box Mechanic
Blacksmith-Welder	Letter Carrier
Building Equipment Mechanic	LSM Operator
Carpenter	Machinist
Carrier	Mail Handler
Cleaner, Custodian	Maintenance Mechanic
Clerk Stenographer	Mark Up Clerk
Data Conversion Operator	Mason
Distribution Clerk	Mechanic Helper
Electronic Technician	Motor Vehicle Operator
Elevator Mechanic	Painter
Engineman	Plumber
Fireman	Scale Mechanic
Garageman-Driver	Security Guard

Professional

Accounting Technician	Electronic Engineer
Architect/Engineer	Transportation Specialist
Budget Assistant	Industrial Engineer
Computer Programmer	Technical Writer
Computer System Analyst	Stationary Engineer

Management

Administrative Manager	Postmaster-Branch
Foreman of Mail	Safety Officer
General Foreman	Schemes Routing Officer
Labor Relations Representative	Supervisor-Accounting
Manager-Bulk Mail	Supervisor-Customer Service
Manager-Distribution	System Liaison Specialist
Manager-Station/Branch	Tour Superintendent

CHAPTER TEN
Employment For
People with Disabilities

Seven percent of the total federal civilian workforce, over 199,000 employees, have disabilities.[1] Opportunities exist at all levels of government and in hundreds of occupations. The *Americans with Disabilities Act* (ADA) and Executive Order 13217 have increased awareness of hiring options by federal managers and those seeking employment. Both programs along with agency outreach efforts have expanded government employment opportunities for disabled persons.

Agencies have direct hire authority for trial appointments.

The Office of Personnel Management (OPM) established a comprehensive online portal to help the disabled explore and find employment in the federal sector. Its site at http://www.opm.gov/disability provides simple and straightforward guidance for both job seekers and federal managers, plus provides comprehensive resources and guidance for all concerned.

Informative and Helpful Site:

www.opm.gov/disability

CHAPTER OBJECTIVES

- Understand managers' hiring options
- Review types of appointments
- Learn about special accommodations *(includes testing arrangements and on-the-job assistance)*
- Review job resources *(periodicals with job ads, job hotlines, Internet Web sites, placement services, and association list)*

---

[1] Table 498, Federal Employees-Summary Characteristics

The federal government offers special noncompetitive appointments — special emphasis hiring options — for people with physical or mental disabilities. There are distinct advantages for managers to hire individuals under special emphasis hiring appointments. Managers are able to hire individuals under special appointments within days, where it may take as long as several months to fill positions under the competitive process. Secondly, federal managers are tasked with specific performance targets, called *"critical job elements" (CJEs),* for maintaining workforce diversity. All agencies are required by law to develop outreach efforts to identify qualified candidates to meet agency workforce diversity goals.

This chapter explains the various hiring options for people with disabilities. Individuals seeking appointments with the federal government must be proactive and begin networking with local agencies, contacting listed resources, and aggressively seeking out all available federal employment opportunities.

FEDERAL MANAGERS' RESPONSIBILITIES

Federal agency managers and supervisors are responsible for the employment and advancement of people with disabilities.[2] This includes recruitment, hiring, training, career development, mentoring support and considering reasonable accommodations when requested.

Career development and promotion opportunities, training, awards, and other similar programs must be an integral part of an agency's responsibilities toward employees with disabilities. Federal employers are required to make reasonable accommodations to the known physical or mental limitations of a qualified applicant or employee with a disability, unless the agency can demonstrate that the accommodation(s) would impose an undue hardship on the agency. Absent undue hardship, agencies must remove physical barriers as a matter of reasonable accommodation to particular employees for whom necessary facilities are inaccessible.

Agencies are required to establish procedures to ensure that the employment and advancement of people with disabilities meets affirmative action program objectives, diversity planning, special emphasis, and accountability. They must also ensure that there are no personnel or management policies, practices or procedures which unnecessarily restrict hiring, placement, and advancement of people with disabilities.

It is illegal for a federal agency to discriminate in employment against qualified individuals with disabilities. Anyone who believes he or she has been subjected to discrimination on the basis of disability may file a complaint with the employing agency's equal employment opportunity (EEO) office.[3]

---

[2] Employment Guide for People With Disabilities in the Federal Government

[3] EEOC's MD-110 and 29 CFR, Part 1614. EEO complaint process.

Agencies have direct hire authority to hire disabled employees under Schedule A appointments. Therefore interested parties must contact individual agencies to determine what's available. Refer to the agency lists in Appendix C and the common resources listed in Chapter Three. Additional special hiring programs exist for disabled veterans. Refer to Chapter Seven for complete details.

Selective Placement Program Coordinators

Most federal agencies have a Selective Placement Program Coordinator, Special Emphasis Manager (SEP) for Employment of Adults with Disabilities, or equivalent, who helps agency management recruit, hire and accommodate people with disabilities at that agency. SEP managers develop, manage and evaluate the agency's Affirmative Employment Program for Individuals with Disabilities.

One of their primary responsibilities is to help persons with disabilities get information about current job opportunities, types of jobs in the agency and how these jobs are filled, and reasonable accommodation. SEP coordinators are subject to change due to transfers, retirements, and promotions. It is best to locate the most up-to-date contacts online at **www.apps.opm.gov/sppc_directory/**. The directory can be searched by agency or state. The SEP contacts are a primary resource for you to use to locate agencies in your area and potential employment prospects.

Many federal managers and HR specialists that you contact in the federal sector may not be aware of who their SEP contact is or that they even exist. You best bet is to contact the agency SEP first, and when you do talk to local HR specialists or managers, let them know who their agency SEP is and provide them with their contact information. The SEP serves a dual role, providing assistance to both disabled job seekers and managers.

Typical SEP Coordinator Directory Listing (by agency)

Agricultural Marketing Service
Todd Birkenruth
EEO Specialist
Civil Rights Program Office
Room 3074
1400 Independence Ave., SW
Washington, DC 20240

Phone: (202) 720-0583
Email: todd.birkenruth@usda.gov

THE REHABILITATION ACT OF 1973

Section 501 of the Rehabilitation Act of 1973, as amended (29 U.S.C. Section 791) prohibits discrimination on the basis of disability in federal employment and requires the federal government to engage in affirmative action for people with disabilities. The law:

- Requires federal employers not to discriminate against qualified job applicants or employees with disabilities. Persons with disabilities should be employed in all grade levels and occupational series commensurate with their qualifications. Federal employers should ensure that their policies do not unnecessarily exclude or limit persons with disabilities because of a job's structure or because of architectural, transportation, communication, procedural, or attitudinal barriers.

- Requires employers to provide "reasonable accommodations" to applicants and employees with disabilities unless doing so would cause undue hardship to the employers. Such accommodations may involve, for example, restructuring the job, reassignment, modifying work schedules, adjusting or modifying examinations, providing readers or interpreters, and acquiring or modifying equipment and/or facilities (including the use of adaptive technology such as voice recognition software).

- Prohibits selection criteria and standards that tend to screen out people with disabilities, unless such procedures have been determined through a job analysis to be job-related and consistent with business necessity, and an appropriate individualized assessment indicates that the job applicant cannot perform the essential functions of the job, with or without reasonable accommodation.

- Requires Federal agencies to develop affirmative action programs for hiring, placement, and advancement of persons with disabilities. Affirmative action must be an integral part of ongoing agency personnel management programs.

HIRING OVERVIEW

In addition to competing for a position by applying through a vacancy announcement, the federal government's Selective Placement programs include special hiring authorities for hiring people with disabilities. You may apply for employment directly to agencies, which may use these authorities to streamline the appointment of people with disabilities. If you are interested in being considered under these special authorities, you should contact a state vocational rehabilitation agency or, if you are a veteran, a Department of Veterans Affairs vocational rehabilitation counselor, and request his/her assistance. Links to both groups can be found in the resources section of this chapter. You should ask the counselor to provide you with a "certification" statement that identifies you as a person with a disability and that describes your ability to perform the essential duties of the position in which you are interested. Then, once you have obtained this certification statement, you should contact the federal agency where you wish to work. Ask for the Selective Placement or Disability Employment coordinator or their equivalent.[4]

HIRING OPTIONS

The federal government provides opportunities for qualified persons with physical and mental disabilities. Applicants with handicaps must be considered fairly for all jobs in which they are able to perform the job duties efficiently and safely. To be eligible for these noncompetitive, Schedule A appointments, a person must meet the definition for being disabled. The person must have a severe physical, cognitive, or emotional disability; have a history of having such disability; or be perceived as having such disability. In addition, the person must obtain a certification letter from a state Vocational Rehabilitation Office or the Department of Veterans Affairs to be eligible for appointment under these special authorities.

Applicants with handicaps must be considered fairly for all jobs in which they are able to perform the job duties efficiently and safely.

Disabled veterans may also be considered under special hiring programs for disabled veterans with disability ratings from the Department of Veterans Affairs of 30 percent or more.

Agency human resource management departments encourage federal managers to give people with disabilities full and fair consideration, and to make accommodations when necessary. Although the majority of employees with handicaps obtain their jobs through competitive procedures, there are some for whom ordinary procedures do not function fairly or accurately. The competitive process is explained in Chapters Two and Three. To meet the needs of those with severe impairments agencies may appoint, on a permanent, time-limited, or temporary basis persons with certified mental retardation, severe physical disabilities, or psychiatric disabilities if they meet the conditions described below.

Proof of disability

The disabled applicant must present proof of his or her mental retardation, severe physical disability, or psychiatric disability prior to appointment. Agencies may accept, as proof of an individual's mental retardation, severe physical disability, or psychiatric disability, appropriate documentation (e.g., records, statements, or other appropriate information) issued from a licensed medical professional (e.g., a physician or other medical professional duly certified by a state, the District of Columbia, or a U.S. territory, to practice medicine); a licensed vocational rehabilitation specialist (i.e., state or private); or any federal agency, state agency, or an agency of the District of Columbia or a U.S. territory that issues or provides disability benefits.

---

[4] Federal Employment of People With Disabilities — OPM Web site

Certification of job readiness

Certification that the individual is likely to succeed in the performance of the duties of the position for which he or she is applying is required. Certification of job readiness may be provided by any entity specified in the previous paragraph. In cases where certification has not been provided, the hiring agency may give the individual a temporary appointment under this authority to determine the individual's job readiness. The agency may also accept, at the agency's discretion, service under another type of temporary appointment in the competitive or excepted services as proof of job readiness

APPOINTMENT TYPES

Permanent or time-limited employment options

Permanent or time-limited appointment is based upon proof of disability and certification of job readiness, or demonstration of job readiness through a temporary appointment.

Temporary employment options

Temporary appointments are based upon proof of disability as noted in the previous paragraphs. Temporary appointments are used when it is necessary to observe the applicant on the job to determine whether the applicant is able or ready to perform the duties of the position. When an agency uses this option to determine an individual's job readiness, the hiring agency may convert the individual to a permanent appointment whenever the agency determines the individual is able to perform the duties of the position or the individual has a certification of job readiness and the work is of a temporary nature.

Noncompetitive conversion to the competitive service

Agencies may noncompetitively convert an employee to the competitive service who completed two years of satisfactory service in a nontemporary appointment under this authority of Executive Order 12125 as amended by Executive Order 13124 and Sec. 315.709. Disabled workers may receive credit for time spent on a temporary appointment towards the two-year requirement.

CONVERSION TO CAREER OR CAREER-CONDITIONAL

A disabled employee who is appointed under 5 CFR Parts 213 and 315 may have his or her appointment converted to a career or career-conditional appointment when he or she:

1. Completes two or more years of satisfactory service, without a break of more than 30 days, under a nontemporary appointment;

2. Is recommended for such conversion by his or her supervisor;

3. Meets all requirements and conditions governing career and career-conditional appointment except those requirements concerning competitive selection from a register and medical qualifications; and

4.   Is converted without a break in service of one workday.

Employees who are converted under these regulations becomes career-conditional employees, with a few exceptions, or career employee if he completed three years of substantially continuous service in a temporary appointment.

TEMPORARY LIMITED APPOINTMENTS

Temporary appointments are made when the need for the position is short-term and not expected to last for more than one year. Temporary jobs are filled through competitive procedures with a requirement for public notice. Under limited circumstances, agencies may use "outside-the-register" procedures. Agencies may also give noncompetitive temporary appointments to individuals who qualify for positions and have a specific noncompetitive eligibility such as reinstatement or veterans readjustment appointment (VRA) (5 CFR 316.402).

Time Limits: Appointments are not to exceed one year; a one-year extension is allowed.

TERM APPOINTMENTS

Term appointments are made when the need for an employee's services will last for a period of more than one year, but no more than four years. Reasons for term appointments may include, but not be limited to, project work, extraordinary workload, and uncertainty of future funding. Term positions are filled through competitive procedures with the requirement for public notice.

These positions may also be filled by qualified individuals based on specific noncompetitive eligibility such as reinstatement and veterans readjustment appointment (VRA) (5 CFR Part 316.302).

Time Limits: Appointments are made for more than one year but not more than four years.

Conversion: This authority does not contain a provision for conversion to a permanent appointment when the term expires.

STUDENT VOLUNTEER PROGRAM

Agencies may provide educationally-related work assignments for student volunteers on a non-pay basis. (5 CFR 308.103)

Requirements: The student is enrolled at least half-time in a high school, trade school, vocational institute, university, or other accredited educational institution, and the school permits the participation of the student in a program established to provide educational experience.

Time Limits: No time limits have been established for these appointments, as long as the student continues to meet program requirements.

COMPETITIVE VERSUS EXCEPTED SERVICE

People with disabilities may start their federal career in an Excepted Service temporary appointment, while most federal jobs are in the Competitive Service. Congress excepted certain jobs, hiring authorities and groups from the Competitive Service procedures. In the Competitive Service, individuals must compete for positions through examination. Review the discussion on competitive and excepted service in Chapter Two.

UNPAID WORK EXPERIENCE

Most rehabilitation organizations include on-the-job training and job placement programs for participants. Vocational rehabilitation centers work with federal agencies to place people with disabilities in jobs that provide meaningful work experience. Agencies benefit from the services provided by these workers and they get an opportunity to evaluate a prospective employee.

Federal regulations limit unpaid services from a person with disabilities to those who are clients of a state *Office of Vocational Rehabilitation* (OVR). Applicants must be enrolled in an OVR program. Signed agreements must be initiated between the rehabilitation center and the federal agency. Agencies can negotiate these agreements individually with local Vocational Rehabilitation Facilities. Once an agreement is initiated, the agreement covers all participants. Individuals accepted into these programs don't receive any compensation from the government; however, many sponsors provide a small stipend to the worker.

Federal regulations limit unpaid services from a person with disabilities to those who are clients of a state OVR.

SPECIAL ACCOMMODATIONS

When appropriate, OPM uses special examination (testing) procedures for applicants who are physically handicapped to assure that their abilities are properly and fairly assessed.[5] Special testing arrangements are determined on an individual basis depending on the applicant's disability. For example: readers, examinations in Braille, tape, or large print for visually impaired competitors; interpreters for test instructions and modifications of parts of tests for hearing-impaired competitors.

Accommodations on the Job

When federal agencies hire a person with disabilities, efforts are made to accommodate the individual to remove or modify barriers to his or her ability to effectively perform the essential duties of the position. Agencies may, for example: (1) provide interpreter service for the hearing impaired, (2) use readers for the visually impaired, (3) modify job duties, (4) restructure work sites, (5) alter work schedules, and (6) obtain special equipment or furniture.

---

[5]U.S. OPM, Office of Affirmative Employment Programs, ES-5 (GPO 0-157-269).

The Rehabilitation Act of 1973, as amended, requires federal agencies to provide reasonable accommodations to qualified employees or applicants with disabilities, unless doing so would cause an undue hardship to the agency. (An undue hardship means that a specific accommodation would require significant difficulty or expense.) A reasonable accommodation is any change to a job, the work environment, or the way things are usually done that allows an individual with a disability to apply for a job, perform the essential job functions, or enjoy equal access to benefits available to other individuals in the workplace.

Federal agencies are required to develop written procedures for providing reasonable accommodation. You may gain greater understanding of your specific situation and alternatives available to you by reading the agency's reasonable-accommodation procedures. Different agencies place responsibility for reasonable-accommodation in different offices. Contact the agency's personnel office, reasonable-accommodation coordinator, civil rights office, or EEO office to request a copy of the agency's written procedures.[6]

COMMON JOB SOURCES

This section presents resources that can be used to locate federal job announcements for people with disabilities. After reviewing the listed resources, refer to Appendix D for a complete list of federal occupations. A number of the periodicals and directories listed in this chapter are available at libraries. Many newsletter and periodical publishers will send complimentary review copies of their publications upon request.

Resource headings include job openings, placement services, directories, and general information. Job openings include publications with job ads, job hot lincs, and Internet Web sites. The general information section lists related books, pamphlets, and Internet fact sheets. All job sources are listed alphabetically. For additional resources refer to Chapter Three's listings.

JOB OPENINGS

Job Listings and Information Services

ABILITY Jobs & Resumes — 8941 Atlanta Ave., Huntington Beach, CA 92646, 949-854-8700, e-mail info@abilityjobs.com. ABILITY provides information on new technologies, the "Americans with Disabilities Act," employment opportunities for people with disabilities and more. Posting your resume or searching job postings are free. ABILITY also offers **JobAccess** to recruit qualified individuals with disabilities. Locate job opportunities on the Web site at www.jobaccess.org/.

---

[6] Reasonable-accommodation policy per Executive Order 13164

Disabilities Resource Center — www.disability.gov/

A comprehensive federal government online resource designed to provide people with disabilities with quick and easy access to the information they need. The site provides access to disability-related information and programs available across the government on numerous subjects, including benefits, civil rights, community life, education, employment, housing, health, technology and transportation.

CAREERS & The DisAbled (Equal Opportunity Publications) — 445 Broad Hollow Rd, Suite 425, Melville, NY 11747, 631-421-9421, e-mail:info@eop.com, Web site: http://eop.com. This company publishes a number of excellent target audience publications. Call for subscription rates. A résumé matching service is also available to subscribers.

Diversity Services — www.diversity-services.com

Diversity Services was created to address the issues of diversity in today's ever-changing workplace. Diversity Services builds bridges to create workforce inclusion of all qualified individuals regardless of race, age, sexual orientation, or disability.

Federal People with Disabilities — www.opm.gov/disability/

This information includes Federal and state laws as well as other governmental and non-governmental sites. However, this site is not designed to address or respond to individual circumstances. Individual inquiries should be addressed to the current or potential employing agency.

Federaljobs.net — www.federaljobs.net

This career center assists visitors with their federal government job search and guides them through the process. Search this site for key words and phrases. Includes a listing of over 200 federal agency employment Web sites that you can visit for up-to-date job listings and agency information.

JAN — Job Accommodation Network www.jan.wvu.edu/

A free consulting service designed to increase the employability of people with disabilities by providing individualized worksite accommodations, technical assistance regarding the ADA and other disability related legislation, and educating callers about self-employment options. The Job Accommodation Network (JAN) is a service of the U.S. Department of Labor Office of Disability Employment Policy, hosted by West Virginia University. This site is a wealth of information for job seekers. You can call **1-800-526-7234, voice and 877-781-9403 TTY.**

JobAccess — www.jobaccess.org

This site helps employers recruit qualified individuals with disabilities. The goal of JobAccess is to enable people with disabilities to enhance their professional lives by providing a dedicated system for finding employment. People with disabilities can locate viable employment opportunities at this Web site.

National Business and Disability Council — www.business-disability.com

The National Business and Disability Council links employers and college graduates with disabilities. It offers a free national résumé database, job search, career events and internship information. E-mail jtowles@abilitiesonline.org for additional information.

State Vocational & Rehabilitation Agencies *(2 resources listed)*

www.parac.org/svrp.html, http://askjan.org/cgi-win/TypeQuery.exe?902

The Rehabilitation Council and the JAN Network both offer a list of state vocational and rehabilitation agencies and contact information for disabled persons. These services can include counseling, evaluation, training and job placement. There are also services for the sight and hearing impaired. Visit this site for direct links to state Vocational and Rehabilitation Agencies. Call or write the office nearest you.

The ARC of the United States, 800-433-5255

1010 Wayne Ave., Suite 650, Silver Spring, MD 20910. National organization that you may find helpful in seeking job leads, placement, training, or assistance in the employment process such as résumé writing and interviewing techniques. You can join their online job registry at http://www.thearc.org.

Unemployment Offices Listings by State

www.servicelocator.org/OWSLinks.asp

This site offers Internet Web links to all 50 state unemployment offices. Visit this site to find the unemployment office nearest you.

Job Hotlines

Department of Veterans Affairs, 800-827-1000

The Department of Veterans Affairs supports a nationwide employment training program for veterans with service-connected disabilities who qualify for vocational rehabilitation. Regional or local offices are listed under federal government agencies in the telephone directory.

JAN — Job Accommodation Network, 800-526-7234 (V/TTY)

The Job Accommodation Network (JAN) is *not* a job placement service, but an international toll-free consulting service that provides information about job accommodations and the employability of people with disabilities. JAN is a service of the President's Committee on Employment of People with Disabilities. It also provides information regarding the Americans with Disabilities Act (ADA). Visit the Web site at www.janweb.icdi.wvu.edu/.

USA JOBS by Phone — Federal government job hotline, **703-724-1850** or TDD 978-461-8404. Operated by the Office of Personnel Management. Phone answers 24 hours a day. Provides federal employment information for most occupations. Easy-to-use online voice prompts and voice commands allow access with any touch tone or rotary dial telephone.

PLACEMENT SERVICES

State Vocational and Rehabilitation Agencies

www.askjan.org/cgi-win/TypeQuery.exe?902

State vocational and rehabilitation agencies coordinate and provide a number of services for disabled persons. These services can include counseling, evaluation, training and job placement. Many of the OVR and VA rehabilitation centers offer job placement services. Associations also offer services including job placement to their members. Refer to the association list that follow and contact local OVR and VA facilities in your area to identify available job placement services.

DIRECTORIES

ADA Technical Assistance & Resource Manual www.ada.gov/publicat.htm

Encyclopedia of Associations — Internet www.gale.cengage.com/. Lists thousands of associations and it is available at most larger libraries. Use this resource to identify associations for your specific disability. This resource is also available in two additional formats including CD ROM and online. Most large libraries carry this title in their reference section.

Selective Placement Program Coordinators www.apps.opm.gov/sppc_directory/

Most federal agencies have a Selective Placement Program Coordinator, Special Emphasis Manager (SEP) for Employment of Adults with Disabilities who helps agency management recruit, hire and accommodate people with disabilities at that agency. They help persons with disabilities get information about current job opportunities, types of jobs in the agency and how these jobs are filled, and reasonable accommodation.

ASSOCIATIONS

Associations and Organizations

The following is a list of associations and organizations that offer numerous services to people with physical or mental impairments. Many offer job placement services, on-site accessibility surveys, job analysis, and advice and support to the group represented. Contact individual listings for details.

American Cancer Society — 1-800-ACS-2345 or 1-866-228-4327 for TTY, www.cancer.org. Refers employers to organizations offering help in recruiting qualified individuals with disabilities, and community programs offering consultation and technical assistance to cancer patients, survivors, and their families.

American Council of the Blind — 2200 Wilson Boulevard, Suite 650, Arlington, VA 22201, Phone: (202) 467-5081 (800) 424-8666, www.acb.org/. Provides information on topics affecting the employment of individuals who are blind, including job seeking strategies, job accommodations, electronic aids, and employment discrimination. Provides information on job openings for individuals who are blind and visually impaired. Offers free legal assistance.

American Speech-Language-Hearing Association — 2200 Research Boulevard, Rockville, MD 20850-3289; 301-296-5700, www.asha.org/. Information and technical assistance on overcoming communication barriers.

The ARC 1 — 660 L Street, NW, Suite 301, Washington, DC 20036, (800) 433-5255, www.thearc.org/. (Formerly Association for Retarded Citizens of the United States). The country's largest voluntary organization committed to the welfare of all children and adults with mental retardation and their families.

Arthritis Foundation — P.O. Box 7669, Atlanta, GA 30357; 800-283-7800, www.Arthritis.org/. Helps people with arthritis and lupus obtain employment.

Disabled American Veterans — 3725 Alexandria Pike, Cold Springs, KY 41076; 877-426-2838, www.dav.org/. Provides information on recruitment sources for veterans with disabilities. Offers a broad range of services.

Epilepsy Foundation of America — 8301 Professional Place, Landover, MD 20785; 800-332-1000 (Voice/TDD), www.efa.org/. Maintains a network of local employment assistance programs, which provide education and support to employers on epilepsy and employment issues, including employment referrals.

Helen Keller National Center for Deaf-Blind Youths and Adults — 141 Middle Neck Rd., Sands Point, NY 11050; 516-944-8900 (voice/TDD). Visit the Web site at www.helenkeller.org/. Provides job placement for deaf-blind individuals, and on-site support services for employers and employees.

Mental Health America — 2000 N. Beauregard Street, 6th Floor, Alexandria, VA 22311, Phone (800) 969-6642. Visit www.nmha.org. Mental Health America (formerly known as the National Mental Health Association) is a leading non-profit dedicated to helping all people live mentally healthier lives. They provide valuable services to promote mental wellness for the health and well-being of the nation.

National Center for Learning Disabilities — 381 Park Ave. South, Suite 1401, New York, NY 10016; 888-575-7373, www.ncld.org/. Provides information, referral, public education and outreach programs on the learning-disabled. Offers job placement and publishes a quarterly newsletter.

National Down Syndrome Congress — 1370 Center Drive, Suite 102, Atlanta, GA 30338. Phone, 800-232-6372, www.ndsccenter.org/. Provides general information on Down syndrome and the employment of individuals with Down syndrome.

National Multiple Sclerosis Society — 733 Third Avenue, New York, NY 10017. Phone: 1-800-344-4867. www.nationalmssociety.org. The society helps those with MS with the challenges of living with the disease. It funds MS research, provides services to MS patients, offers professional education and other helpful services.

National Spinal Cord Injury Association — 1 Church Street #600, Rockville, MD 20850. Phone, (800) 962-9629, visit www.spinalcord.org/. The mission of the National Spinal Cord Injury Association (NSCIA) is to enable people with spinal cord injury and disease (SCI/D) to achieve their highest level of independence, health, and personal fulfillment by providing resources, services, and peer support.

Spina Bifida Association of America — 4590 MacArthur Blvd. NW, Suite 250, Washington, DC 20007-4226. Phone, 1-800-621-3141, 202-944-3295. Visit the Web site at www.sbaa.org/. SBAA serves as the nation's only voluntary health agency dedicated to enhancing the lives of those with spina bifida and those whose lives they touch. SBA has a presence in more than 125 communities nationwide.

United Cerebral Palsy Association — 380 Washington Avenue, Roosevelt, NY 11575-1899, 516) 378-2000, www.ucpn.org/. The United Cerebral Palsy Association's mission is to advance the independence, productivity and full citizenship of people with disabilities through an affiliate network.

Books, Pamphlets, and Brochures

JAN (Job Accommodation Network) — It will send out an informational brochure upon request. Most of the pamphlets can be reviewed online at the Web site, www.janweb.icdi.wvu.edu. Call 1-800-526-7234 for free consulting and information about job accommodations and the employability of people with disabilities.

Most of the associations listed in this chapter provide information upon request or provide online pamphlets, databases, and directories to assist members. Visit the association relevant to your diagnosis and register online to join the organization. Upon registration you will have significant resources and contacts available to assist you with your job search.

CHAPTER ELEVEN
Law Enforcement and
Homeland Security Careers

The Department of Homeland Security (DHS) is constantly changing to better manage its diverse mission. DHS is now the third largest executive Department with 188,983 employees including 3,700 working overseas. Homeland Security consolidated 22 agencies from various departments to unify the war on terror.[1]

Homeland Security has had a significant impact on federal law enforcement careers in general, and many law enforcement functions were transferred to DHS when it was formed after September 11, 2001. The federal government employs over 180,000 law enforcement personnel in more than 40 job series (see Table 11-1). Most federal agencies employ law enforcement specialists in one capacity or another. Work in law enforcement is not limited to investigative, police, compliance and security positions. There are tens of thousands of federal employees working in occupations that provide direct support to these groups.

Over 180,000 law enforcement personnel work for Uncle Sam.

CHAPTER OBJECTIVES

✎   Explore federal law enforcement occupations

✎   Learn about opportunities with Homeland Security

✎   Determine job qualifications *(review several qualification standards for the largest occupations)*

✎   Locate hiring agencies *(TSA security screeners, agents, investigators, FBI, CIA, Secret Service, and others)*

✎   Review typical working conditions, employment, training requirements, job outlook, and earnings

---

[1]U.S. Department of Homeland Security Annual Performance Plan 2009

213

The Department of Homeland Security transferred functions from the Departments of the Treasury, Justice, HHS, Defense, FBI, Secret Service, GSA, Energy, Agriculture, Transportation and the U.S. Coast Guard. The new organization was originally composed of five major Directorates, listed below. Agencies in parentheses were originally responsible for the listed service:

- **Border and Transportation Security**

  o   U.S. Customs Service (Treasury)
  o   Immigration& Naturalization Service (Justice)
  o   Federal Protective Service
  o   Transportation Security (Transportation)
  o   Federal Law Enforcement Training Center (Justice)
  o   Animal & Plant Health Inspection Service (Agriculture)
  o   Office for Domestic Preparedness (Justice)

- **Emergency Preparedness and Response**

  o   Federal Emergency Management Agency (FEMA)
  o   Strategic National Stockpile & National Disaster Medical System (HHS)
  o   Nuclear Incident Response Team (Energy)
  o   Domestic Emergency Support Team (Justice)
  o   National Domestic Preparedness Office (FBI)

- **Information Analysis and Infrastructure Protection**

  o   Federal Computer Incident Response Center (GSA)
  o   National Communications System (Defense)
  o   National Infrastructure Protection Center (FBI)
  o   Energy Security and Assurance Program (Energy)

- **Science and Technology**

  o   CBRN Countermeasures Program (Energy)
  o   Environmental Measurement Laboratory (Encrgy)
  o   National BW Defense Analysis Center (Defense)
  o   Plum Island Animal Disease Center (Agriculture)

- **Management**

The Secret Service and the Coast Guard are also with the DHS. They report directly to the secretary. In addition, the Immigration and Naturalization Service (INS) adjudications and benefits programs report directly to the deputy secretary as the U.S. Citizenship and Immigration Service.

LAW ENFORCEMENT

Many federal investigative jobs have age requirements, and applicants must be at least 21 years of age and under the age of 37 at the time of appointment. Other positions state that you must be 21 years of age and be a U.S. citizen. Age require may vary between agencies. Each job announcement lists the required qualifications for that position. If you want to work in law enforcement, and you are over age 37, your options are limited; you may have to consider a support position that does not have an age limit.[2]

Federal Bureau of Investigation (FBI) agents are the Government's principal investigators, responsible for investigating violations of more than 200 categories of Federal law and conducting sensitive national security investigations. Agents may conduct surveillance, monitor court-authorized wiretaps, examine business records, investigate white-collar crime, or participate in sensitive undercover assignments. The FBI investigates a wide range of criminal activity, including organized crime, public corruption, financial crime, bank robbery, kidnapping, terrorism, espionage, drug trafficking, and cybercrime.

There are many other Federal agencies that enforce particular types of laws. U.S. Drug Enforcement Administration (DEA) agents enforce laws and regulations relating to illegal drugs. U.S. marshals and deputy marshals provide security for the Federal courts and ensure the effective operation of the judicial system. Bureau of Alcohol, Tobacco, Firearms, and Explosives agents enforce and investigate violations of Federal firearms and explosives laws, as well as Federal alcohol and tobacco tax regulations. The U.S. Department of State Bureau of Diplomatic Security special agents are engaged in the battle against terrorism.

The Department of Homeland Security also employs numerous law enforcement officers within several different agencies, including Customs and Border Protection, Immigration and Customs Enforcement, and the U.S. Secret Service. U.S. Border Patrol agents protect more than 8,000 miles of international land and water boundaries. Immigration inspectors interview and examine people seeking entry into the United States and its territories. Customs inspectors enforce laws governing imports and exports by inspecting cargo, baggage, and articles worn or carried by people, vessels, vehicles, trains, and aircraft entering or leaving the United States. Federal Air Marshals provide air security by guarding against attacks targeting U.S. aircraft, passengers, and crews. U.S. Secret Service special agents and U.S. Secret Service uniformed officers protect the President, the Vice President, their immediate families, and other public officials. Secret Service special agents also investigate counterfeiting, forgery of Government checks or bonds, and fraudulent use of credit cards.

Other Federal agencies employ police and special agents with sworn arrest powers and the authority to carry firearms. These agencies include the Postal

---

[2] Bureau of Labor Statistics, Occupational Outlook Handbook, 2010 - 2011 edition

Service, the Bureau of Indian Affairs Office of Law Enforcement, the Forest Service, and the National Park Service.

U.S. Drug Enforcement Administration (DEA) agents enforce laws and regulations relating to illegal drugs. Not only is the DEA the lead agency for domestic enforcement of federal drug laws, but it also has sole responsibility for coordinating and pursuing U.S. drug investigations abroad. Agents may conduct complex criminal investigations, carry out surveillance of criminals, and infiltrate illicit drug organizations using undercover techniques.

U.S. marshals and deputy marshals protect the federal courts and ensure the effective operation of the judicial system. They provide protection for the federal judiciary, transport federal prisoners, protect federal witnesses, and manage assets seized from criminal enterprises. They enjoy the widest jurisdiction of any federal law enforcement agency and are involved to some degree in nearly all federal law enforcement efforts. In addition, U.S. marshals pursue and arrest federal fugitives.

Bureau of Alcohol, Tobacco, Firearms, and Explosives agents regulate and investigate violations of federal firearms and explosives laws, as well as federal alcohol and tobacco tax regulations.

The U.S. Department of State *Bureau of Diplomatic Security special agents* are engaged in the battle against terrorism. Overseas, they advise ambassadors on all security matters and manage a complex range of security programs designed to protect personnel, facilities, and information. In the United States, they investigate passport and visa fraud, conduct personnel security investigations, issue security clearances, and protect the secretary of state and a number of foreign dignitaries. They also train foreign civilian police and administer a counter-terrorism reward program.

The Department of Homeland Security employs numerous law enforcement officers under several different agencies, including *Customs and Border Protection, Immigration and Customs Enforcement,* and the *U.S. Secret Service. U.S. Border Patrol agents* protect more than 8,000 miles of international land and water boundaries. Their missions are to detect and prevent the smuggling and unlawful entry of undocumented foreign nationals into the United States; to apprehend those persons violating the immigration laws; and to interdict contraband, such as narcotics.

Immigration inspectors interview and examine people seeking entrance to the United States and its territories. They inspect passports to determine whether people are legally eligible to enter the United States. Immigration inspectors also prepare reports, maintain records, and process applications and petitions for immigration or temporary residence in the United States.

Customs inspectors enforce laws governing imports and exports by inspecting cargo, baggage, and articles worn or carried by people, vessels, vehicles, trains, and aircraft entering or leaving the United States. These inspectors examine, count, weigh, gauge, measure, and sample commercial and noncommercial cargoes entering and leaving the United States. Customs inspectors seize prohibited or smuggled articles; intercept contraband; and apprehend, search, detain, and arrest violators of U.S. laws. *Customs agents* investigate violations, such as narcotics smuggling, money laundering, child pornography, and customs fraud, and they enforce the Arms Export Control Act. During domestic and foreign investigations, they develop and use informants; conduct physical and electronic surveillance; and examine records from importers and exporters, banks, couriers, and manufacturers. They conduct interviews, serve on joint task forces with other agencies, and get and execute search warrants.

Federal Air Marshals provide air security by fighting attacks targeting U.S. airports, passengers, and crews. They pose as ordinary passengers and board flights of U.S. air carriers to locations worldwide.

U.S. Secret Service special agents protect the president, vice president, and their immediate families; presidential candidates; former presidents; and foreign dignitaries visiting the United States. Secret Service agents also investigate counterfeiting, forgery of government checks or bonds, and fraudulent use of credit cards.

Other federal agencies employ police and special agents with sworn arrest powers and the authority to carry firearms. These agencies include the Postal Service, the Bureau of Indian Affairs Office of Law Enforcement, the Forest Service, and the National Park Service.

WORKING CONDITIONS

Law enforcement work can be very dangerous and stressful. In addition to the obvious dangers of confrontations with criminals, officers need to be constantly alert and ready to deal appropriately with a number of other threatening situations. Many law enforcement officers witness death and suffering resulting from accidents and criminal behavior. A career in law enforcement may take a toll on officers' private lives.

Uniformed officers, detectives, agents, and inspectors are usually scheduled to work 40-hour weeks, but paid overtime is common. Shift work is necessary because protection must be provided around the clock. Junior officers frequently work weekends, holidays, and nights. Police officers and detectives are required to work at any time their services are needed and may work long hours during investigations. In most jurisdictions, whether on or off duty, officers are expected to be armed and to exercise their arrest authority whenever necessary.

The jobs of some federal agents such as U.S. Secret Service and DEA special agents require extensive travel, often on very short notice. They may relocate a number of times over the course of their careers. Some special agents in agencies such as the Border Patrol work outdoors in rugged terrain for long periods and in all kinds of weather.

EMPLOYMENT

There are approximately 180,000 law enforcement workers in the federal government. There are many more in support occupations such as administrative officers, clerks, logistics specialists, etc. The Justice Department is the largest employer of (GS-1811) criminal investigators, employing 24,448. The Department of Homeland Security is the second largest employer of this series with 10,671 criminal investigators. Total criminal investigator employment is 43,810. Correctional officers (GS-0007) are employed by two agencies — the Department of Justice has 17,580 officers, and Interior employs the remaining 136. All Internal Revenue officers (GS-1169) are employed by the Treasury Department.

Airport screeners and immigration inspection occupations are now in the GS-1802 job series.

Table 11-1 lists the major occupations, the total number employed in parentheses, the largest employing agency, and number of workers employed. There are two significant changes to this table since the last edition was published. Airport screeners, originally classified under the GS-0019 job series, and immigration inspection, originally classified under the GS-1816 series, are both included in the GS-1802 Compliance, Inspection, and Support series. Use Table 11-1 to identify viable opportunities and then visit those agencies' recruiting sites.

You can use the job series or titles on the following table to search for job vacancy announcements on www.usajobs.gov. This site allows job series or occupational title searches and also offers e-mail notification for specific job series announcements. You can register on this site for free e-mail notification for job vacancies and compile your federal style résumé online. Also, visit the specific agency Web sites where law enforcement jobs are posted. Not all agencies advertise on OPM's Web site. You will find abundant information, and in some cases, online testing and applications on several law enforcement agency Web sites. Go to www.federaljobs.net/law.htm for more links to federal agency recruitment sites.

Homeland Security advertises most jobs through OPM's Web site at www.usajobs.opm.gov. However, it does offer some online applications for specific jobs on www.dhs.gov and provides informative applicant study guides, career information, and videos. U.S. Immigration and Customs Enforcement (ICE) site at www.ice.gov offers career information for federal Air Marshal, Office of Intelligence, Detention and Removal, Air and Marine Operations, and Office of Investigations.

Table 11-1 does not list support occupations that are available, such as a number of occupations under general administration, clerical, office services, communications, IT professionals, chemistry and biological science. A number of positions in these occupations are recruited in support of most law enforcement organizations. Also, check out the Skills Index in Appendix E to locate other agencies that hire law enforcement specialists.

	TABLE 11-1		
	Law Enforcement Occupations		
Job Series (GS)	Title	Total Employment	Largest Employing Department
0006	Correctional Administration	1,742	Justice (1,670)
0007	Correctional Officer	17,866	Justice (17,580)
0025	Park Ranger	6,424	Interior (5,777)
0072	Fingerprint Identification	577	Justice (516)
0080	Security Administration	13,048	Defense (8,106)
0083	Police Officer	14,562	Defense (8,106)
0101	Social Science	10,341	Defense (2,838)
0132	Intelligence	10,918	Defense (4,880)
0180	Psychology	6,951	Vet. Admin. (4,320)
0249	Wage & Hour Compliance	72	Labor (72)
0390	Telecomm. Processing	361	Interior (152)
1169	Internal Revenue Officer	5,934	Treasury (5,934)
1397	Document Analysis	102	Justice (47)
1801	General Insp., Investigation	33,311	Homeland Security (24,079)
1802*	Compliance Insp.& Support	53,658	Homeland Security (49,656)
1810	General Investigation	3,380	Agriculture (1786)
1811	Criminal Investigation	43,810	Justice (24,471)
1822	Mine Safety & Health	1,423	Labor (1,419)
1889	Import Specialist	1,070	Homeland Security (1,048)
1896	Border Patrol Agent	20,337	Homeland Security (20,337)
2121	Railroad Safety	461	Transportation (461)
2151	Radio Dispatching	1,254	Defense (957)
2181	Aircraft Operations	2,907	Defense (2,523)

Employment statistics from OPM's September 2010 Central Personnel data File
* Airport screeners and immigration inspection are now under the GS-1802 job series.

TRAINING AND QUALIFICATIONS OVERVIEW

Federal civil service regulations govern the appointment of law enforcement officers, police and detectives. Candidates must be U.S. citizens, usually at least 21 years of age, and must meet rigorous physical and personal qualifications. In the federal government, candidates must be at least 21 years of age but less than 37 years of age at the time of appointment. Physical examinations for entrance into law enforcement often include tests of vision, hearing, strength, and agility. Eligibility for appointment usually depends on performance in competitive written examinations and previous education and experience. Federal agencies typically require a college degree. Candidates should enjoy working with people and meeting the public.

It should be noted that qualifications and training requirements are subject to change. Visit agency web sites, that are listed starting on page 224, for specific requirements including age limitations. Agencies may have age limitation waivers and there is a standing waiver for military VRA appointments.

Because personal characteristics such as honesty, sound judgment, integrity, and a sense of responsibility are especially important in law enforcement, candidates are interviewed and their character traits and backgrounds are investigated. In some agencies, candidates are interviewed by a psychiatrist or a psychologist, or given a personality test. Most applicants are subjected to lie detector examinations or drug testing. Some agencies subject current employees to random drug testing as a condition of continuing employment.

Before their first assignments, officers usually go through a period of training. In federal departments, recruits get training in their agency's academy, often for 12 to 14 weeks. Training includes classroom instruction in constitutional law and civil rights, state laws and local ordinances, and accident investigation. Recruits also receive training and supervised experience in patrol, traffic control, use of firearms, self-defense, first aid, and emergency response.

Police officers usually become eligible for promotion after a probationary period ranging from six months to three years. In the federal sector the probationary period is one year. Promotion may enable an officer to become a detective or specialize in one type of police work, such as working with juveniles. Promotions to corporal, sergeant, lieutenant, and captain usually are made according to a candidate's position on a promotion list, as determined by scores on a written examination and on-the-job performance.

The FBI has the largest number of special agents. To be considered for appointment as an FBI agent, an applicant must be either a graduate of an accredited law school or a college graduate with a major in accounting, fluency in a foreign language, or three years of related full-time work experience. All new agents undergo 20 weeks of training at the FBI academy on the U.S. Marine Corps base in Quantico, Virginia.

Applicants for special agent jobs with the Secret Service and the Bureau of Alcohol, Tobacco, and Firearms must have a bachelor's degree or a minimum of three years' related work experience. Prospective special agents undergo 11 weeks of initial criminal investigation training at the Department of Homeland Security's Federal Law Enforcement Training Center in Glynco, Georgia, and another 17 weeks of specialized training with their particular agencies.

Applicants for special agent jobs with the U.S. Drug Enforcement Administration (DEA) must have a college degree and either one year of experience conducting criminal investigations, one year of graduate school, or have achieved at least a 2.95 grade point average while in college. DEA special agents undergo 14 weeks of specialized training at the FBI Academy in Quantico, Virginia.

U.S. Border Patrol agents must be U.S. citizens, younger than 37 years of age at the time of appointment, possess a valid driver's license, and pass a three-part examination on reasoning and language skills. A bachelor's degree or previous work experience that demonstrates the ability to handle stressful situations, make decisions, and take charge is required for a position as a Border Patrol agent. Applicants may qualify through a combination of education and work experience.

Postal inspectors must have a bachelor's degree and one year of related work experience. It is desirable that they have one of several professional certifications, such as that of certified public accountant. They also must pass a background suitability investigation, meet certain health requirements, undergo a drug screening test, possess a valid state driver's license, and be a U.S. citizen between 21 and 36 years of age when hired.

Law enforcement agencies are encouraging applicants to take post-secondary school training in law enforcement-related subjects. Many entry-level applicants for police jobs have completed some formal post-secondary education and a significant number are college graduates. Many junior colleges, colleges, and universities offer programs in law enforcement or administration of justice. Other courses helpful in preparing for a career in law enforcement include accounting, finance, electrical engineering, computer science, and foreign languages. Physical education and sports are helpful in developing the competitiveness, stamina, and agility needed for many law enforcement positions. Ability to speak, understand, read and write in a foreign language is an asset in many federal agencies.

Continuing training helps police officers, detectives, and special agents improve their job performance. Through police department academies, regional centers for public safety employees established by the states, and federal agency training centers, instructors provide annual training in self-defense tactics, firearms, use-of-force policies, crowd-control techniques, sensitivity and communications skills, relevant legal developments, and advances in law enforcement equipment. Many agencies pay all or part of the tuition for officers to work toward degrees in criminal justice, police science, administration of justice, or public administration, and pay higher salaries to those who earn such a degree.

JOB OUTLOOK

The opportunity for public service through law enforcement work is attractive to many because the job is challenging and involves much personal responsibility. Furthermore, law enforcement officers, if their positions qualify for the Law Enforcement Officer (LEO) retirement program, can retire after 20 years of service at age 50, or 25 years of service at any age. Because of relatively attractive salaries and benefits, the number of qualified candidates exceeds the number of job openings in federal law enforcement agencies, resulting in increased hiring standards and selectivity by employers. Competition is expected to remain keen for the higher- paying jobs with state and federal agencies and police departments in more affluent areas. Applicants with college training in police science, military police experience, or both should have the best opportunities.

Employment of police and detectives is expected to increase about as fast as the average for all occupations through 2014. A more security-conscious society and concern about drug-related crimes should contribute to the increasing demand for police services. Employment growth at the federal level is currently being driven by the war on terror; however, employment will be tempered by continuing budgetary constraints faced by law enforcement agencies.

EARNINGS

Police and sheriff's patrol officers had median annual wages of $51,410 in May 2008. The middle 50 percent earned between $38,850 and $64,940. The lowest 10 percent earned less than $30,070, and the highest 10 percent earned more than $79,680. Median annual wages were $46,620 in Federal Government, $57,270 in State government, $51,020 in local government and $43,350 in educational services.

The following statistics are form May 2008. Median annual wages of **police and detective supervisors** were $75,490. The middle 50 percent earned between $59,320 and $92,700. The lowest 10 percent earned less than $46,000, and the highest 10 percent earned more than $114,300. Median annual wages were $89,930 in Federal Government, $75,370 in State government, and $74,820 in local government.

Median annual wages of **detectives and criminal investigators** were $60,910. The middle 50 percent earned between $45,930 and $81,490. The lowest 10 percent earned less than $36,500, and the highest 10 percent earned more than $97,870. Median annual wages were $73,170 in Federal Government, $53,910 in State government, and $55,930 in local government.

Median annual wages of **fish and game wardens** were $48,930. The middle 50 percent earned between $37,500 and $61,290. The lowest 10 percent earned less than $30,400, and the highest 10 percent earned more than $81,710. Median annual wages were $48,960 in Federal Government, $50,440 in State government, and $35,810 in local government.

Median annual wages of **parking enforcement workers** were $32,390. The middle 50 percent earned between $25,400 and $42,000. The lowest 10 percent earned less than $20,510, and the highest 10 percent earned more than $50,470. Median annual wages were $33,130 in local government and $27,640 in educational services.

Median annual wages of **transit and railroad police** were $46,670. The middle 50 percent earned between $37,640 and $57,830. The lowest 10 percent earned less than $31,300, and the highest 10 percent earned more than $72,700. Median annual wages were $49,370 in State government, $43,720 in local government, and $56,300 in rail transportation.

Federal law provides special salary rates to Federal employees who serve in law enforcement. Additionally, Federal special agents and inspectors receive law enforcement availability pay (LEAP)—equal to 25 percent of the agent's grade and step—awarded because of the large amount of overtime that these agents are expected to work. Salaries were slightly higher in selected areas where the prevailing local pay level was higher. Because Federal agents may be eligible for a special law enforcement benefits package, applicants should ask their recruiter for more information.

EMPLOYMENT RESOURCES

Further information about employment opportunities with specific agencies is included here. Use the information and resources provided in Chapter Three and Appendix C and E of this book to research opportunities with all agencies. Also, visit *www.federaljobs.net* for direct links to hundreds of resources and agency employment Web sites.

Department of Homeland Security

FBI Special Agent — Information is available from the nearest FBI office. The address and phone number are listed in the local telephone directory. Apply online at www.fbi.gov and explore careers.

Immigration and Customs Inspectors — Inspectors are stationed nationwide at air, land, and sea ports of entry. Visit the Web site at www.cbp.gov for complete information including a *"Career Finder"* tool that allows you to apply online through the Department of Homeland Security. Phone: 1-877-CBP-5511.

Intelligence Operations Specialist — Analyzes intelligence from DHS operating components, state and local partners, and other Intelligence Community (IC) agencies into Homeland Security assessments; ensuring analytic intelligence support to DHS elements that addresses the secretary's top priorities, serving as the primary interface between the IC and customers at state/local/tribal/territorial levels and in the private sector on Homeland Security issues; and coordinating intelligence analytic operations between I&A and DHS operating components as an integrated DHS intelligence enterprise. Locate vacancies at www.usajobs.gov. The Department of Defense is the largest employer of this career field.

Security Screeners — Transportation Security Administration (TSA) This administration is in charge of the Airport Security Screener program. The TSA was transferred from the Department of Transportation to Homeland Security in 2002. Visit the Web site at www.tsa.gov/join/index.shtm.

U.S. Secret Service Special Agents — Information is available from: U.S. Secret Service, 950 H St. NW, Washington, DC 20223. Web site: www.dhs.gov/.

Department of the Interior

Park Ranger — Park Rangers supervise, manage and perform work in the conservation and use of resources in national parks and other federally-managed areas. Park Rangers carry out various tasks associated with forest or structural fire control and they also operate campgrounds, including such tasks as assigning sites, replenishing firewood, performing safety inspections, providing information to visitors, and leading guided tours. Contact regional offices for employment information and visit www.usajobs.gov for job vacancy announcements. Career information is available at www.doi.gov/public/findajob.cfm.

Department of Justice

DEA Special Agent — Information is available from the nearest DEA office, or call **(800) DEA-4288.** Internet, www.justice.gov/dea/index.htm. This Web site offers an assessment tool to help you determine what special agent jobs you may qualify for. The toll free phone line announces job openings and will forward your call to a recruiting officer if you select that option.

Deputy Marshal — Information is available from the United States Marshals Service, Human Resource Division, Washington, DC 20530. Phone 202-616-0682 or visit the Web site at www.justice.gov/marshals/.

Bureau of Prisons - Central Office, 320 First St. NW, Washington, DC 20534. Phone: 202-307-3189 or www.bop.gov/. The bureau is under the Department of Justice and consists of 114 institutions, 6 regional offices, a central office, two staff training centers, and 28 community corrections offices to care for 193,000 federal offenders. Approximately 85 percent of these inmates are confined in Bureau-operated correctional facilities or detention centers. Visit the online facility locator at www.bop.gov/DataSource/execute/dsFacilityLoc to explore employment opportunities in your area.

> *Correctional Officers with the Department of Justice (GS-0007)* — Job hotline at 202-514-3397. There are 17,580 correctional officers working for Justice. Correctional officers enforce the rules and regulations governing the operation of a correctional institution. This includes the confinement, safety, health, and protection of inmates, as well as supervising the various work assignments of inmates. On occasion, correctional officers are required to use firearms, and may at times require arduous physical exertion to subdue unruly inmates who may be armed or assaultive.

CIA Agents — Information is available at https://www.cia.gov/careers/index.html. Its mission is to provide our nation's first line of defense by collecting information, producing timely threat analysis, and conducting covert action at the direction of the president.

Department of the Treasury

IRS Special Agent — Agents combine their accounting skills with law enforcement skills to investigate financial crimes. Special Agents are duly sworn law enforcement officers who are trained to "follow the money." No matter what the source, all income earned, both legal and illegal, has the potential of becoming involved in crimes which fall within the investigative jurisdiction of the IRS Criminal Investigation. Because of the expertise required to conduct these complex financial investigations, IRS Special Agents are considered the premier financial investigators for the federal government.

Criminal Investigators – Investigate potential criminal violations of the Internal Revenue Code, and related financial crimes.

Visit www.irs.gov/compliance/enforcement/ to explore all IRS enforcement careers. You can also call the main number at 202-622-5000.

Treasury Department Office Human Resource Numbers:

Bureau of Public Debt: (304) 480-6144
United States Mint: (800) USA-MINT

Not all occupations are included in the above listed resources. Research all occupations and agencies using Appendix C and Chapter Three of this book plus visit www.federaljobs.net/federal.htm for direct links to over 140 federal agency recruitment sites.

Table 11-1 lists the major law enforcement occupations and job classification series that you can use to search OPM's online federal job vacancy database at www.usajobs.gov and other job listing services that are listed in Chapter Three. Not all federal jobs are listed on OPM's Web site. Visit the 140 federal agency recruitment sites noted above to locate even more jobs.

Security Screening Positions

The Transportation Security Administration (TSA) constantly reviews screening procedures to ensure that measures are targeted to counter potential threats. Originally, the TSA was under the Department of Transportation. When Homeland Security was established, all TSA functions and personnel transferred to HLS. Originally screeners were in the job series 0019, now GS-1802.

Job vacancies are available at www.tsa.gov/join/careers/. Individuals can call 877-872-7990 for additional information. All interested applicants are encouraged to fully review job vacancy announcements and Frequently Asked Questions on the TSA Web site prior to applying.

QUALIFICATION STANDARDS
FOR TWO MAJOR OCCUPATIONS

This section presents the federal qualification standards for two of the larger occupations: Correctional Officer GS-0007 and Criminal Investigator GS-1811.[3] The qualification standards are used by agency personnel department to develop the job announcements that you will see on USAJOBS and through other listing sites. They are also the primary guides that human resource departments use to rate your application. Review these standards closely for the occupation you are interested in to determine if you meet the basic qualification for the position. Visit http://federaljobs.net to locate qualification standards for all other occupations.

IMPORTANT

Read the entire standard before deciding whether or not you qualify. For example, look at education in the first standard. At first glance it appears that a four year B.S. degree is required for the position. You must have a four year degree **OR** three years of experience and they tell you exactly what experience qualifies. It may help to have a four year degree, but experience is also acceptable for some jobs. Many applicants stop reading after they see a degree requirement and think they don't qualify.

READ THE ENTIRE STANDARD — FRONT TO BACK

CORRECTIONAL OFFICER GS-0007

EDUCATION AND EXPERIENCE REQUIREMENTS

EDUCATION

Undergraduate Education: Successful completion of a full four-year course of study in any field leading to a bachelor's degree, in an accredited college or university, is qualifying for GS-5 level positions.

Graduate Education: One full academic year of graduate education with major study in criminal justice, social science, or other field related to the position is qualifying for GS-7. Graduate education may be prorated according to the grade level of the position to be filled; however, it is not qualifying for positions above GS-7.

OR

---

[3] Excerpted from "Operations Manual, Qualifications Standards for General Schedule Positions, 2000."

EXPERIENCE

General Experience (for GS-5 positions): Three years of general experience, one year of which was equivalent to at least GS-4, are qualifying for positions at the GS-5 level. This experience must have demonstrated the aptitude for acquiring knowledge, skills, and abilities required for correctional work, and, in addition, demonstrate the possession of personal attributes important to the effectiveness of correctional officers, such as:

- Ability to meet and deal with people of differing backgrounds and behavioral patterns.
- Ability to be persuasive in selling and influencing ideas.
- Ability to lead, supervise, and instruct others.
- Sympathetic attitude toward the welfare of others.
- Ability to reason soundly and to think out practical solutions to problems.
- Ability to make decisions and act quickly, particularly under stress.
- Poise and self-confidence, and ability to remain calm during emergency situations.

Qualifying general experience may have been gained in work such as:

- Social case work in a welfare agency or counseling in other types of organizations.
- Classroom teaching or instructing.
- Responsible rehabilitation work, e.g., in an alcoholic rehabilitation program.
- Supervising planned recreational activities or active participation in community action programs.
- Management or supervisory work in a business or other organization that included directing the work flow and/or direct supervision of others.
- Sales work, other than taking and filling orders as in over-the-counter sales.

Specialized Experience (for positions above GS-5): One year of specialized experience equivalent to at least the next lower level in the normal line of progression is qualifying for positions at grade GS-6 and above. Specialized experience must have equipped the applicant with the particular knowledge, skills, and abilities to perform successfully the duties of the position to be filled. Experience may have been gained in work such as police officer, mental health counselor in a residential facility, or detention officer.

EMPLOYMENT INTERVIEW

The personal qualities and characteristics of the applicant are the most critical of all the requirements for correctional officer positions. The applicant must be willing to perform arduous and prolonged duties on any of three shifts. In addition, the applicant must possess certain personal qualities in order to relate to inmates effectively in a correctional setting. These include empathy, objectivity, perceptiveness, resourcefulness, adaptability and flexibility, stability, and maturity.

Before appointment, candidates may be required to appear before a panel of specialists in correctional administration for an employment interview to determine the extent to which the candidates possess these and other qualities necessary to perform correctional officer duties adequately. The interview will also serve to acquaint applicants with further details of, and the environment surrounding, the position. A determination by the panel that a person who is otherwise qualified does not possess such personal characteristics to the required degree may result in removal of his/her application from further consideration.

MEDICAL REQUIREMENTS

The Department of Justice, Bureau of Prisons, has established the following medical requirements for correctional officer positions:

General: The duties of these positions involve unusual mental and nervous pressure, and require arduous physical exertion involving prolonged walking and standing, restraining of prisoners in emergencies, and participating in escape hunts. Applicants must be physically capable of performing efficiently the duties of these positions, and be free from such defects or disease as may constitute employment hazards to themselves or others. The duties of a correctional officer are arduous, and sound health as well as physical fitness is required.

Vision: Must have at least 20/30 vision with or without correction. If only one eye is present or functional, the examining health care practitioner shall determine if an applicant can safely perform the physical ability test, the firearms component, and the self-defense component at the training center.

Hearing: Must be capable of hearing conversational voice, with or without a hearing aid, in at least one ear, as measured by normal findings in the decibel ranges of 500, 1000, 2000. This determination is made via a hearing booth test.

Mental/Emotional Stability: Must display mental and emotional stability. The examining health care practitioner shall evaluate mental and emotional stability based upon a thorough medical/psychiatric history as well as a current medical/psychiatric examination. Additionally, any history of psychiatric hospitalizations and outpatient psychiatric treatments shall be considered when evaluating an applicant's mental health.

Active Disease: Active diseases that are infectious and may be spread by routine means, such as handshakes, skin contact, and breathing, preclude an applicant from employment. Once this disease is cured or is considered by the examining health care practitioner to be no longer infectious, the applicant may be considered for employment. Active disease processes or conditions cannot (solely on the basis of the existence of such process, disease, condition, impairment or disability) exclude an otherwise qualified applicant from consideration for employment (i.e., HIV positive, AIDS, cancer, epilepsy, diabetes, heart disease, and loss or injury of one or more limbs).

Disability: Similarly, history of a disease, medical condition, or impairment, particularly if deemed a permanent "disability," cannot, solely on the basis of the existence of such disease, condition, or impairment, exclude an otherwise qualified applicant from consideration for employment. If the applicant is otherwise qualified and can, with or without reasonable accommodation, safely perform the essential functions of the position, the physical ability tests, the firearms component, and the self-defense component, then the individual may be considered for employment.

CRIMINAL INVESTIGATING SERIES GS-1811

Use these individual occupational requirements in conjunction with the "Group Coverage Qualification Standard for Administrative and Management Positions." Individual occupational requirements for Treasury Enforcement Agent positions are identified separately. Visit http://federaljobs.net to view the entire Group Coverage Qualification Standard for Administrative and Management Positions.

MEDICAL REQUIREMENTS

The duties of positions in this series require moderate to arduous physical exertion involving walking and standing, use of firearms, and exposure to inclement weather. Manual dexterity with comparatively free motion of finger, wrist, elbow, shoulder, hip, and knee joints is required. Arms, hands, legs, and feet must be sufficiently intact and functioning in order that applicants may perform the duties satisfactorily. Sufficiently good vision in each eye, with or without correction, is required to perform the duties satisfactorily. Near vision, corrective lenses permitted, must be sufficient to read printed material the size of typewritten characters. Hearing loss, as measured by an audiometer, must not exceed 35 decibels at 1000, 2000, and 3000 Hz levels. Since the duties of these positions are exacting and responsible, and involve activities under trying conditions, applicants must possess emotional and mental stability. Any physical condition that would cause the applicant to be a hazard to himself/herself or others is disqualifying.

CRIMINAL INVESTIGATOR / GS-1811

Treasury Enforcement Agent

Use these individual occupational requirements in conjunction with the "Group Coverage Qualification Standard for Administrative and Management Positions."

EDUCATION

Undergraduate and Graduate Education:

All Treasury Enforcement Agent (TEA) positions in Treasury bureaus and offices, except Internal Revenue Service (IRS) Special Agent positions: Major study—any field of study in an accredited college or university.

IRS Special Agent positions: Major study—any field of study that included or was supplemented by at least 15 semester hours in accounting, and nine semester hours from among the following or closely related fields: finance, economics, business law, tax law, or money and banking.

OR

EXPERIENCE

General Experience (for GS-5 positions):

TEA positions except IRS Special Agent: Successful, responsible experience in the criminal investigative or law enforcement fields that required knowledge and application of laws relating to criminal violations, and the ability to deal effectively with individuals or groups in stressful or controversial situations, collect and assemble pertinent facts for investigations, and prepare clear, concise written reports.

IRS Special Agent positions: Successful, responsible accounting and business experience that required knowledge and application of accounting and auditing principles and general business practices, and that demonstrated the ability to analyze and comprehend accounting and bookkeeping records, financial statements, related reports and automated systems.

Nonqualifying General Experience: Experience as a uniformed law enforcement officer where the principal duties consisted of investigations and arrests involving traffic violations, minor felonies, misdemeanors, and comparable offenses; or in which the major duties involved guarding and protecting property, preventing crimes, and/or legal research without the application of investigative techniques.

Specialized Experience (for positions above GS-5):

TEA positions except IRS Special Agent: Experience in or related to investigation of criminal violations that provided the specific knowledge, skills, and abilities to perform successfully the duties of the position. Examples of qualifying specialized experience include:

- Leadership or membership of a military intelligence or criminal investigative team or component in which the principal duties consisted of security investigation, intelligence gathering, or criminal prosecution.

- Analyzing or evaluating raw investigative data and preparing comprehensive written investigative reports.

- Investigating complex claims involving suspected crimes or alleged fraud.

- Investigating criminal cases requiring the use of recognized investigative methods and techniques and that may have included appearing in court to present evidence.

- Supervising or conducting interviews or interrogations that involved eliciting evidence, data, or surveillance information.

- Law enforcement work in which 50 percent or more of the time involved criminal investigations requiring the use of surveillance, undercover, or other criminal detection methods or techniques.

- Investigating computerized business and/or accounting systems and forming sound conclusions as to related criminal business practices and compliance with federal laws and regulations.

- Investigative work that required rapid, accurate judgments and sound decision-making in applying regulations, instructions, and procedures.

- Successful completion of formalized programs of in-service training for any of the above.

IRS Special Agent positions: Specialized experience required for IRS Special Agent positions is essentially the same as that described above for other TEA positions, except that the experience must have been acquired in investigative work related to the accounting, auditing, business, or commercial practices of subjects investigated.

CERTIFICATE AS A CERTIFIED PUBLIC ACCOUNTANT (CPA)

Proof of possession of a CPA certificate (certificate number and date of issuance) obtained through written examination in a state, territory, or the District of Columbia meets the GS-5 level requirements for positions requiring accounting know-ledge. Applicants with such certificates may also qualify for higher grade levels based on their education and/or experience.

PERSONAL QUALITIES

Appointment is conditional on a satisfactory report of character and background investigation, including a tax audit. This investigation is conducted in order to secure evidence of candidates' loyalty to the U.S. government, honesty, and integrity. For some positions, a top secret security clearance will be required.

INTERVIEW

Applicants who pass the written test, as required, and who meet the experience or educational requirements will be required to appear for an interview at the time of consideration for appointment. The interview is to evaluate observable personal qualifications essential for successful performance of the duties of the position, such as poise, tact, and ability in oral expression. An otherwise qualified applicant who is found to lack the personal qualifications necessary for successful performance of the duties of the position will be removed from further consideration.

MOTOR VEHICLE OPERATION

Applicants must possess a valid automobile driver's license at the time of appointment. Candidates must qualify after appointment for authorization to operate motor vehicles in accordance with applicable OPM regulations and related Department of the Treasury requirements.

USE OF FIREARMS

All positions require basic and periodic qualification in the use of firearms; proficiency with standard issue firearms must be demonstrated for successful completion of training. All agents are required to carry a handgun in the performance of duties.

MAXIMUM ENTRY AGE

The date immediately preceding an individual's 37th birthday is the maximum entry age for original appointment to a position within the Department of the Treasury as a law enforcement officer as defined in title 5 U.S.C. 8331(20) or in 5 U.S.C. 8401(17). Consideration will be restricted to candidates who have not yet reached age 37 at the time of referral for positions.

MEDICAL REQUIREMENTS

General: The duties of these positions require moderate to arduous physical exertion involving walking and standing, use of firearms, and exposure to inclement weather. Manual dexterity with comparatively free motion of fingers, wrists, elbows, shoulders, hips and knee joints is required. Arms, hands, legs, and feet must function sufficiently in order for applicants to perform the duties satisfactorily.

Vision: For all positions, near vision, corrected or uncorrected, must be sufficient to read larger type 2 at 14 inches. Normal depth perception and peripheral vision are required, as is the ability to distinguish shades of color by color plate tests. For all positions covered by this standard, applicants who have undergone refractive surgery (i.e., surgery to improve distant visual acuity) must meet Treasury-approved requirements which include documentation that they have passed specific exam and protocol testing. Visual acuity requirements for each bureau listed below are expressed in terms of the Snellen vision test:

U.S. Secret Service — Uncorrected distant vision must test 20/60 in each eye, and corrected distant vision must test 20/20 in each eye.

Bureau of Alcohol, Tobacco and Firearms — Uncorrected distant vision must test 20/100 in each eye, and corrected distant vision must test 20/20 in one eye, 20/30 in the other.

All other bureaus — Uncorrected distant vision must test 20/200, and corrected distant vision must test 20/20 in one eye, 20/30 in the other.

Hearing: Hearing loss, as measured by an audiometer, must not exceed 30 decibels (A.S.A. or equivalent I.S.O.) in either ear in the 500, 1000, and 2000 Hz ranges. Applicants must be able to hear the whispered voice at 15 feet with each ear without the use of a hearing aid.

Special Medical Requirements: Since the duties of these positions are exacting and involve the responsibility for the safety of others under trying conditions, applicants must possess emotional and mental stability. Any condition that would hinder full, efficient performance of the duties of these positions or that would cause the individual to be a hazard to himself/herself or to others is disqualifying.

Appointment will be contingent upon a candidate's passing a pre-employment medical examination and drug test to ascertain possession of the physical and emotional requirements for the position. For certain positions in-volving particularly arduous or hazardous duties, there are specific medical requirements where a direct relationship exists between the condition and the duties of the position being filled. Certain diseases or conditions resulting in indistinct speech may be disqualifying. Any chronic disease or condition affecting the respiratory system, the cardiovascular system, the gastrointestinal, musculoskeletal, digestive, nervous, endocrine or genitourinary systems that would impair full performance of the duties of the position is disqualifying. Prior to completion of the one-year probationary period following initial appointment, an incumbent may be required to undergo a physical examination and meet the same medical requirements as those for appointment. Supervisory positions excepted, these med-ical requirements must be met in service placement actions, including reinstatement of former employees and transfers from positions not covered by this standard. The presence of medical conditions that would be aggravated by the environmental conditions of these positions will ordinarily disqualify an applicant for appointment.

CHAPTER TWELVE
Employment Secrets

Why is it that some who land jobs with Uncle Sam have half the experience, education, and special qualifications that you have — and you're still looking? Many who approach the federal sector lose out because they didn't take the time to understand the federal hiring process. Others get frustrated by the required paperwork and give up prematurely. Decades later they will regret their impatience and wish they had done what it takes to land a high-paying and benefit-loaded government job.

The secret to success is that the harder you work the luckier you get.

If you take the time to understand the differences between the private and public sectors, thoroughly complete your application package, and seek out all available job vacancies, your chances for employment will increase substantially. Job applicants who successfully land government jobs have to deal with the application process throughout their careers. During my 35-plus years of government service I submitted over 14 application packages while working for the Departments of Defense and Transportation. My last federal application, for a senior management position, was over 60 pages long.

CHAPTER OBJECTIVES

- Achieve *"Best Qualified"* résumé/application ratings
- Learn how to improve your chances
- Identify job options *(apply for all job series that you can qualify for)*
- Understand the *"Keys to Success"*

APPLY EARLY

It pays to start your employment search early for federal jobs, well in advance of the time you will be available for employment. Applications can take six to eight weeks or even longer for processing. It can take even longer than that if written tests are required. From the time you first identify an opening to actual interviews and hiring can still take up to six months in some cases even under recent hiring reform initiatives.

All individuals interested in federal employment should start researching the system, identifying jobs, visiting agency Web sites, and preparing for tests — if required — months in advance.

> Most federal agencies have Internet Web sites. Over 80 percent of all federal jobs are advertised by individual agencies with the majority posted on USAJobs. However, visit agency Web sites to locate **ALL** job vacancies in your area. A comprehensive list of federal agency employment Web sites is available in this book with direct online links located on http://federaljobs.net.

YOUR APPLICATION AND RÉSUMÉ

Review Chapter Six to learn how to evaluate job announcements and complete your federal style résumé. There are a number of application methods used by agencies including the traditional paper copy résumé, online résumé builder submissions, and standard forms. You should also be familiar with the OF-612 optional application form and the OF-306. All forms listed in the job announcement must be submitted with your package.

The most popular application method today is the federal style résumé, for a number of reasons. First, most people are familiar with résumés and secondly, with the increase in online submissions, the résumé format makes the most sense because it is easy to copy and paste from your federal style résumé into online résumé builders.

DON'T SUBMIT A PRIVATE SECTOR RÉSUMÉ

Many applicants submit a private sector résumé, which is insufficient for federal jobs. The major differences between the federal style résumé and private sector is explained in Chapter Six and you will find sample résumés to assist you with yours. The differences are significant. Considerably more detail is required for the federal style résumé and if you don't provide the exact information requested your application may be rejected. At the very least you risk not being placed in the highest category rating and less likely to be referred to the selecting official.

Details, Details, and More Details

First and foremost, when applying for any federal job **READ** the job announcement front to back. The job announcement will explain everything you need to know to apply for that specific job. Every job announcement is unique, so don't assume because you read one for the exact same job series and grade that the requirements are the same for this new job. This is especially true for the required key *Duties, Responsibilities* and *Specialized Experience*. Each advertised job has specific requirements such as proficiency and experience with computer software, equipment, programs, reporting systems, skills, and other factors.

When applying for any federal job read the job announcement front to back.

Achieve "Best Qualified" Ratings and Be Referred for Interviews by:

✓   Reading the job announcement completely — front to back

✓   Using a highlighter to mark key words and phrases listed on the job announcement under Duties, Responsibilities and Specialized Experience.

✓   Tailoring your résumé, competencies/KSAs, and Occupational Questionnaire by incorporating the key words and phrases identified in the previous step into your work descriptions and competencies.

I can't stress enough the importance of tailoring your federal style résumé to the job announcement's key duties, responsibilities and specialized experience. If you do as suggested above you will improve your chances of being referred for interviews. Everything is about ranking factors and showing rating officials through your detailed work descriptions that you deserve to be placed in the "Best Qualified" group.

Another factor to consider is that most résumés — over 90 percent or more — are now submitted online through federal résumé builders. I suggest completing your federal style résumé offline on your desktop computer rather than going straight to a résumé builder. You need quality time to compose and tailor your résumé, and many of the online résumé builder and submission programs have time limits and other constraints.

APPLY FREQUENTLY

Many job hunters send in an application for only one job announcement. Seek out all available job vacancies and continue to send in applications with every opportunity. Don't limit yourself to www.usajobs.gov. This excellent site does advertise about 80 percent or more of all federal jobs; however, you may be passing up job opportunities in your own back yard by not visiting individual agency recruitment sites in your area. Visit www.federaljobs.net/federal.htm, this book's companion Web site, for direct links to over 140 federal agency recruiting sites.

Review the Agency Skills Index in Appendix D to locate agencies that utilize your skills and college degrees. For example, if you have a degree in archeology you will discover that the Departments of Agriculture and Defense hire over 1,000 in the GS-0193 Archeology job series. Identify all job series that you can possibly qualify for. If you are having difficulty identifying job series that fit your training, experience, and abilities, review the qualification standards for those positions online at www.federaljobs.net/quals2.htm.

You will find that you may qualify for many different jobs. Don't overlook Wage Grade (WG) positions. When searching for vacancies online, review job announcements for all the job series that interest you. You will be surprised by how many you qualify for.

Consider the electronics technician field. For example, all of the following job series require basic electronic technician skills:[1]

GS-856	Electronics Technician
GS-802	Electronics Engineering Technician
GS-2101	Transportation Specialist (FAA System Specialists)

WG-2500 — Wire Communications Equip/Installation/Maintenance Family

WG-2502	Telephone Mechanic
WG-2504	Wire Communications Cable Splicing
WG-2508	Communications Line Installing/Repairing
WG-2511	Wire Communications Equipment Install/Repair

WG-2600 — Electronic Equipment Installation and Maintenance Family

WG-2602	Electronic Measurement Equipment Mechanic
WG-2604	Electronic Mechanic
WG-2606	Electronic Industrial Controls
WG-2698	Electronic Digital Computer Mechanic

WG-2800	Electrical Installation Maintenance Family (4 occupations)
WG-3300	Instrument Work Family (5 occupations)
WG-4800	General Maintenance Family (7 occupations)

Over 40 Electronic Related Jobs Are Listed Under Various Wage Grade Families

---

[1] Publication TS-56, March 1990, Part 3, Definitions of Trades and Labor Job Families and Occupations.

GETTING IN THE FRONT DOOR

Getting in is half the battle. If you want to enter a specific career field with an agency and there are currently no openings, apply for other related jobs with that agency. For instance, if you qualify for a logistics/supply position and they have a lower graded opening that you meet the qualifications for, it may be to your benefit to apply and get on board. Agencies often advertise in-house first to offer qualified workers opportunities for advancement. You may have a good chance to bid on other jobs if you have the qualifications and a good track record. However, other factors such as time -in-grade must be considered before making this choice.

Example: Sue was applying for and was highly qualified for a GS-11 Family Support Specialist, but her application never reached the selecting official because she was blocked by an individual claiming vet preference. She decided to just get her foot in the door by accepting a GS-5 clerk position and then apply as an internal candidate. Unfortunately, due to time in grade restrictions, she will not qualify for a GS-11 internal candidate position for several years because she is required to spend up to a year at each intervening grade.

"There are two things to aim at in life: first, to get what you want; and after that to enjoy it. Only the wisest of people achieve the second."

LOCATE ALL JOB VACANCIES

Locate announcements from all sources including OPM's USAJOBS, individual agency Web sites, www://federaljobs.net, and other services listed in Chapter Three. Listings on www.federaljobs.net can be searched by occupation or agency and the results show ALL federal and private sector job vacancies in your area to improve your chances of finding employment.

Identify local agency offices and conduct informational interviews as discussed in Chapter Four and send them a copy of your federal style résumé along with a short cover letter. In the letter thank them for the interview and let them know what jobs you are interested in. This is a good way to introduce yourself and your qualifications to a perspective employer. The more contacts you make the better. This is especially important if you qualify for a special hiring programs such as the Veterans Recruitment Appointment (VRA) or disability pro-grams.

Visit www.federaljobs.net/federal.htm, this book's companion Web site, for direct links to over 140 federal agency recruiting sites. Consider subscribing to *Federal Career Opportunities* (www.fedjobs.com) published by Federal Research Services. Online job vacancy listing services compile job vacancies from over 200 federal personnel offices. **The larger the area of consideration the better your chances**. Choice jobs with certain agencies often require an applicant to accept a job in a not-so-desirable location. Often, agencies have to advertise jobs to the general public because the area isn't desirable and they can't get in-house applicants. Once hired, you may have an opportunity to apply to more desirable locations after you are trained and have the required agency experience.

During my early government career I accepted a job with an agency in a small town of 3,056 inhabitants in central Pennsylvania. After completing the required initial training and receiving required system certifications I was able to successfully relocate to the area of my choice. It took me three years to gain the training and experience needed to apply for jobs in other areas. When I did relocate, the agency paid for the complete move, including real estate expenses.

One important fact to remember: In most cases **your first move is at your expense**. If you are willing to relocate you will be responsible for the cost of the move. Initial relocation might be negotiable for certain hard to fill vacancies. However, if you relocate to other areas after your first year of employment the government might pick up the tab. The moving allowances are generous. If you own a home and are relocated, agencies often buy your house from you at close to market rates, pay to move your household goods, and pay real estate costs including certain closing costs at your new location. On top of this, you may be allowed up to 60 to 90 days of temporary housing expenses at your new location, 64 hours of leave for the move, and a house hunting trip.

CAUTION

Don't jump blindly at an employment offer. Many agencies have difficulty filling jobs in high-cost-of-living areas such as New York, Los Angeles, and Washington, D.C. Investigate the cost of living in the area you are selected for before saying yes. If you can't afford to live in the area you may have to turn down the initial offer.

"LOOK BEFORE YOU LEAP"

TRAINING AND EXPERIENCE

Often, applicants neglect to add valuable work experience and training to their application package. Most HR specialists and announcements requests that you go back 10 years for your work history. Go back as many years as needed to capture related education and experience. For example, if you were a supply specialist in the military in 1990, and you are applying for a supply/logistics position, then by all means add your military experience and training to your application. I suggest that you always add your military experience no matter how far back it may be.

Many agencies require supplemental occupational questionnaires or in rare cases today qualification forms. If you are applying for an electronics position these questionnaires and forms often capture your math, electronics training and specific experience background. List all of your math training back through high school. Trigonometry and algebra are required for many electronics positions. If you had these subjects in high school and you don't list them you might not be rated eligible for the position.

NETWORKING

Networking is a term used to define the establishment of a group of individuals who assist one another for mutual benefit. You can establish your own network by talking to personnel specialists, contacting regional agency employment departments, conducting informational interviews, and bidding on all applicable job announcements. By following the guidelines outlined in the book and using your innate common sense your chances of success are magnified tenfold.

Use the more than 1,000 contacts presented in this book to begin your personal employment network. Add to this information individual contacts that you make with local agencies.

KEYS TO SUCCESS

There are six basic ingredients to successfully finding federal employment for qualified applicants:

- Understand the differences between the private and federal sectors.
- Seek out all job vacancies and bid on multiple positions.
- Completely read and analyze each job announcement.
- Package a professional federal style résumé.
- Don't give up when you receive your first rejection.
- Prepare for interviews.

You can learn from rejections by contacting the selecting official and/or the HR specialist. Ask what training and/or experience would have enhanced your application package for future positions. If the selecting official or HR specialist suggests obtaining certain education, training or experience, work to achieve their recommendations. A rejection may also be due to things beyond your control such as funding restrictions, a hiring freeze, or your selection may have been blocked by a military member claiming veterans' preference.

You may discover that you did have the specific skills needed. However, you either neglected to capture required key words and phrases (skills needed) in your work descriptions or didn't include critical work history in your application. This happens frequently. It doesn't pay to debate your qualifications over spilled milk. The job has already been filled. Thank the selecting official for his candor and time, then revise your bid for the next opening.

Write the selecting official a **BRIEF** letter of thanks and explain that you neglected to incorporate the recommended skills in the original application. Send him or her a copy of your revised application for future reference. **Managers appreciate dealing with rational and mature individuals, and you will be remembered.**

I used the Individual Development Plan (IDP) process throughout my federal career to target promotions and to work with management to obtain valuable career-enhancing lateral assignments and temporary details. You can do the same once hired. Visit http://fedcareer.info to learn how to target your career goals and achieve them. During my tenure as a manager for the Federal Aviation Administration I encouraged employees seeking promotions to develop viable IDPs in concert with management to achieve their career goals.

It took me two years to land my first competitive federal civil service job. I was not aware of the employment options available at that time. Today there are many options available through special emphasis hiring, direct hire authority, student employment, veterans' preference, and internships, to name a few. Add to this list the more than 1,000 job resources provided throughout this book. Take advantage of as many of the programs as you qualify for to enhance your career search. Don't give up or get overly frustrated with the paperwork that is required when applying for federal employment. Look at the long-term view and remind yourself that if you do the paperwork — and do it right — you can end up with a high-paying, benefit-loaded job for the rest of your career.

If you should get frustrated, and many do, just think of this: The average annual total compensation in 2010 for federal civilian workers was **$123,049,** compared to **$61,051** for the private sector.[2] The benefits are outstanding and according to the Congressional Budget Office, *Characteristics and Pay of Federal Civilian Employees* report, federal employees' benefits ranged between 26 percent and 50 percent of pay based on time in service, the employee's age, and retirement system. Federal jobs are well worth the time and effort that you **INVEST** in the process.

Finally, I must add that it is unwise to get angry with the process; instead of getting mad, **GET INVOLVED**.

> *"We grow great by dreams. All
> big men are dreamers.
> They see things in the soft haze of a
> spring day or in the red fire of a
> long winter's evening. Some of
> us let these dreams die, but others
> nourish and protect them, nurse
> them to the sunshine and light
> which come always to those who
> sincerely hope that their dreams
> will come true."*
>
> **— Woodrow Wilson**

---

[2] Bureau of Economic Analysis, National Income & Product Account Tables 6.2D and 6.5D, 2010.

APPENDIX A
Job Hunter's Checklist

WHAT TO DO NOW

☐ Review the federal occupations lists in Appendix C and the skills index in Appendix D. These appendices provide lists of specific federal jobs that you may qualify for.

☐ Review Chapter One for an overview of the federal hiring system.

> ✔ Visit **USAJOBS** at http://usajobs.gov and link direct to over 140 federal agency recruitment sites at http://federaljobs.net/federal.htm. If you don't have access to the Internet, call **USAJOBS by phone** at 703-724-1850 or TTY 978-461-8404. However, you will need a vacancy number. The best way to obtain a vacancy number for a specific job is online or directly from a federal human resource department. Many libraries now have online access capabilities. Obtain job announcements for specific job series *(online or by phone)*.

> ✔ Review the application process in Chapter Six, including the sample job announcement and résumés.

☐ Contact regional and local agency personnel offices. See Appendix B for office addresses, Web sites, and phone numbers.

> ✔ Review agency career information online.
> ✔ Visit http://federaljobs.net for direct links to over 140 agency employment Web sites.
> ✔ Talk with agency personnel offices to determine when they will be hiring and obtain information on special hiring programs.
> ✔ Obtain local government office phone numbers from your phone directory. Look under "U.S. Government."

> Applications will only be accepted for open job announcements. If you are applying for an analyst position and no openings exist, they will not accept your application.

☐   Visit **Federal Jobs Network** at http://federaljobs.net/, this book's companion Web site for updates to *The Book of U.S. Government Jobs*. If hiring programs are modified, or Web site addresses or contact information change, those changes will be posted on this site. You can also link direct to hundreds of federal agency employment sites.

☐   Review Chapter Three's listings to identify job announcement resources including Internet Web site addresses. Also review:

✔   Chapter Three for Student Hiring Programs.

✔   Chapter Seven for Veterans Hiring Programs.

✔   Chapter Eight for overseas job resources.

✔   Chapter Nine for postal jobs.

✔   Chapter Ten for job resources for people with disabilities.

✔   Chapter Eleven for Homeland Security and law enforcement jobs.

☐   Locate your high school and college transcripts, military records, awards, and professional licenses. Collect past employment history; salary, addresses, phone numbers, dates employed, etc.

☐   Visit your local library for these resources:

✔   *The United States Government Manual* — This book provides agency descriptions, addresses, contacts and basic employment information.

✔   *The Occupational Outlook Handbook* — If your library doesn't have this publication, check with a local college placement office. It is also available online at http://bls.gov/. This handbook is a nationally recognized source of career information and includes detailed descriptions of working conditions for over 250 jobs.

✔ *Computer access* – Visit your local library if you need to research careers, find job announcements, and apply using online resume builders.

✔ You will find this book in most large libraries. If you don't have the cash to purchase a copy, visit your local library's reference department and ask for a copy of the book. *The Book of U.S. Government Jobs* is recommended by **Library Journal**.

WHAT'S AVAILABLE

☐ Call local agencies listed in the phone directory. Also visit local federal buildings. Request informational interviews per guidance in Chapter Four. Visit the following sites to locate job announcements:

✔ http://www.usajobs.gov *(OPM Sponsored — approximately 70 percent of all federal jobs are advertised on this site. Average 20,000 daily listings.)*

✔ http://federaljobs.net/federal.htm *(Companion Web site for this book; direct links to over 140 federal agency recruiting sites.)*

☐ Research the agencies in Appendix B of this book, including agency Web sites. Department Web sites are listed in Chapter Three.

☐ Consider subscribing to Federal Research Services' *Federal Career Opportunities* at www.fedjobs.com. This company publishes online databases and bi-weekly listings of job vacancies from over 200 federal personnel offices.

☐ Review Chapters Three, Seven, Eight, Nine, and Ten.

APPLYING FOR A JOB

☐ Locate job announcements instantly online. Each announcement lists all required information and in most cases you apply online through one of several résumé builders. Most agencies require online résumé submissions and allow you to draft and archive your federal style résumé online.

☐ Review Chapter Six and follow the guidance for completing your federal style résumé. Chapter Six provides guidance on the federal style résumé and takes you step-by-step through the application process. You'll learn how to tailor and write a professional federal résumé and application using key words and phrases noted in the job announcement.

☐ If no vacancies exist for your specialty, visit http://www.usajobs.gov/ and agency Web sites frequently. Jobs can be advertised for very short periods.

You can register on USAJOBS to compile and save your online résumé and for e-mail notification for specific job openings. Job vacancies can be located through USAJOBS, direct from local agencies, agency Web sites, various non-federal job listing services, local state employment offices, or through various publications.

❑   Contact individual agencies. The more contacts, the greater your chance of finding open announcements and special emphasis programs.

❑   Complete ALL requested application information. Follow the step-by-step instructions presented in Chapter six and in the job announcement.

❑   Retain a copy of each job announcement that you applied for, along with a copy of your submitted application package. You will need to review them prior to the interview.

❑   Submit your application online or send in your completed résumé and application to the address specified on the announcement. You must submit or send in your application package by the closing date of the bid.

RESULTS

Your application will be processed and results returned to you within several weeks. You will receive a *Notice of Rating or Notice of Results* informing you of your eligibility by mail. If rated eligible, your name will be placed on the list of eligible applicants for that position. Your name and application will be forwarded to a selecting official for consideration.

THE INTERVIEW

❑   Prepare for the interview. Review Chapter Four's Employment Interviewing section.

APPENDIX B
Federal Agency Contact List

═══

This appendix provides a functional summary and general employment information for the three branches of the government and for 18 federal departments under the executive branch. Larger independent agencies are also listed.

The information and statistics provided in this appendix were extracted from the U.S. Government Manual 2009/2010, Federal Civilian Workforce Statistics Employment and Trends as of September 2010, the Federal Career Directory, and the Central Personnel Data File, Office of Workforce Information. The agency summaries include Internet Web site addresses and specific employment contact information when available. Many listings also include a summary of occupations employed by that organization. Use this Appendix in conjunction with Appendix C to target specific agencies that employ individuals in your occupational group. Also, explore related occupations that you may be qualified for. The more occupations and job series that you target, the better your chances are for employment.

Notice

If you're unable to reach an agency at the listed number, call directory assistance by dialing the area code plus 555-1212. For directory assistance in the metropolitan Washington, D.C., area call (202) 555-1212, for northern Virginia (703) 555-1212, and (301) 555-1212 for agencies located in Maryland in close proximity to the District of Columbia. You can also locate phone numbers at www.info.gov/phone.htm.

LEGISLATIVE BRANCH

The Congress of the United States was created by Article 1, Section 1, of the Constitution. All legislative powers are vested in Congress, which consists of the Senate and House of Representatives. The Legislative branch has 33,754 employees.

The Senate is composed of 100 members, two from each state. Senators are elected for a six-year term. The House of Representatives is made up of 435 representatives. Each state elects representatives based on population distribution. The more populous the state the more representatives it has.

The vice president of the United States is the presiding officer of the Senate. The following offices are under the Legislative branch (the number employed by each office is noted in parentheses):

Congress	(18,155)
Architect of the Capitol	(2,507)
United States Botanic Garden	(63)
Government Accountability Office	(3,191)
Government Printing Office	(2,378)
Library of Congress	(3,871)
Congressional Budget Office	(238)

ARCHITECT OF THE CAPITOL

U.S. Capitol Building, Washington, DC 20515 (202)-228-1793, www.aoc.gov

The Architect of the Capitol is responsible for the care and maintenance of the Capitol building and nearby buildings and grounds.

UNITED STATES BOTANIC GARDEN

Office of the Director, 245 First St. SW., Washington, DC 20024
(202) 225-6670, www.usbg.gov

The United States Botanic Garden collects and grows various vegetable productions of this and other countries for exhibition and public display, student study, scientists, and garden clubs.

GOVERNMENT ACCOUNTABILITY OFFICE

441 G St. NW., Washington, DC 20548
(202) 512-3000, www.gao.gov

The Accountability Office is the investigative arm of Congress and is charged with examining matters related to the receipt & disbursement of public funds.

GOVERNMENT PRINTING OFFICE

732 North Capitol Street NW., Washington, DC 20401
(202) 512-0000, www.gpo.gov

This office prints, binds, and distributes the publications of Congress as well as the executive departments. Employment is primarily in administrative, clerical and technical fields.

LIBRARY OF CONGRESS
Recruitment & Placement Office
101 Independence Ave. SE,
Washington, DC 20540
(202) 707-5000, www.loc.gov

The Library of Congress is the national library of the United States, offering diverse materials for research including comprehensive historical collections.

CONGRESSIONAL BUDGET OFFICE
Second & D Streets SW,
Washington, DC 20515
(202) 226-2600, www.cbo.gov

Provides Congress with assessments of the economic impact of the congressional budget.

JUDICIAL BRANCH

Article III, Section 1, of the Constitution of the United States provides that "the judicial power of the United States shall be vested in one Supreme Court, and in such inferior courts as the Congress may from time to time ordain and establish." The Supreme Court was established on September 24, 1789. This branch employs 33,760 legal professionals, clerks, administrative personnel, secretaries, and other related specialties. The following offices are under this branch:

Supreme Court of the United States
Lower Courts
Special Courts
Administrative Office of the United States Courts
Federal Judicial Center
United States Sentencing Commission

THE SUPREME COURT
One First Street NE,
Washington, DC 20543
(202) 479-3000, www.supremecourtus.gov

Composed of the chief justice and eight associate justices, who are nominated by the president of the United States.

LOWER COURTS
Administrative Office of the U.S. Courts,
Thurgood Marshall Federal Judiciary Bldg.
One Columbus Circle NE,
Washington, DC 20544
(202) 502-2600

The 12 circuits include all states. There are 89 district offices located throughout the country. Consult your local telephone book for offices located near you. Includes Court of Appeals, U.S. District Courts, Territorial Courts, Court of International Trade, and the Judicial Panel on Multidistrict Litigation.

SPECIAL COURTS
Clerk's Office, U.S. Court of Federal Claims
717 Madison Place NW.,
Washington, DC 20005
(202) 357-6400

Consists of the U. S. Claims Court, Court of International Trade, Court of Military Appeals, United States Tax Court, Temporary Emergency Court of Appeals, Court of Veterans Appeals, and others.

ADMINISTRATIVE OFFICE OF U.S. COURTS

Thurgood Marshall Federal Judiciary Bldg.
One Columbus Circle NE,
Washington, DC 20544
(202) 502-2600, www.uscourts.gov

Charged with the nonjudicial, administrative business of U.S. courts. Includes the following divisions; Bankruptcy, Court Admin, Defender Services, Financial Management, General Counsel, Magistrates, Personnel, Probation, and Statistical Analysis.

FEDERAL JUDICIAL CENTER

Thurgood Marshall Federal Judiciary Bldg.
One Columbus Circle NE,
Washington DC 20002-8003
(202) 502-4000, www.fjc.gov

The Federal Judiciary Center is the agency for policy research and continuing education.

U.S. SENTENCING COMMISSION

Suite 2-500, South Lobby,
One Columbus Circle NE,
Washington DC 20002-8002
(202) 502-4500, www.ussc.gov

U.S. Sentencing Commission develops sentencing guidelines and policies for the federal courts.

EXECUTIVE BRANCH

The president is the administrative head of the Executive branch and is responsible for numerous agencies as well as 14 executive departments. The administration of this vast bureaucracy is handled by the president's Cabinet, which includes the heads of the 15 executive departments. The Executive branch consists of 1,879,679 employees distributed among the 15 departments and numerous independent agencies. The following offices, departments, and over 63 independent agencies are under the Executive branch (The number employed by each office is noted in parentheses):

Executive Office of the President	(1,769)
The White House Office	(423)
Office of Management and Budget	(517)
Council of Economic Advisors	(24)
National Security Council	(63)
Office of Policy Development	(30)
U. S. Trade Representative	(234)
Council on Environmental Quality	(24)
Office of Science & Technology Policy	(27)
Office of Administration	(226)
Office of the Vice President	(21)
Office of National Drug Control Policy	(92)

THE WHITE HOUSE OFFICE
1600 Pennsylvania Avenue NW,
Washington, DC 20500
(202) 456-1414, www.whitehouse.gov

This office assists the president in the performance of the many duties and responsibilities of the office. The staff facilitates and maintains communication with Congress, agencies, and the public.

OFFICE OF MANAGEMENT & BUDGET
Executive Office Building
Washington, DC 20503
(202) 395-3080, www.whitehouse.gov/omb

Evaluates, formulates, and coordinates management procedures and program objectives among federal departments and agencies. Employment inquiries: (202) 395-1088.

NATIONAL SECURITY COUNCIL
Eisenhower Executive Office Building
Washington, DC 20504
(202) 456-1414, www.whitehouse.gov/nsc

Advises the president with respect to the integration of domestic, foreign, and military policies relating to national security.

OFFICE OF POLICY DEVELOPMENT
Eisenhower Executive Office Bldg.,
Room 469
Washington, DC 20502
(202) 456-5594, www.whitehouse.gov/dpc

Advises the president in the formulation, evaluation, and coordination of long-range domestic and economic policy.

U.S. TRADE REPRESENTATIVE
600 17th Street NW,
Washington, DC 20508

(202) 395-3230, www.ustr.gov

Responsible for the direction of all trade negotiations of the United States and for the formulation of trade policy for the United States.

COUNCIL OF ECONOMIC ADVISORS
1800 G St. NW,
Washington DC 20502
(202) 395-5084, www.whitehouse.gov/cea

Analyzes the National Economy to provide policy recommendations to the president.

COUNCIL ON ENVIRONMENTAL QUALITY
722 Jackson Place NW,
Washington, DC 20503
(202) 395-5750, www.whitehouse.gov/ceq

Develops and recommends to the president national environmental quality policies.

OFFICE OF SCIENCE & TECHNOLOGY
Executive Office Bldg.
725 17th St. NW, Washington, DC 20502
(202) 456-7116, www.ostp.gov

Provides scientific, engineering, and technological analysis and judgment for the president in major policy, plans, and programs.

OFFICE OF NATIONAL DRUG CONTROL POLICY

Executive Office of the President,
Washington, DC 20503
(202) 395-6700, www.ondcp.gov

Assists the president in policies and objectives in the national drug control strategy. Employment: (202) 395-6695

OFFICE OF ADMINISTRATION
Eisenhower Executive Building
1650 Pennsylvania Ave. NW,
Washington, DC 20503
(202) 456-2861, www.whitehouse.gov/oa

Provides administrative support to all units within the Executive Office of the President.

OFFICE OF THE VICE PRESIDENT
Eisenhower Executive Office Building
Washington, DC 20501
(202) 456-7549

The executive functions of the vice president include participation in Cabinet meetings and, by statute, membership on the National Security Council and the Board of Regents of the Smithsonian Institution.

THE 15 EXECUTIVE DEPARTMENTS

Agriculture	(108,291)
Commerce	(49,162)
Defense — nonmilitary	(644,299)
Education	(4,536)
Energy	(16,625)
Health & Human Services	(61,163)
Homeland Security	(188,983)
Housing & Urban Development	(10,041)
Interior	(79,048)
Justice	(116,901)
Labor	(16,640)
State	(11,890)
Transportation	(57,947)
Treasury	(109,900)
Veterans Affairs	(308,814)

DEPARTMENT OF AGRICULTURE
1400 Independence Ave. SW,
Washington, DC 20250
(202) 720-4623, www.usda.gov

This department works to maintain and improve farm income and develop and expand markets abroad for agricultural products. Helps curb and cure poverty, hunger, and malnutrition. Enhances the environment and maintains production capacity through efforts to protect the soil, water, forests, and other natural resources.

General employment inquiries may be sent to the Staffing & Personnel Information Systems Staff, Office of Personnel, Department of Agriculture, Washington, DC 20250.

EMPLOYMENT INFORMATION — Employment opportunities within the Food & Consumer Service can be researched by contacting the national headquarters in Washington, D.C., phone (703) 305-2286. Regional offices are located in Atlanta, Chicago, Dallas, San Francisco, Denver, Boston, and N.J. For these locations look up the Department of Agriculture, Food & Nutrition Services in the above cities' phone directory or obtain addresses from the headquarters in Washington, D.C.

Field meat and poultry inspector units are located throughout the country in hundreds of metropolitan areas. Employment opportunities exist at hundreds of locations that are administered from the central offices. Persons interested in employment in the Food Safety and Inspection Service should contact the Food Safety and Inspection Service, Beltsville, Maryland, 20705, Phone (301) 344-4755, E-mail: mphotline.fsis@usda.gov. Internet Web site: www.fsis.usda.gov

DEPARTMENT OF COMMERCE (DOC)
Fourteenth Street and Constitution Ave. NW,
Washington, DC 20230
(202) 482-2000, www.doc.gov, Employment: (202) 482-5138
Employment Web site: www.commerce.gov/about-commerce/careers

This department promotes the nation's international trade, economic growth, and technological advancement. The Department of Commerce provides assistance and information to increase America's competitiveness in the world economy, administers programs to prevent unfair foreign trade competition, provides research and support for the increased use of scientific engineering and technological development. Other responsibilities include the granting of patents and registration of trademarks, development of policies, and conducting various research projects.

DOC OFFICES, AGENCIES AND BUREAUS

- **BUREAU OF INDUSTRY AND SECURITY** — The mission of this bureau is to advance U.S. national security, foreign policy, and economic objectives. For additional information contact the Bureau of Industry and Security, Office of Public Affairs, Room 3897, 14th St. And Constitution Ave. NW, Washington DC 20230. Phone (202) 482-2721, www.bis.doc.gov

- **ECONOMIC & STATISTICS ADMINISTRATION** — This bureau provides a picture of the U. S. economy and includes the Bureau of the Census and the Bureau of Economic Analysis. For additional information contact the Economic & Statistics Administration, Dept. of Commerce, Washington, DC 20230. Phone (202) 482-3727, www.esa.doc.gov

- **ECONOMIC DEVELOPMENT ADMINISTRATION** — This agency was created to generate new jobs, to help protect existing jobs, and to stimulate commercial and industrial growth in economically distressed areas. For further information contact the Economic Development Administration, Department of Commerce, Washington, DC 20230. Phone (202) 482-2309, www.eda.gov

- **INTERNATIONAL TRADE ADMINISTRATION** — The International Trade Administration was established to strengthen the international trade and investment position of the United States. There are numerous district offices located throughout the country. A listing of district offices and specific employment information can be obtained through the International Trade Administration, Department of Commerce, Washington, DC 20230. Phone (202) 482-3917, www.trade.gov

- **MINORITY BUSINESS DEVELOPMENT AGENCY** — This agency was created to assist minority enterprise in achieving effective and equitable participation in the American free enterprise system. Provides management and technical assistance to minority firms on request, primarily through a network of minority business development centers. For additional information contact the Office of the Director, Minority Business Development Agency, Department of Commerce, Washington, DC 20230. Phone (202) 482-5061, www.mbda.gov

- **NATIONAL INSTITUTE OF STANDARDS AND TECHNOLOGY** — Conducts research for the nation's physical and technical measurement systems as well as scientific and technological measurement systems. For additional information contact the National Institute of Standards and Technology, 100 Bureau Dr. Gaithersburg, MD 20899. Phone, (301) 975-6478, e-mail: inquiries@nist.gov, or visit their web site at www.nist.gov

- **NATIONAL OCEANIC AND ATMOSPHERIC ADMINISTRATION (NOAA)** — NOAA's mission is to explore, map, and chart the global ocean and its living resources and to manage, use, and conserve those resources. Predicts atmospheric conditions, ocean, sun, and space environment. Maintains weather stations including an electronic maintenance staff to service weather radar systems and other related weather equipment. For additional information contact the National Oceanic and Atomospheric Administration, Department of Commerce, 401 Constitution Avenue, NW, Washington DC 20230. Phone (202) 482-4190, www.noaa.gov. For a listing of offices in your state visit http://www.legislative.noaa.gov/NIYS/index.html

- **NATIONAL TECHNICAL INFORMATION SERVICE** — Operates a clearinghouse of scientific and technical information for U.S. businesses. For additional information contact the National Technical Information Service, 5301 Shawnee Rd., Alexandria VA 22312. Phone (703) 605-6050, www.ntis.gov

- **NATIONAL TELECOMMUNICATIONS AND INFORMATION ADMINISTRATION** — This agency was established to develop communication plans and policies, serve as advisor on telecommunication policy, and other various responsibilities. For further information contact the National

Telecommunications and Information Administration, Department of Commerce, Washington DC 20230, Phone (202) 482-1551, www.ntia.doc.gov

- **UNITED STATES PATENT AND TRADEMARK OFFICE** — Examines hundreds of thousands of patents and trademarks each year. Sells copies of issued patents and trademark registrations, records and indexes documents transferring ownership, maintains a scientific library and searches over 40 million documents. Office of Public Affairs, Patent and Trademark Office, 600 Dulaney St., Alexandria VA 22314. Phone (571)-272-8400, www.uspto.gov

DEPARTMENT OF DEFENSE (DOD)

Office of the Secretary, The Pentagon,
Washington, DC 20301-1155
(703) 545-6700, www.defenselink.mil

Responsible for providing the military forces needed to deter war and protect the security of the United States. Major elements are the Army, Navy, Marine Corps, and Air Force, consisting of close to 1.5 million men and women on active duty. In case of emergency, they are backed up by 1 million reserve forces members. In addition, there are about 675,744 Defense Department civilian employees.

The DOD is composed of the Office of the Secretary of Defense; the military departments and the military services within those departments; the Organization of the Joint Chiefs of Staff; the unified and specified combatant commands; the Armed Forces Policy Council; the Defense agencies, and various DOD field facilities. This executive branch department is the largest civilian employer. The jobs are located through the United States and at several hundred installations overseas.

For overseas locations and employment contacts see Chapter Seven. The jobs in the United States are distributed throughout every state plus the District of Columbia. The majority of military installations hire civilian personnel. Many are hired off of Office of Personnel Management's federal registers, and others are special appointments for hiring veterans, spouses and family members of military personnel, the handicapped, minorities and others.

Locate military installations in your area in the yellow pages of your phone directory under government. Also, the blue pages in the white page telephone directory provide comprehensive listings of government offices including military installations in your area.

> **EMPLOYMENT INFORMATION -** Additional employment information can be obtained by writing to Washington Headquarters Services, 2521 S. Clark St, Suite 4000, Arlington VA 22202. Phone (703) 604-6219, website: https://storm.psd.whs.mil/

DEPARTMENT OF EDUCATION

400 Maryland Ave. SW,
Washington, DC 20202
(800) USA-LEARN, www.ed.gov

The Department of Education is the Cabinet-level department that establishes policy for, administers, and coordinates most federal assistance to education. Total employment within this department is less than 5,000. There are 10 regional offices, located in Atlanta, Boston, Chicago, Dallas, Denver, Kansas City, New York, Philadelphia, San Francisco, and Seattle.

>   **EMPLOYMENT INFORMATION** – Employment inquiries and applications should be directed to the Human Resources Group at the above address. Phone (202) 401-0553.

DEPARTMENT OF ENERGY

1000 Independence Ave. SW,
Washington, DC 20585
(202) 586-5000, www.energy.gov

The Department of Energy provides a balanced national energy plan through the coordination and administration of the energy functions of the federal government. The department is responsible for long-term, high-risk research and development of energy technology; the marketing of federal power, energy conservation; the nuclear weapons program, energy regulatory programs, and a central energy data collection and analysis program.

The majority of the department's energy research and development activities are carried out by contractors who operate government-owned facilities. Management and administration of these government-owned, contractor operated facilities are the major responsibility of this department.

>   **EMPLOYMENT INFORMATION** – Employment inquiries and applications should be directed to the Office of Human Capital Management. Phone (202) 586-1234.

DEPARTMENT OF HEALTH AND HUMAN SERVICES (HHS)

200 Independence Ave. SW,
Washington, DC 20201
(202) 619-0257, www.hhs.gov

The Department of Health and Human Services employs 61,163 persons and touches the lives of more Americans than any other federal agency. This department advises the president on health, welfare, and income security plans, policies, and programs of the federal government. These programs are administered through five operating divisions:

the Social Security Administration, the Health Care Financing Administration, the Office of Human Development Services, the Public Health Service, and the Family Support Administration.

ADMINISTRATION, SERVICES AND OTHER OFFICES

- **ADMINISTRATION FOR CHILDREN AND FAMILIES** — Provides national leadership and direction to plan, manage, and coordinate the nationwide admin-istration of comprehensive and supportive programs for vulnerable children and families. Contact the Office of Human Resource Management, Administration for Children and Families, 370 L'Enfant Promenade SW, Washington, DC 20447. Phone (202) 401-9200, www.acf.hhs.gov

- **AGENCY FOR HEALTHCARE RESEARCH & QUALITY** — The research arm of the Public Health Service. They work with the private sector and other public organizations to help consumers make better informed choices. 540 Gaither Rd., Rockville, MD 20850. Phone (301) 427-1889, Email: info@ahrq.gov , www.ahrq.gov

- **AGENCY FOR TOXIC SUBSTANCES & DISEASE REGISTRY** — This agency is charged with prevention of exposure to toxic and hazardous substances. For further information contact the Agency for Toxic Substances & Disease Registry, MS E-61, 4770 Buford Hwy. NE, Atlanta, GA 30341, Phone (770) 488-0604, www.atsdr.cdc.gov

- **CENTER FOR DISEASE CONTROL AND PREVENTION** — CDC is the federal agency charged with protecting the public health of the nation by providing leadership and direction in the prevention and control of diseases and other conditions. Contact the CDC at 1600 Clifton Road NE, Atlanta, GA 30333. Phone (404) 639-3311, www.cdc.gov

- **CENTERS FOR MEDICARE & MEDICAID SERVICES** — These centers administer Medicare, Medicaid, and related programs. Contact the Dept. of Health & Human Services, 7500 Security Blvd, Baltimore MD 21244, Phone (410) 786-3000, www.cms.gov

- **FOOD AND DRUG ADMINISTRATION (FDA)** — The FDA's programs are designed to achieve the objective of consumer protection. FDA, 5600 Fishers Lane, Rockville, MD 20857. Phone (888) 463-6332. Career info www.hhs.gov/careers. Website: www.fda.gov

- **HEALTH RESOURCES & SERVICES ADMINISTRATION** — Ensures delivery of health care to under served communities. Contact the Office of Communications, Health Resources & Services Administration, 5600 Fishers Ln, Rockville MD 20857. Phone (301) 443-3376, www.hrsa.gov

- **INDIAN HEALTH SERVICE** — Provides a comprehensive health services delivery system for American Indians and Alaska Natives. Contact the Management Policy & Internal Control Staff, Indian Health Services, Suite 625A, 801 Thompson Ave., Rockville, MD 20852. Phone (301) 443-2650 www.ihs.gov

- **NATIONAL INSTITUTES OF HEALTH** — NIH seeks to expand fundamental knowledge about the nature and behavior of living systems, to apply that knowledge to extend the health of human lives, and to reduce the burdens resulting from disease and disability. Contact the National Institutes of Health, 1 Center Dr, Bethesda MD 20892, Phone (301) 496-4000, www.nih.gov. For employment information visit www.jobs.nih.gov.

- **SUBSTANCE ABUSE & MENTAL HEALTH SERVICES ADMINISTRATION** — This agency funds and administers grant programs and contracts that support substance abuse treatment and mental health services. Contact this agency at 1 Choke Cherry Rd, Rockville MD 20857, Phone (240) 276- 2130, www.samhsa.gov

DEPARTMENT OF HOMELAND SECURITY (DHS)
Washington, DC 20528
(202) 282-8000, www.dhs.gov

Homeland Security employs 154,100 federal workers, and the department's mission is to protect the United States using state-of-the-art intelligence information. DHS was established by the Homeland Security Act of 2002, (6 U.S.C. 101) to consolidate the functions of 22 agencies under one vast network to protect the United States.

The Department of Homeland Security transferred functions from the Department of the Treasury, Justice, HHS, Defense, FBI, Secret Service, GSA, Energy, Agriculture, Transportation, and the U.S. Coast Guard. The organization is composed of five major directorates:

Policy Directorate

U.S. Customs Service
US Citizenship & Immigration Service
Federal Protective Service
Transportation Security
Federal Law Enforcement Training Center
Animal & Plant Health Inspection Service
Office for Domestic Preparedness

Federal Emergency Management Agency

Federal Emergency Management Agency (FEMA)
Strategic National Stockpile & National Disaster Medical System

Nuclear Incident Response Team
Domestic Emergency Support Team
National Domestic Preparedness Office

National Preparedness & Programs Directorate

Federal Computer Incident Response Center
National Communications System
National Infrastructure Protection Center
Energy Security and Assurance Program

Science and Technology

CBRN Countermeasures Program
Environmental Measurement Laboratory
National BW Defense Analysis Center
Plum Island Animal Disease Center

Management

EMPLOYMENT INFORMATION — Homeland Security advertises most jobs through OPM's Web site at http://usajobs.opm.gov. However, some online applications are accepted for specific jobs on their site at http://www.dhs.gov and they offer informative applicant study guides, career information, and videos. Their U.S. Immigration and Customs Enforcement (ICE) site at http://ice.gov provides career information for Federal Air Marshals, Office of Intelligence, Detention and Removal, Air and Marine Operations, and their Office of Investigations.

DEPARTMENT OF HOUSING AND URBAN DEVELOPMENT (HUD)
451 Seventh St. SW,
Washington, DC 20410
(202) 708-1422, www.hud.gov

This department employs 9,935 persons and is the federal agency responsible for programs concerned with the nation's housing needs, the development and preservation of the nation's communities, and the provisions of equal housing opportunity.

The department administers the Federal Housing Administration mortgage insurance programs, rental assistance programs for lower income families; the Government National Mortgage Association (GNMA) mortgage-backed securities programs and other programs. Regional offices are located in Boston, New York City, Philadelphia, Atlanta, Fort Worth, Kansas City, Denver, San Francisco, and Seattle.

EMPLOYMENT INFORMATION — General employment inquiries should be directed to the Office of Human Resources, (202) 708-0408; or visit the website at hud.gov/jobs/index.cfm

DEPARTMENT OF THE INTERIOR
1849 C St. NW,
Washington, DC 20240
(202) 208-3100, www.doi.gov

The nation's principal conservation agency employs 72,274 persons. The Department of the Interior has responsibility for most of our nationally owned public lands and natural resources. This includes fostering the wisest use of our land and water resources, protecting our fish and wildlife, preserving the environmental and cultural values of our national parks and historical places, and providing for the enjoyment of life through outdoor recreation.

BUREAUS, SERVICES AND OTHER OFFICES

- **U.S. FISH & WILDLIFE SERVICE** — This service is composed of a headquarters office in Washington, D.C., seven regional offices in the lower 48 states and Alaska, a regional research structure, and a variety of field units and installations. These include 550 national wildlife refuges, 64 fishery resource offices, 70 national fish hatcheries, 81 ecological services field stations, and a nationwide network of wildlife law enforcement agents. Office of Public Affairs, Fish and Wildlife Service, Department of the Interior, 1849 C St. NW, Washington, DC 20240. Phone (703) 358-2220, Headquarters Personnel Office: (703) 358-1743, www.fws.gov.

- **NATIONAL PARK SERVICE** — The National Park Service has a service center in Denver and a center for production of exhibits in Harpers Ferry, W.Va.. There are 391 units in the national parks, monuments, scenic parkways, river ways, seashores, lakeshores, recreation areas, reservoirs, and historic sites. This service develops and implements park plans and staffs the area offices. Phone (202) 208-6843. Internet, www.nps.gov.

  EMPLOYMENT INFORMATION – Direct inquiries to the Personnel Office, National Parks Service, Department of the Interior, Washington, DC 20240. **Applications for temporary employment** must be received between September 1 and January 15 and should be sent to the Division of Human Resources, National Parks Service, 1849 C St. NW, Washington, DC 20240. Phone (202) 354-1927. Schools interested in the recruitment program should write to the address above or call (202) 354-1927.

- **BUREAU OF LAND MANAGEMENT** — This service has responsibility for programs associated with public land management; operations management and leasing for minerals on public lands. Contact the bureau for employment information at Department of the Interior, LS-406, 1849 C St. NW, Washington DC 20240. Phone (202) 452-5125, Employment Info (202) 452-5072, Internet, www.blm.gov.

- **U.S. GEOLOGICAL SURVEY** — The primary responsibilities of this service are to identify the nation's land, water, energy, and mineral resources. U.S. Geological Survey, Dept. of the Interior, 12201 Sunrise Valley Drive, Reston, VA 20192. Phone 703-648-4000. E-mail: ask@usgs.gov, Visit USGS jobs at www.usgs.gov/ohr/oars.

- **OFFICE OF SURFACE MINING RECLAMATION & ENFORCEMENT** — Protects the environment from the detrimental effects of coal mining. Office of Surface Mining Reclamation and Enforcement, Dept. of the Interior, Washington, DC 20240. Phone (202) 208-2694, www.osmre.gov.

- **MINERALS MANAGEMENT SERVICE** — Assesses the nature and recoverability of minerals including environmental review for Outer Continental Shelf lands. Mineral Management Service, Dept. of the Interior, Room 5417, MS 5438, 1849 C St. NW, Washington, DC 20240. Ph (202) 208-3985. Website www.mms.gov.

- **BUREAU OF INDIAN AFFAIRS** — The mission of the BIA is to fulfill its trust responsibilities and promote self determination of federally recognized tribal governments. For information contact the Office of the Assistant Secretary, Bureau of Indian Affairs, Dept. of the Interior, 1849 C St. NW, Washington, DC 20240. Phone (202) 208-3710.

- **BUREAU OF RECLAMATION** — The largest water supplier and second largest hydroelectric power supplier in the US. Bureau of Reclamation, Dept. of the Interior, Washington, DC 20240. Phone (202) 513-0575. Internet, www.usbr.gov.

DEPARTMENT OF JUSTICE
950 Pennsylvania Avenue NW,
Washington, DC 20530
(202) 514-2000, www.usdoj.gov
Agency Wide Employment HOTLINE: 202-514-3397

The Department of Justice employs 106,781. It is the largest law firm in the nation and serves as counsel for its citizens. It represents them in enforcing the law in the public interest. This department conducts all suits in the Supreme Court in which the United States is concerned. The attorney general supervises and directs these activities, as well as those of the U.S. attorney and U.S. marshals in the various districts around the country.

DIVISIONS — DEPARTMENT OF JUSTICE

ANTITRUST — Responsible for promoting and maintaining competitive markets by enforcing the federal antitrust laws. This division has field offices at the federal buildings in Atlanta, Chicago, Cleveland, Dallas, New York, Philadelphia, and San Francisco.

Contact the FOIA Unit, Antitrust Division, Department of Justice, 325 Seventh St. NW, Washington DC 20530. Phone (202) 514-2692.

CIVIL — Litigation involves cases in federal district courts, the U.S. Courts of Appeals, the U.S. Claims Court, etc This division represents the United States, its departments and agencies, members of Congress, Cabinet officers, and other federal employees. There are three field office facilities. The Commercial Litigation Branch has two field offices. For employment information contact the Civil Division, Tenth Street & Pennsylvania Ave. NW, Washington, DC 20530. Phone, 202-514-3301.

CRIMINAL — Formulates criminal law enforcement policies, enforces and exercises general supervision over all federal criminal laws except those assigned to the other divisions. Contact Criminal Division, Dept. of Justice, Tenth St. & Pennsylvania Ave. NW, Washington DC 20530. Phone (202) 514-2601.

ENVIRONMENT AND NATURAL RESOURCES DIVISION - Enforces criminal and civil environmental laws to protect the U.S. and its environment. Environment and Natural Resources Division, Dept. of Justice, Tenth St. and Pennsylvania Ave. NW, Washington, DC 20530. Phone (202) 514-2701.

NATIONAL SECURITY DIVISION — Develops and enforces criminal laws related to national counterterrorism and counterespionage. Contact the National Security Division, Dept. of Justice, Tenth St. & Pennsylvania Ave NW, Washington DC 20530, Phone (202) 514-5600, www.usdoj.gov/nsd. Employment: www.justice.gov/careers/careers.html

TAX DIVISION — Ensures fair tax enforcement of federal tax laws in both the state and federal court systems. Contact the Tax Division, Dept. of Justice, Tenth St. & Pennsylvania Ave. NW, Washington, DC 20530. Phone (202) 514-2901. Internet www.usdoj.gov/tax. Employment: http://www.justice.gov/tax/career_opp.htm

BUREAUS AND SERVICES

- **FEDERAL BUREAU OF INVESTIGATION (FBI)**
  935 Pennsylvania Ave, NW
  Washington, DC 20535
  (202) 324-3000, www.fbi.gov,

  The FBI is the principal investigative arm of the U.S. Department of Justice. It is charged with gathering and reporting facts, locating witnesses, and compiling evidence in cases involving federal jurisdiction. The bureau's investigations are conducted through 58 field offices.

  EMPLOYMENT INFORMATION – Direct inquiries to the Director, Federal Bureau of Investigation, Washington, DC 20535. You can also contact any of the 58 field offices. Consult your local telephone directory for the office nearest you. Employment website: http://www.fbijobs.gov/

- **BUREAU OF PRISONS**
  320 First St. NW,
  Washington, DC 20534
  (202) 307-3198, www.bop.gov

  Responsible for maintaining secure, safe, and humane correctional institutions for individuals placed in the care and custody of the attorney general. Maintains and staffs all federal penal and correctional institutions.

  > **EMPLOYMENT INFORMATION** – Direct inquiries to the Bureau of Prisons, Central Office, 320 First St. NW, Washington, DC 20534, 202-307-3082 or to any regional or field office. Visit the career site at http://www.bop.gov/jobs/index.jsp

- **BUREAU OF ALCOHOL, TOBACCO, FIREARMS, AND EXPLOSIVES**
  650 Massachusetts Ave. NW,
  Washington DC 20226
  (202) 927-8500, www.atf.gov

  The ATF is responsible for regulating the firearms and explosives industries. Visit the ATF career website at http://www.atf.gov/careers/

- **OFFICE OF JUSTICE PROGRAMS**
  810 Seventh St. NW,
  Washington DC 20531
  (202) 307-0703, www.ojp.usdoj.gov

  The OJP provides Federal leadership and assistance to make the national justice system more efficient and effective in preventing and controlling crime.

- **OFFICE ON VIOLENCE AGAINST WOMEN**
  800 K St. NW,
  Washington DC 20530
  (202) 307-6026, www.ovw.usdoj.gov

  This office was established to reduce violence against women and is responsible for administering assistance for community programs designed to end domestic violence, sexual assault, and stalking crimes.

- **UNITED STATES MARSHALS SERVICE**
  Washington, DC 20530
  (202) 307-9000, www.usmarshals.gov

The presidentially appointed marshals and their support staff of just over 4,300 deputy marshals and administrative personnel operate from 427 office locations in all 94 federal judicial districts nationwide, from Guam to Puerto Rico and from Alaska to Florida.

EMPLOYMENT WEBSITE – www.usmarshals.gov/careers/index.html

- **DRUG ENFORCEMENT ADMINISTRATION**
  600-700 Army Navy Drive
  Arlington, VA 22202
  (202) 307-1000, www.dea.gov

The Drug Enforcement Administration is the lead federal agency in enforcing narcotics and controlled substances laws and regulations. The administration has offices throughout the United States and in 62 foreign countries. Special agents conduct criminal investigations and prepare for the prosecution of violators of the drug laws. Entry level is at the GS-7 or GS-9 grade with progression to GS-12 in three years.

This administration uses accountants, engineers, computer scientists, language majors, chemists, history majors, mathematicians, and other specialties for special agents. Investigators, intelligence research and administrative positions are also filled.

EMPLOYMENT INFORMATION – Contact or direct inquiries to the Office of Personnel at the address listed above or call the job hotline at 202-514-3397. Visit the employment website at http://www.justice.gov/dea/resources/job_applicants.html

DEPARTMENT OF LABOR
200 Constitution Ave. NW,
Washington, DC 20210
(202) 693-5000, www.dol.gov

The Department of Labor was created to foster, promote and develop the welfare of the wage earners of the United States, to improve their working conditions, and to advance their opportunities for profitable employment. The department administers a variety of federal labor laws guaranteeing workers the right to safe and healthful working conditions.

This department has 16,195 employees and ranks 12th out of the 15 departments in total number of employees. Yet the Department of Labor affects every worker in the United States through one of its many internal components: the Pension and Welfare Benefits Administration, Office of Labor-Management Standards, Office of Administrative Law Judges, Benefits Review Board, Bureau of International Labor Affairs, Bureau of Labor

Statistics, Women's Bureau, Employment Standards Administration, Employment and Training Administration, Mine Safety and Health Administration, Veterans' Employment and Training Service, and Occupational Safety and Health Administration (OSHA).

> **EMPLOYMENT INFORMATION** — Personnel offices use lists of eligibles from the clerical, scientific, technical, and general examinations of the Office of Personnel Management. Inquiries and applications may be directed to the address listed above or consult your telephone directory (under U.S. Government Department of Labor) for field offices nearest you. Also visit the DOL employment website at http://www.dol.gov/dol/jobs.htm

DEPARTMENT OF STATE
2201 C St. NW,
Washington, DC 20520
(202) 647-4000, www.state.gov

The Department of State advises the president in the formulation and execution of foreign policy. The department's primary objective is to promote the long-range security and well-being of the United States.

There are hundreds of staffed facilities internationally including U.S. embassies, missions, consulates general, U.S. Liaison offices and consular agencies throughout the world , manned by several thousand Foreign Service officers of the Department of State. The State Department's total employment exceeds 34,000 full time employees assigned stateside and overseas in administrative, personnel, management, engineering, communications electronics, security, and career Foreign Service officer positions.

> **EMPLOYMENT INFORMATION** — **For Foreign Service Opportunities contact**: Foreign Service, Recruitment Division, HR/REE, Room H-518, 2401 E St. NW, Washington, DC 20522. Phone (202) 261-8888, www.careers.state.gov. **For Civil Service Opportunities**: Use the same Web site or phone (202) 663-2176 for the job vacancy hotline. Also visit http://www.state.gov/careers/ for DOS opportunities.

DEPARTMENT OF TRANSPORTATION (DOT)
Central Employment Information Office
400 Seventh St. SW,
Washington, DC 20590
(202) 366-4000, www.dot.gov

The Department of Transportation employs 53,865 persons and establishes the nation's overall transportation policy. There are 11 administrations, whose jurisdiction includes highway planning, urban mass transit, railroads, aviation, and the safety of waterways, ports, highways, and pipelines. **For Employment opportunities:** Contact the Transportation Administrative Service Center DOT Connection, Room PL-402,1200 New

Jersey Ave. SE, Washington DC 20590. Phone (202) 366-9391 or (800) 525-2878. Visit the DOT Career site at http://careers.dot.gov/index.htm.

ADMINISTRATIONS & OFFICES OF THE DOT

Federal Aviation Administration
Federal Highway Administration
Federal Railroad Administration
National Highway Traffic Safety Administration
Federal Transit Administration
St. Lawrence Seaway Development Corporation
Maritime Administration
Research and Innovative Technology Administration
Pipeline and Hazardous Materials Safety Administration
Federal Motor Carrier Safety Administration
Surface Transportation Board

- **FEDERAL AVIATION ADMINISTRATION (FAA)**
  800 Independence Ave. SW,
  Washington, DC 20591
  (202) 366-4000, www.faa.gov

The administration is charged with regulating air commerce, controlling navigable airspace, promoting civil aeronautics, research and development, installing and operating air navigation facilities, air traffic control, and environmental impact of air navigation.

> **EMPLOYMENT INFORMATION:** Entry level engineers start at the FV-5/7/9 grade depending on college grades and work experience. The FAA is now an excepted agency and their pay system is determined by a core compensation pay band system. Engineers progress to the FV-11 or 12 pay grade. Air traffic control specialists start at an equivalent FG-7 pay grade and can progress through an equivalent FV-14 grade and higher. Electronics technicians typically start in the F or G band (equivalent to the FV 9/11) and journeyman specialists are in the H band, which is greater than a typical GS-12 grade. A large number of administrative, clerical, and personnel specialists are also needed. Internet, http://www.faa.gov/jobs/

- **FEDERAL HIGHWAY ADMINISTRATION**
  1200 New Jersey Ave. SE,
  Washington, DC 20590
  (202) 366-0650, www.fhwa.dot.gov

This agency is concerned with the total operation and environment of highway systems. Civil/highway engineers, motor carrier safety specialists, accountants, contract specialists, computer programmers, and administrative and clerical skills are needed.

EMPLOYMENT INFORMATION — Major occupations include Civil and Highway Engineer, Motor Carrier Safety Specialists, Accountants, Contract Specialists, Computer Programmers, Administrative, Clerical and Transportation Specialists. www.fhwa.dot.gov/vacancy/index.htm

- **FEDERAL RAILROAD ADMINISTRATION**
Office of Personnel
1120 Vermont Ave. NW,
Washington, DC 20590
(202) 493-6000, www.fra.dot.gov

The Federal Railroad Administration enforces railroad safety, conducts research and development, provides passenger and freight services, and staffs and maintains the Transportation Test Center.

> **EMPLOYMENT INFORMATION** — Major occupations include economist, contract specialist, accountant, attorney, law clerk, administrative and clerical. www.fra.dot.gov/Pages/456.shtml

- **NATIONAL HIGHWAY TRAFFIC SAFETY ADMINISTRATION**
Office of Personnel
1200 New Jersey Ave. SE,
Washington, DC 20590
(202) 366-9550, (888) 327-4236 (toll free), www.nhtsa.gov

The National Highway Traffic Safety Administration was established to reduce the number of deaths, injuries, and economic losses resulting from traffic accidents on national highways.

> **EMPLOYMENT INFORMATION** — Major occupations include attorney advisor, law clerk, highway safety specialist, mathematical statistician, mechanical engineer, safety standard engineer, and administrative and clerical. www.nhtsa.gov/Jobs

- **FEDERAL TRANSIT ADMINISTRATION**
1200 New Jersey Ave. SE,
Washington, DC 20590
(202) 366-4043, www.fta.dot.gov

Its mission is to assist in the development of improved mass transportation, to encourage the planning and establishment of area wide urban mass transit systems, and to provide assistance to state and local governments in financing such systems.

EMPLOYMENT INFORMATION — Transportation specialist, civil engineer, general engineer, contract specialist, and administrative and clerical.

- **RESEARCH & INNOVATIVE TECHNOLOGY ADMINISTRATION**
1200 New Jersey Ave. SE,
Washington, DC 20590
(202) 366-7582, www.rita.dot.gov

This administration consists of the Office of Hazardous Materials Transportation, office of Pipeline Safety, Office of Civil Rights, Office of the Chief Counsel, the Transportation Systems Center in Cambridge, Massachusetts, Office of Emergency Transportation, Office of Aviation Information Management, and the Office of Administration.

EMPLOYMENT INFORMATION — Major occupations include transportation specialist, general engineer (pipeline), mechanical engineer, chemical engineer, writer/editor, and administrative and clerical. Job website, www.rita.dot.gov/jobs.html

- **MARITIME ADMINISTRATION**
1200 New Jersey Ave. SE,
Washington, DC 20590
(202) 366-5807, (888) 996-2723 (toll free), www.marad.dot.gov

- **PIPELINE & HAZARDOUS MATERIALS SAFETY ADMINISTRATION**
1200 New Jersey Ave. SE,
Washington, DC 20590
(202) 366-4433, www.phmsa.dot.gov
Employment, www.phmsa.dot.gov/careers

- **FEDERAL MOTOR CARRIER SAFETY ADMINISTRATION**
1200 New Jersey Ave. SE,
Washington, DC 20590
(202) 366-2519, www.fmcsa.dot.gov
Employment, www.fmcsa.dot.gov/about/other/jobs/workforus.htm

- **SURFACE TRANSPORTATION BOARD**
395 E St. SW,
Washington DC 20423,
(202) 245-0245, www.stb.dot.gov
Employment, www.stb.dot.gov/stb/about/jobs.html

DEPARTMENT OF THE TREASURY
1500 Pennsylvania Ave. NW,
Washington, DC 20220
(202) 622-2000, www.treas.gov
Employment, www.treasury.gov/careers/Pages/default.aspx

The Department of the Treasury employs 106,925 persons and performs four basic functions: formulating and recommending economic, financial, tax, and fiscal policies; serving as financial agent for the US Government; enforcing the law; and manufacturing coins and currency.

BUREAUS, SERVICES, and OFFICES OF THE TREASURY

Internal Revenue Service
Bureau of Alcohol, Tobacco, & Trade
Bureau of Engraving and Printing
Financial Management Service
U.S. Mint
Office of the Comptroller of the Currency
Bureau of the Public Debt
Office of Thrift Supervision

- **INTERNAL REVENUE SERVICE (IRS)**
  1111 Constitution Ave. NW,
  Washington, DC 20224
  (202) 622-5000, www.irs.gov

  The Internal Revenue Service has more than 100,000 employees and is the largest organization in the Department of the Treasury. Approximately 7,000 of these employees work in Washington, D.C. Others are employed in hundreds of offices throughout the U.S. There is an IRS office in or near most large towns.

  EMPLOYMENT INFORMATION — Almost every major field of study has some application to the work of the IRS. A substantial number of positions are in accounting, business administration, finance, economics, criminology, and law. There are also a number of persons whose college major was political science, public administration, education, liberal arts, or other fields not directly related to business or law. Career Site http://jobs.irs.gov/home.html?navmenu=menu2

- **BUREAU OF ALCOHOL & TOBACCO TAX & TRADE BUREAU**
  1310 G St. NW.,
  Washington, DC 20220
  (202)927-5000, www.ttb.gov

  The bureau is responsible for enforcing and administering the existing federal laws and Tax Code provisions related to the production and taxation of alcohol and tobacco products. It also collects all excise taxes on the manufacture of firearms and ammunition.

- **BUREAU OF ENGRAVING & PRINTING**
  14th and C Streets SW,
  Washington, DC 20228
  (202) 874-3019, www.moneyfactory.com

  The Bureau of Engraving & Printing designs, prints, and finishes a large variety of security products including Federal Reserve notes, U.S. postage stamps, Treasury securities, and certificates. The bureau is the largest printer of security documents in the world; over 40 billion documents are printed annually. The bureau's headquarters and most of its production operations are located in Washington, D.C. A second currency plant is in Fort Worth, Texas.

  > **EMPLOYMENT INFORMATION** — Selections are highly competitive. Major occupations include police officer, computer specialist, engineer, contract specialist, engraver, production manager, security specialist, accountant, auditor, and administrative and clerical positions. Phone 202-874-2633 for information. Website, www.moneyfactory.gov/careers.html

- **U.S. MINT**
  801 Ninth St. NW,
  Washington, DC 20220
  (202) 354-7200, www.usmint.gov

  The United States Mint employs some 2,300 employees at six locations including Washington, D.C. Field facilities are located in Philadelphia, Denver, San Francisco, West Point, N.Y., and Fort Knox, Ky. The U.S. Mint produces bullion and domestic and foreign coins, distributes gold and silver, and controls bullion.

- **BUREAU OF PUBLIC DEBT**
  999 E St. NW,
  Washington, DC 20239-0001
  (202) 504-3500, www.publicdebt.treas.gov

  The bureau administers the public debt by borrowing money through the sale of United States Treasury securities. The sale, service, and processing of Treasury securities involves the Federal Reserve Banks and their branches, which serve as fiscal agents of the Treasury. This bureau also manages the U.S. Savings Bond program.

> **EMPLOYMENT INFORMATION** — The major occupations include accountant, operating accountant, computer systems analyst, computer programmer, computer analyst. Employment inquiries: Bureau of the Public Debt, Division of Human Resources, Recruitment and Classification Branch, Parkersburg, WV 26106. Phone (304) 480-6144. Employment Site, www.publicdebt.treas.gov/careers/careers_with_us.htm

DEPARTMENT OF VETERANS AFFAIRS
810 Vermont Ave. NW,
Washington, DC 20420
(202) 273-4900, www.va.gov

The Department of Veterans Affairs employs 239,299 persons and operates programs to benefit veterans and members of their families. Benefits include compensation payments for disabilities or death related to military service; pensions; education and rehabilitation; home loan guaranty; burial; and a medical care program incorporating nursing homes, clinics, and medical centers.

> **EMPLOYMENT INFORMATION** — The VA employs physicians, dentists, podiatrists, optometrists, nurses, nurse anesthetists, physician assistants, expanded function dental auxiliaries, registered respiratory therapists, certified respiratory therapists, licensed physical therapists, occupational therapists, pharmacists, and licensed practical or vocational nurses under the VA's excepted merit system. This does not require civil service eligibility.

> Other major occupations include accounting, all B.S. and B.A. majors, architecture, business, computer science, engineering, law, statistics, and numerous administrative and clerical positions. There are hundreds of national Veterans Affairs facilities within the United States. Consult your local telephone directory for the facility nearest you or search the VA Web site at www.va.gov/jobs.

INDEPENDENT AGENCIES (Partial List)

African Development Foundation
1400 I St. NW, Suite 1000
Washington, DC 20005
(202) 673-3916, www.usadf.gov

Broadcasting Board of Governors
330 Independence Ave. SW,
Washington, DC 20237
(202) 203-4545, www.bbg.gov

Central Intelligence Agency
Office of Personnel
Washington, DC 20505
(703) 482-0623, www.cia.gov
Careers, www.cia.gov/careers/index.html

Commission on Civil Rights
624 Ninth St., NW,
Washington, DC 20425
(202) 376-7700, www.usccr.gov

Commodity Futures Trading Commission
1155 21st St. NW,
Washington, DC 20581
(202) 418-5000, www.cftc.gov

Consumer Product Safety Commission
Division of Personnel Management
4330 East West Hwy.
Bethesda, MD 20814
(301) 504-7923, www.cpsc.gov

Corp. for National & Community Service
1201 New York Ave. NW,
Washington, DC 20525
(202) 606-5000, www.nationalservice.gov

Defense Nuclear Facilities Safety Board
Suite 700, 625 Indiana Ave. NW,
Washington, DC 20004
(202) 694-7000, www.dnfsb.gov

Environmental Protection Agency
1200 Pennsylvania Ave. NW,

Washington, DC 20460
(202) 272-0167, www.epa.gov
Employment, www.epa.gov/careers

Equal Opportunity Commission
1801 L Street NW,
Washington, DC 20507
202-663-4900, TTY, 202-663-4494
Employment, (202) 663-4306, www.eeoc.gov

Farm Credit Administration
1501 Farm Credit Drive
McLean, VA 22102-5090
(703) 883-4000
Employment (703) 883-4135, www.fca.gov

Federal Communications Commission
445 12th St. SW,
Washington, DC 20554
(888) 225-5322, Employment (202) 418-0130
www.fcc.gov

Federal Deposit Insurance Corporation
550 17th St. NW,
Washington, DC 20429
(703) 562-222, www.fdic.gov

Federal Election Commission
999 E St. NW,
Washington, DC 20463
(202) 694-1100 or (800) 424-9530
www.fec.gov

Federal Housing Finance Board
1700 G Street NW,
Washington, DC 20552
(866) 796-5595, www.fhfb.gov

Federal Labor Relations Authority
1400 K Street NW,
Washington, DC 20005
(202) 218-7770, Employment (202) 218-7963
www.flra.gov, www.flra.gov/jobs

Federal Maritime Commission
800 North Capitol St. NW,
Washington, DC 20573-0001
(202) 523-5707, Employment (202) 523-5773, www.fmc.gov

Federal Mine Safety & Health Commission
601 New Jersey Ave. NW, Suite 9500
Washington, DC 20001-2021
202-434-9900, www.fmshrc.gov

Federal Reserve System
20th St. and Constitution Ave. NW,
Washington, DC 20551
202-452-3000, www.federalreserve.gov

Federal Retirement Thrift Investment Board
1250 H Street NW,
Washington, DC 20005
(202) 942-1600, www.tsp.gov

Federal Trade Commission
600 Pennsylvania Ave. NW,
Washington, DC 20580
(202) 326-2222, Employment 202-326-2021
www.ftc.gov

General Services Administration
1800 F St. NW,
Washington, DC 20405
(202) 708-5082, www.gsa.gov
Employment, Email GSAjobs@gsa.gov

Inter-American Foundation
901 N. Stuart St, 10th Floor
Arlington, VA 22203
(703) 306-4301, www.iaf.gov

Merit Systems Protection Board
Personnel Division
5th Floor, 1615 M St. NW,
Washington, DC 20419
(202) 653-7200, www.mspb.gov

NASA, NASA Headquarters
300 E St. SW,
Washington, DC 20546
(202) 358-0000, Employment 877-677-2123
www.nasa.gov

National Archives and Records Admin.
8601 Adelphi Rd.
College Park, MD 20740
(866) 272-6272, www.archives.gov
Employment (800) 827-4898

National Credit Union Administration
Office of Human Resources
1775 Duke St.
Alexandria, VA 22314-3428
(703) 518-6300, www.ncua.gov

National Endowment for the Humanities
1100 Pennsylvania Ave. NW,
Washington, DC 20506
(202) 606-8400, www.neh.gov

National Endowment for the Arts
1100 Pennsylvania Ave. NW,
Washington, DC 20506
(202) 682-5400, www.arts.gov

National Labor Relations Board
Personnel Operations
1099 14th St. NW,
Washington, DC 20570
(202) 273-1000, www.nlrb.gov

National Mediation Board
1301 K Street NW, Suite 250 East,
Washington, DC 20005
(202) 692-5000, www.nmb.gov

National Railroad Passenger Corporation
60 Massachusetts Ave. NE,
Washington, DC 20002
(202) 906-3000, www.amtrak.com

National Science Foundation
Division of Personnel Management

4201 Wilson Blvd.
Arlington, VA 22230
(703) 292-5111, www.nsf.gov

National Transportation Safety Board
490 L'Enfant Plaza SW,
Washington, DC 20594
(202) 314-6000, www.ntsb.gov

Nuclear Regulatory Commission
Washington, DC 20555
(301) 415-7000, www.nrc.gov

Occupational Safety and Health Review Commission
1120 20th St. NW,
Washington, DC 20036-3457
(202) 606-5050, www.oshrc.gov

Office of the Director of National Intelligence
Washington DC, 20511
(703) 733-8600, www.dni.gov

Office of Government Ethics
1201 New York Ave. NW, Suite 500
Washington, DC 20005
(202) 482-9300, www.usoge.gov

Office of Personnel Management (OPM)
1900 E. St. NW,
Washington, DC 20415
(202) 606-1800,
Employment (202) 606-2400
www.opm.gov

Office of Special Counsel
1730 M St. NW, Suite 218
Washington, DC 20036-4505
(800) 872-9855, www.osc.gov

Peace Corps
1111 20th St. NW,
Washington, DC 20526
(800) 424-8580, www.peacecorps.gov

Pension Benefit Guaranty Corporation
1200 K St. NW,
Washington, DC 20005
(202) 326-4000, www.pbgc.gov

Postal Regulatory Commission
901 New York Ave. NW,
Washington, DC 20268-0001
(202) 789-6800, www.prc.gov

Railroad Retirement Board
844 N. Rush St.
Chicago, IL 60611-2092
(312) 751-4777, www.rrb.gov

Securities and Exchange Commission
100 F St. NE,
Washington, DC 20549
(202) 551-7500, Employment 202-942-7500
www.sec.gov

Selective Service System
Arlington, VA 22209-2425
(703) 605-4000, www.sss.gov

Small Business Administration
409 Third St. SW,
Washington, DC 20416
202-205-6600, www.sba.gov

Social Security Administration
6401 Security Blvd.
Baltimore, MD 21235
(410) 965-1234, www.ssa.gov

United States International Trade Commission
500 E St. SW,
Washington, DC 20436
(202) 205-2000, www.usitc.gov

United States Postal Service
475 L'Enfant Plaza SW,
Washington, DC 20260
(202) 268-2000, www.usps.gov

APPENDIX C
Federal Occupation List

The government's classification system includes an occupational structure which groups similar jobs together. There are 23 occupational groups comprising 441 different white-collar occupations under the General Schedule (GS): GS-000 through GS-2200. Each occupational group is further subdivided into specific numerical codes (for example: GS-856, Electronics Technician, GS-318, Secretary Series, etc.). The Wage Grade (WG) Trades and Labor Schedule offers an additional 36 occupational families: WG-2500 through WG-9000.

This Appendix presents a comprehensive listing of both GS and WG occupational groups, families and related series. First, locate the occupational group or groups in which you have specific knowledge, skill, and/or training. Then review each job series under the primary occupation group or family.[1]

More than a quarter of white-collar workers had an occupation in the General Administrative, Clerical and Office Services group. The other four large white-collar groups are: Medical, Hospital, Dental and Public Health; Engineering and Architecture; Accounting and Budget; and Business and Industry.

Certain white-collar occupations are concentrated in particular federal agencies. The Department of Agriculture employs the majority of Biological Science employees and almost all Veterinary Medical Science workers. The Department of Health and Human Services was the major employer of the Social Science, Psychology and Welfare group and the Legal and Kindred group.. The Veterans Administration employed almost three-quarters of the Medical, Hospital, Dental and Public Health group. The Department of Commerce employed the vast majority of the Copyright, Patent and Trademark group. The Department of Transportation employs most Transportation group employees. The Library of Congress and Department of Defense together employed over half of the Library and Archives group. The Departments of Homeland Security, Treasury and Justice together employed the majority of the Investigative group. The Department of Defense was the major employer in all the other white collar occupational groups.

---

[1] References for the General Schedule Occupational Groups and Series are the Handbook of Occupational Groups & Series, published by the U.S. Office of Personnel Management, and Pamphlet PB97-170591.

GENERAL SCHEDULE (GS) OCCUPATIONAL GROUPS

GS-000: MISCELLANEOUS — This group includes all classes of positions, the duties of which are to administer, supervise, or perform work which cannot be included in other occupational groups either because the duties are unique, or because they are complex and come in part under various groups.

GS-100: SOCIAL SCIENCE, PSYCHOLOGY, AND WELFARE GROUP — This group includes all classes of positions, the duties of which are to advise on, administer, supervise, or perform research or other professional and scientific work, subordinate technical or related clerical work in one or more of the social sciences; in psychology; in social work; in recreational activities; or in the administration of public welfare and insurance programs.

GS-200: PERSONNEL MANAGEMENT & INDUSTRIAL RELATIONS GROUP — This group includes all classes of positions, the duties of which are to advise on, administer, supervise, or perform work involved in the various phases of personnel management and industrial relations.

GS-300: GENERAL ADMIN, CLERICAL, & OFFICE SERVICES GROUP — This group includes all classes of positions the duties of which are to administer, supervise, or perform work involved in management analysis; stenography, typing, correspondence, and secretarial work; mail and file work; the operation of office appliances; the operation of communications equipment, use of codes and ciphers, and procurement of the most efficient communications services; the operation of microform equipment, peripheral equipment, duplicating equipment, mail processing equipment, and copier/duplicating equipment; and other work of a general clerical and administrative nature.

GS-400: BIOLOGICAL SCIENCE GROUP — This group includes all classes of positions, the duties of which are to advise on, administer, supervise, or perform research or other professional and scientific work or subordinate technical work in any of the fields of science concerned with living organisms, their distribution, characteristics, life processes, and adaptations and relations to the environment; the soil, its properties and distribution, and the living organisms growing in or on the soil; and the management, conservation, or utilization thereof for particular purposes or uses.

GS-500: ACCOUNTING AND BUDGET GROUP — This group includes all classes of positions, the duties of which are to advise on, administer, supervise, or perform professional, technical, or related clerical work of an accounting, budget administration, related financial management, or similar nature.

GS-600: MEDICAL, HOSPITAL, DENTAL, & PUBLIC HEALTH GROUP — This group includes all classes of positions, the duties of which are to advise on, administer, supervise, or perform research or other professional and scientific work, subordinate technical work, or related clerical work in the several branches of medicine, surgery, and dentistry or in related patient care services such as dietetics, nursing, occupational therapy, physical therapy, pharmacy, and others.

GS-700: VETERINARY MEDICAL SCIENCE GROUP — This group includes all classes of positions, the duties of which are to advise and consult on, administer, manage, supervise, or perform research or other professional and scientific work in the various branches of veterinary medical science.

GS-800: ENGINEERING AND ARCHITECTURE — This group includes all classes of positions, the duties of which are to advise on, administer, supervise, or perform professional, scientific, or technical work concerned with engineering or architectural projects, facilities, structures, systems, processes, equipment, devices, material or methods. Positions in this group require knowledge of the science or art, or both, by which materials, natural resources, and power are made useful.

GS-900: LEGAL AND KINDRED GROUP — This group includes all classes of positions, the duties of which are to advise on, administer, supervise, or perform professional legal work in the preparation for trial and the trial and argument of cases, the presiding at formal hearings afforded by a commission, board, or other body having quasi-judicial powers, as part of its administrative procedure, the administration of law entrusted to an agency, the preparation or rendering of authoritative or advisory legal opinions or decisions to other federal agencies or to administrative officials of own agency, the preparation of various legal documents; and the performance of other work requiring training equivalent to that represented by graduation from a recognized law school and in some instances requiring admission to the bar; or quasi-legal work which requires knowledge of particular laws, or of regulations, precedents, or departmental practice based thereon, but which does not require such legal training or admission to the bar.

GS-1000: INFORMATION AND ARTS GROUP — This group includes positions which involve professional, artistic, technical, or clerical work in (1) the communication of information and ideas through verbal, visual, or pictorial means, (2) the collection, custody, presentation, display, and interpretation of art works, cultural objects, and other artifacts, or (3) a branch of fine or applied arts such as industrial design, interior design, or musical composition. Positions in this group require writing, editing, and language ability; artistic skill and ability; knowledge of foreign languages; the ability to evaluate and interpret informational and cultural materials; the practical application of technical or aesthetic principles combined with manual skill and dexterity; or related clerical skills.

GS-1100: BUSINESS AND INDUSTRY GROUP — This group includes all classes of positions, the duties of which are to advise on, administer, supervise, or perform work pertaining to and requiring a knowledge of business and trade practices, characteristics and use of equipment, products, or property, or industrial production methods and processes, including the conduct of investigations and studies; the collection, analysis, and dissemination of information; the establishment and maintenance of contracts with industry and commerce; the provision of advisory services; the examination and appraisement of merchandise or property; and the administration of regulatory provisions and controls.

GS-1200: COPYRIGHT, PATENT, AND TRADEMARK GROUP — This group includes all classes of positions, the duties of which are to advise on, administer, supervise, or perform professional scientific, technical, and legal work involved in the cataloging and registration of copyright, in the classification and issuance of patents, in the registration of trade-marks, in the prosecution of applications for patents before the Patent Office, and in the giving of advice to government officials on patent matters.

GS-1300: PHYSICAL SCIENCE GROUP — This group includes all classes of positions, the duties of which are to advise on, administer, supervise, or perform research or other professional and scientific work or subordinate technical work in any of the fields of science concerned with matter, energy, physical space, time, nature of physical measurement, and fundamental structural particles; and the nature of the physical environment.

GS-1400: LIBRARY AND ARCHIVES GROUP — This group includes all classes of positions, the duties of which are to advise on, administer, supervise, or perform professional and scientific work or subordinate technical work in the various phases of library archival science.

GS-1500: MATHEMATICS AND STATISTICS GROUP — This group includes all classes of positions, the duties of which are to advise on, administer, supervise, or perform research or other professional and scientific work or related clerical work in basic mathematical principles, methods, procedures, or relationships, including the development and application of mathematical methods for the investigation and solution of problems; the development and application of statistical theory in the selection, collection, classification, adjustment, analysis, and interpretation of data; the development and application of mathematical, statistical, and financial principles to programs or problems involving life and property risks; and any other professional and scientific or related clerical work requiring primarily and mainly the understanding and use of mathematical theories, methods, and operations.

GS-1600: EQUIPMENT, FACILITIES, AND SERVICES GROUP — This group includes positions the duties of which are to advise on, manage, or provide instructions and information concerning the operation, maintenance, and use of equipment, shops, buildings, laundries, printing plants, power plants, cemeteries, or other government facilities, or other work involving services provided predominantly by persons in trades, crafts, or manual labor operations. Positions in this group require technical or managerial knowledge and ability, plus a practical knowledge of trades, crafts, or manual labor operations.

GS-1700: EDUCATION GROUP — This group includes positions which involve administering, managing, supervising, performing, or supporting education or training work when the paramount requirement of the position is knowledge of, or skill in, education, training, or instruction processes.

GS-1800: INVESTIGATION GROUP — This group includes all classes of positions, the duties of which are to advise on, administer, supervise, or perform investigation, inspection, or enforcement work primarily concerned with alleged or suspected offenses against the laws of the United States, or such work primarily concerned with determining compliance with laws and regulations.

GS-1900: QUALITY ASSURANCE, INSPECTION, & GRADING GROUP — This group includes all classes of positions, the duties of which are to advise on, supervise, or perform administrative or technical work primarily concerned with the quality assurance or inspection of material, facilities, and processes; or with the grading of commodities under official standards.

GS-2000: SUPPLY GROUP — This group includes positions which involve work concerned with finishing all types of supplies, equipment, material, property (except real estate), and certain services to components of the federal government, industrial, or other concerns under contract to the government, or receiving supplies from the federal government. Included are positions concerned with one or more aspects of supply activities from initial planning, including requirements analysis and determination, through acquisition, cataloging, storage, distribution, utilization to ultimate issue for consumption or disposal. The work requires a knowledge of one or more elements or parts of a supply system, and/or supply methods, policies, or procedures.

GS-2100: TRANSPORTATION GROUP — This group includes all classes of positions, the duties of which are to advise on, administer, supervise, or perform work which involves two or more specialized transportation functions or other transportation work not specifically included in other series of this group.

GS-2200: INFORMATION TECHNOLOGY GROUP — This group includes administrative positions in the information technology group covering only those positions for which the paramount requirement is knowledge of IT principles, concepts, and methods; e.g., data storage, software applications, and networking.

GENERAL SCHEDULE GROUPS & RELATED SERIES

GS-000 – MISCELLANEOUS OCCUPATIONS GROUP (Not Elsewhere Classified)

Correctional Institution Administration Series	GS-006	Chaplain Series	GS-060
Correctional Officer	GS-007	Clothing Design Series	GS-062
Bond Sales Promotion Series	GS-011	Fingerprint Identification Series	GS-072
Safety and Occupational Health Mgmt Series	GS-018	Security Administration Series	GS-080
Safety Technician Series	GS-019	Fire Protection and Prevention Series	GS-081
Community Planning Series	GS-020	United States Marshal Series	GS-082
Community Planning Technician Series	GS-021	Police Series	GS-083
Outdoor Recreation Planning Series	GS-023	Nuclear Materials Courier Series	GS-084
Park Ranger Series	GS-025	Security Guard Series	GS-085
Environmental Protection Specialist Series	GS-028	Security Clerical Assistance Series	GS-086
Environmental Protection Assistant Series	GS-029	Guide Series	GS-090
Sports Specialist Series	GS-030	Foreign Law Specialist Series	GS-095
Funeral Directing Series	GS-050	General Student Trainee Series	GS-099

GS-100 – SOCIAL SCIENCE, PSYCHOLOGY, AND WELFARE GROUP

Social Science Series	GS-101	Geography Series	GS-150
Social Science Aid and Technician Series	GS-102	Civil Rights Analysis Series	GS-160
Social Insurance Administration Series	GS-105	History Series	GS-170
Unemployment Insurance Series	GS-106	Psychology Series	GS-180
Economist Series	GS-110	Psychology Aide and Technician Series	GS-181
Economics Assistant Series	GS-119	Sociology Series	GS-184
Food Assistance Program Specialist Series	GS-120	Social Work Series	GS-185
Foreign Affairs Series	GS-130	Social Services Aide & Assistant Series	GS-186
International Relations Series	GS-131	Social Services Series	GS-187
Intelligence Series	GS-132	Recreation Specialist Series	GS-188
Intelligence Aide and Clerk Series	GS-134	Recreation Aide and Assistant Series	GS-189
Foreign Agricultural Affairs Series	GS-135	General Anthropology Series	GS-190
International Cooperation Series	GS-136	Archeology Series	GS-193
Manpower Research and Analysis Series	GS-140	Social Science Student Trainee Series	GS-199
Manpower Development Series	GS-142		

GS-200 – PERSONNEL MANAGEMENT AND INDUSTRIAL RELATIONS GROUP

Personnel Management Series	GS-201	Employee Development Series	GS-235
Personnel Clerical and Assistance Series	GS-203	Mediation Series	GS-241
Military Personnel Clerical and Technician Series	GS-204	Apprenticeship and Training Series	GS-243
Military Personnel Management Series	GS-205	Labor Mgmt Relations Examining Series	GS-244
Personnel Staffing Series	GS-212	Contractor Industrial Relations Series	GS-246
Position Classification Series	GS-221	Wage and Hour Compliance Series	GS-249
Occupational Analysis Series	GS-222	Equal Employment Opportunity Series	GS-260
Salary and Wage Administration Series	GS-223	Federal Retirement Benefits Series	GS-270
Employee Relations Series	GS-230	Personnel Management Student Trainee Series	GS-299
Labor Relations Series	GS-233		

GS-300 – GENERAL ADMINISTRATION, CLERICAL, AND OFFICE SERVICES GROUP

Miscellaneous Administration and Program Series	GS-301	Clerk-Typist Series	GS-322
Messenger Series	GS-302	Office Automation Clerical & Assist. Series	GS-326
Miscellaneous Clerk and Assistant Series	GS-303	Computer Operation Series	GS-332
Information Receptionist Series	GS-304	Computer Specialist Series	GS-334
Mail and File Series	GS-305	Computer Clerk and Assistant Series	GS-335
Correspondence Clerk Series	GS-309	Program Management Series	GS-340
Clerk-Stenographer and Reporter Series	GS-312	Administrative Officer Series	GS-341
Work Unit Supervising Series	GS-313	Support Services Administration Series	GS-342
Secretary Series	GS-318	Management and Program Analysis Series	GS-343
Closed Microphone Reporting Series	GS-319	Management Clerical and Assistance Series	GS-344

Logistics Management Series	GS-346	Electric Account. Machine Project Planning	GS-362
Equipment Operator Series	GS-350	Telephone Operating Series	GS-382
Printing Clerical Series	GS-351	Telecommunications Processing Series	GS-390
Data Transcriber Series	GS-356	Telecommunications Series	GS-391
Coding Series	GS-357	General Communications Series	GS-392
Electric Accounting Machine Operation Series	GS-359	Communications Clerical Series	GS-394
Equal Opportunity Compliance Series	GS-360	Admin/ Office Support Student Trainee Series	GS-399
Equal Opportunity Assistance Series	GS-361		

GS-400 – BIOLOGICAL SCIENCES GROUP

General Biological Science Series	GS-401	Range Conservation Series	GS-454
Microbiology Series	GS-403	Range Technician Series	GS-455
Biological Science Technician Series	GS-404	Soil Conservation Series	GS-457
Pharmacology Series	GS-405	Soil Conservation Technician Series	GS-458
Agricultural Extension Series	GS-406	Irrigation System Operation Series	GS-459
Ecology Series	GS-408	Forestry Series	GS-460
Zoology Series	GS-410	Forestry Technician Series	GS-462
Physiology Series	GS-413	Soil Science Series	GS-470
Entomology Series	GS-414	Agronomy Series	GS-471
Toxicology Series	GS-415	Agricultural Management Series	GS-475
Plant Protection Technician Series	GS-421	General Fish and Wildlife Admin. Series	GS-480
Botany Series	GS-430	Fishery Biology Series	GS-482
Plant Pathology Series	GS-434	Wildlife Refuge Management Series	GS-485
Plant Physiology Series	GS-435	Wildlife Biology Series	GS-486
Plant Protection and Quarantine Series	GS-436	Animal Science Series	GS-487
Horticulture Series	GS-437	Home Economics Series	GS-493
Genetics Series	GS-440	Biological Science Student Trainee Series	GS-499

GS-500 – ACCOUNTING AND BUDGET GROUP

Financial Administration and Program Series	GS-501	Voucher Examining Series	GS-540
Financial Clerical and Assistance Series	GS-503	Civilian Pay Series	GS-544
Financial Management Series	GS-505	Military Pay Series	GS-545
Accounting Series	GS-510	Budget Analysis Series	GS-560
Auditing Series	GS-511	Budget Clerical and Assistance Series	GS-561
Internal Revenue Agent Series	GS-512	Financial Institution Examining Series	GS-570
Accounting Technician Series	GS-525	Tax Examining Series	GS-592
Tax Technician Series	GS-526	Insurance Accounts Series	GS-593
Cash Processing Series	GS-530	Financial Management Student Trainee Series	GS-599

GS-600 – MEDICAL, HOSPITAL, DENTAL, AND PUBLIC HEALTH GROUP

General Health Science Series	GS-601	Diagnostic Radiologic Technologist Series	GS-647
Medical Officer Series	GS-602	Therapeutic Radiologic Technologist Series	GS-648
Physician's Assistant Series	GS-603	Medical Instrument Technician Series	GS-649
Nurse Series	GS-610	Medical Technical Assistant Series	GS-650
Practical Nurse Series	GS-620	Respiratory Therapist Series	GS-651
Nursing Assistant Series	GS-621	Pharmacist Series	GS-660
Medical Supply Aide and Technician Series	GS-622	Pharmacy Technician Series	GS-661
Autopsy Assistant Series	GS-625	Optometrist Series	GS-662
Dietitian and Nutritionist Series	GS-630	Restoration Technician Series	GS-664
Occupational Therapist Series	GS-631	Speech Pathology and Audiology Series	GS-665
Physical Therapist Series	GS-633	Orthotist and Prosthetist Series	GS-667
Corrective Therapist Series	GS-635	Podiatrist Series	GS-668
Rehabilitation Therapy Assistant Series	GS-636	Medical Records Administration Series	GS-669
Manual Arts Therapist Series	GS-637	Health System Administration Series	GS-670
Recreation/Creative Arts Therapist Series	GS-638	Health System Specialist Series	GS-671
Educational Therapist Series	GS-639	Prosthetic Representative Series	GS-672
Health Aide and Technician Series	GS-640	Hospital Housekeeping Management Series	GS-673
Nuclear Medicine Technician Series	GS-642	Medical Records Technician Series	GS-675
Medical Technologist Series	GS-644	Medical Clerk Series	GS-679

Medical Technician Series	GS-645	Dental Officer Series	GS-680
Pathology Technician Series	GS-646	Dental Assistant Series	GS-681
Dental Hygiene Series	GS-682	Industrial Hygiene Series	GS-690
Dental Laboratory Aid and Technician Series	GS-683	Consumer Safety Series	GS-696
Public Health Program Specialist Series	GS-685	Environmental Health Technician Series	GS-698
Sanitarian Series	GS-688	Medical and Health Student Trainee Series	GS-699

GS-700 – VETERINARY MEDICAL SCIENCE GROUP

Veterinary Medical Science Series	GS-701	Veterinary Student Trainee Series	GS-799
Animal Health Technician Series	GS-704		

GS-800 – ENGINEERING AND ARCHITECTURE GROUP

General Engineering Series	GS-801	Computer Engineering Series	GS-854
Engineering Technician Series	GS-802	Electronics Engineering Series	GS-855
Safety Engineering Series	GS-803	Electronics Technician Series	GS-856
Fire Protection Engineering Series	GS-804	Biomedical Engineering Series	GS-858
Materials Engineering Series	GS-806	Aerospace Engineering Series	GS-861
Landscape Architecture Series	GS-807	Naval Architecture Series	GS-871
Architecture Series	GS-808	Ship Surveying Series	GS-873
Construction Control Series	GS-809	Mining Engineering Series	GS-880
Civil Engineering Series	GS-810	Petroleum Engineering Series	GS-881
Surveying Technician Series	GS-817	Agricultural Engineering Series	GS-890
Engineering Drafting Series	GS-818	Ceramic Engineering Series	GS-892
Environmental Engineering Series	GS-819	Chemical Engineering Series	GS-893
Construction Analyst Series	GS-828	Welding Engineering Series	GS-894
Mechanical Engineering Series	GS-830	Industrial Engineering Technician Series	GS-895
Nuclear Engineering Series	GS-840	Industrial Engineering Series	GS-896
Electrical Engineering Series	GS-850	Engineering/Architecture Student Series	GS-899

GS-900 – LEGAL AND KINDRED GROUP

Law Clerk Series	GS-904	Legal Clerical and Assistance Series	GS-986
General Attorney Series	GS-905	Tax Law Specialist Series	GS-987
Estate Tax Examining Series	GS-920	General Claims Examining Series	GS-990
Hearings and Appeals Series	GS-930	Workers' Compensation Claims Examining	GS-991
Clerk of Court Series	GS-945	Loss and Damage Claims Examining Series	GS-992
Paralegal Specialist Series	GS-950	Social Insurance Claims Examining Series	GS-993
Pension Law Specialist Series	GS-958	Unemployment Comp. Examining Series	GS-994
Contact Representative Series	GS-962	Dependents and Estates Claims Examining	GS-995
Legal Instruments Examining Series	GS-963	Veterans Claims Examining Series	GS-996
Land Law Examining Series	GS-965	Claims Clerical Series	GS-998
Passport and Visa Examining Series	GS-967	Legal Occupations Student Trainee Series	GS-999

GS-1000 – INFORMATION AND ARTS GROUP

General Arts and Information Series	GS-1001	Music Specialist Series	GS-1051
Interior Design Series	GS-1008	Theater Specialist Series	GS-1054
Exhibits Specialist Series	GS-1010	Art Specialist Series	GS-1056
Museum Curator Series	GS-1015	Photography Series	GS-1060
Museum Specialist and Technician Series	GS-1016	Audiovisual Production Series	GS-1071
Illustrating Series	GS-1020	Writing and Editing Series	GS-1082
Office Drafting Series	GS-1021	Technical Writing and Editing Series	GS-1083
Public Affairs Series	GS-1035	Visual Information Series	GS-1084
Language Specialist Series	GS-1040	Editorial Assistance Series	GS-1087
Language Clerical Series	GS-1046	Information and Arts Student Trainee Series	GS-1099

GS-1100 – BUSINESS AND INDUSTRY GROUP

General Business and Industry Series	GS-1101	Property Disposal Series	GS-1104
Contracting Series	GS-1102	Purchasing Series	GS-1105

Industrial Property Management Series	GS-1103	Procurement Clerical and Technician Series	GS-1106
Property Disposal Clerical and Technician Series	GS-1107	Crop Insurance Administration Series	GS-1161
Public Utilities Specialist Series	GS-1130	Crop Insurance Underwriting Series	GS-1162
Trade Specialist Series	GS-1140	Insurance Examining Series	GS-1163
Commissary Store Management Series	GS-1144	Loan Specialist Series	GS-1165
Agricultural Program Specialist Series	GS-1145	Internal Revenue Officer Series	GS-1169
Agricultural Marketing Series	GS-1146	Realty Series	GS-1170
Agricultural Market Reporting Series	GS-1147	Appraising and Assessing Series	GS-1171
Industrial Specialist Series	GS-1150	Housing Management Series	GS-1173
Production Control Series	GS-1152	Building Management Series	GS-1176
Financial Analysis Series	GS-1160	Business/Industry Student Trainee Series	GS-1199

GS-1200 – COPYRIGHT, PATENT, AND TRADE-MARK GROUP

Patent Technician Series	GS-1202	Patent Attorney Series	GS-1222
Copyright Series	GS-1210	Patent Classifying Series	GS-1223
Copyright Technician Series	GS-1211	Patent Examining Series	GS-1224
Patent Administration Series	GS-1220	Design Patent Examining Series	GS-1226
Patent Advisor Series	GS-1221	Copyright and Patent Student Trainee Series	GS-1299

GS-1300 – PHYSICAL SCIENCES GROUP

General Physical Science Series	GS-1301	Oceanography Series	GS-1360
Health Physics Series	GS-1306	Navigational Information Series	GS-1361
Physics Series	GS-1310	Cartography Series	GS-1370
Physical Science Technician Series	GS-1311	Cartographic Technician Series	GS-1371
Geophysics Series	GS-1313	Geodesy Series	GS-1372
Hydrology Series	GS-1315	Land Surveying Series	GS-1373
Hydrologic Technician Series	GS-1316	Geodetic Technician Series	GS-1374
Chemistry Series	GS-1320	Forest Products Technology Series	GS-1380
Metallurgy Series	GS-1321	Food Technology Series	GS-1382
Astronomy and Space Science Series	GS-1330	Textile Technology Series	GS-1384
Meteorology Series	GS-1340	Photographic Technology Series	GS-1386
Meteorological Technician Series	GS-1341	Document Analysis Series	GS-1397
Geology Series	GS-1350	Physical Science Student Trainee Series	GS-1399

GS-1400 – LIBRARY AND ARCHIVES GROUP

Librarian Series	GS-1410	Archivist Series	GS-1420
Library Technician Series	GS-1411	Archives Technician Series	GS-1421
Technical Information Services Series	GS-1412	Library and Archives Student Trainee	GS-1499

GS-1500 – MATHEMATICS AND STATISTICS GROUP

Actuary Series	GS-1510	Statistical Assistant Series	GS-1531
Operations Research Series	GS-1515	Cryptography Series	GS-1540
Mathematics Series	GS-1520	Cryptanalysis Series	GS-1541
Mathematics Technician Series	GS-1521	Computer Science Series	GS-1550
Mathematical Statistician Series	GS-1529	Math/Statistics Student Trainee Series	GS-1599
Statistician Series	GS-1530		

GS-1600 – EQUIPMENT, FACILITIES, AND SERVICES GROUP

General Facilities and Equipment Series	GS-1601	Steward Series	GS-1667
Cemetery Administration Series	GS-1630	Equipment Specialist Series	GS-1670
Facility Management Series	GS-1640	Equipment/ Facilities Mgmt Student Series	GS-1699
Printing Management Series	GS-1654		
Laundry and Dry Cleaning Plant Mgmt.	GS-1658		

GS-1700 – EDUCATION GROUP

General Education and Training Series	GS-1701	Training Instruction Series	GS-1712
Education and Training Technician Series	GS-1702	Vocational Rehabilitation Series	GS-1715
Educational and Vocational Training Series	GS-1710	Education Program Series	GS-1720
Public Health Educator Series	GS-1725	Instructional Systems Series	GS-1750
Education Research Series	GS-1730	Education Student Trainee Series	GS-1799
Education Services Series	GS-1740		

GS-1800 — INVESTIGATION GROUP

General Insp. Investigation & Compliance Series	GS-1801	Consumer Safety Inspection Series	GS-1862
Compliance Inspection and Support Series	GS-1802	Food Inspection Series	GS-1863
General Investigating Series	GS-1810	Public Health Quarantine Inspection Series	GS-1864
Criminal Investigating Series	GS-1811	Customs Patrol Officer Series	GS-1884
Game Law Enforcement Series	GS-1812	Import Specialist Series	GS-1889
Air Safety Investigating Series	GS-1815	Customs Inspection Series	GS-1890
Immigration Inspection Series	GS-1816	Customs Entry and Liquidating Series	GS-1894
Mine Safety and Health Series	GS-1822	Customs Warehouse Officer Series	GS-1895
Aviation Safety Series	GS-1825	Border Patrol Agent Series	GS-1896
Securities Compliance Examining Series	GS-1831	Customs Aid Series	GS-1897
Agri. Commodity Warehouse Examining Series	GS-1850	Admeasurement Series	GS-1898
Alcohol, Tobacco and Firearms Inspection Series	GS-1854	Investigation Student Trainee Series	GS-1899

GS-1900 – QUALITY ASSURANCE, INSPECTION, AND GRADING GROUP

Quality Assurance Series	GS-1910	Agricultural Commodity Aide Series	GS-1981
Agricultural Commodity Grading Series	GS-1980	Quality Inspection Student Trainee Series	GS-1999

GS-2000 – SUPPLY GROUP

General Supply Series	GS-2001	Packaging Series	GS-2032
Supply Program Management Series	GS-2003	Supply Cataloging Series	GS-2050
Supply Clerical and Technician Series	GS-2005	Sales Store Clerical Series	GS-2091
Inventory Management Series	GS-2010	Supply Student Trainee Series	GS-2099
Distribution Facilities / Storage Mgmt Series	GS-2030		

GS-2100 – TRANSPORTATION GROUP

Transportation Specialist Series	GS-2101	Transportation Loss and Damage Claims	GS-3135
Transportation Clerk and Assistant Series	GS-2102	Examining Series	GS-2136
Transportation Industry Analysis Series	GS-2110	Cargo Scheduling Series	GS-2144
Transportation Rate and Tariff Examining Series	GS-2111	Transportation Operations Series	GS-2150
Railroad Safety Series	GS-2121	Dispatching Series	GS-2151
Motor Carrier Safety Series	GS-2123	Air Traffic Control Series	GS-2152
Highway Safety Series	GS-2125	Air Traffic Assistance Series	GS-2154
Traffic Management Series	GS-2130	Marine Cargo Series	GS-2161
Freight Rate Series	GS-2131	Aircraft Operation Series	GS-2181
Travel Series	GS-2132	Air Navigation Series	GS-2183
Passenger Rate Series	GS-2133	Aircrew Technician Series	GS-2185
Shipment Clerical and Assistance Series	GS-2134	Transportation Student Trainee Series	GS-2199

GS-2200 – INFORMATION TECHNOLOGY GROUP

Information Technology Specialist	GS-2210

WAGE GRADE TRADES AND LABOR JOB FAMILIES AND OCCUPATIONS

The government's Personnel Classification System includes Wage Grade occupations grouped into families of like jobs. The 36 occupational families range from WG-2500 to WG-9000. Each occupational family has its own group number and title which makes it distinctive from every other family grouping. The following is a list of the Wage Grade families.[2]

Each occupational family has a three part identifier: the Pay System, Occupational Group Number, and Title. In the example WG-2500, Wire Communications Equipment Installation and Maintenance Family, WG means the job is in the Wage Grade Schedule (or blue collar) pay system; 2500 is the Occupational Family Number; and Wire Communications Equipment Installation and Maintenance is the Occupational Family Title. Each occupational family lists the individual jobs that comprise the family with their corresponding Job Series Numbers and Titles. A brief description is provided for each of the occupational Wage Grade families and the jobs within that family. There were 201,988 Wage Grade workers in 2007.

WG-2500   Wire Communications Equipment Installation and Maintenance Family

This job family includes occupations involved in the construction, installation, maintenance, repair and testing of all types of wire communications systems and associated equipment which are predominantly electrical-mechanical. Work involved in the installation and repair of communications equipment which requires in-depth knowledge of operating electronic principles should be coded to electronic equipment installation and maintenance family, 2600.

WG-2502	Telephone Mechanic	WG-2508	Communications Line Installing
WG-2504	Wire Communications Cable		and Repairing
	Splicing	WG-2511	Wire Communications Equip.
			Install/Repair

WG-2600   Electronic Equipment Installation and Maintenance Family

This job family includes occupations involved in the installation, repair, overhaul, fabrication, tuning, alignment, modification, calibration, and testing of electronic equipment and related devices, such as radio, radar, loran, sonar, television, and other communications equipment; industrial controls; fire control, flight/landing control, bombing-navigation, and other integrated systems; and electronic computer systems and equipment.

WG-2602	Electronic Measurement Equip.	WG-2698	Electronic Digital
	Mechanic		Computer Mechanic
WG-2604	Electronics Mechanic	WG-2610	Electronic Integrated
WG-2606	Electronic Industrial Controls		Systems Mechanic
	Mechanic		

---

[2]The Wage Grade listing is taken from the Government Printing Office publication TS-PB97-170591.

WG-280   Electrical Installation & Maintenance Family

This job family includes occupations involved in the fabrication, installation, alteration, maintenance, repair, and testing of electrical systems, instruments, apparatus, and equipment.

WG-2800 Electrician	WG-2854 Electrical Equipment Repairing
WG-2810 Electrician (High Voltage)	WG-2892 Aircraft Electrician

WG-3100   Fabric & Leather Work Family

This job family includes occupations involving the fabrication, modification, and repair of clothing and equipment made of (a) woven textile fabrics of animal, vegetable, or synthetic origin; (b) plastic film and filaments; (c) natural and simulated leather; (d) natural and synthetic fabrics; and (e) paper. Work involves use of hand tools and mechanical devices and machines to lay out, cut, sew, rivet, mold, fit, assemble, and attach bindings to articles such as uniforms, rain gear, hats, belts, shoes, briefcases, holsters, equipage articles, tents, gun covers, bags, parachutes, upholstery, mattresses, brushes, etc.

WG-3103 Shoe Repairing	WG-3111 Sewing Machine Operating
WG-3105 Fabric Working	WG-3119 Broom & Brush Making
WG-3106 Upholstering	

WG-3300   Instrument Work Family

This job family includes occupations that involve fabricating, assembling, calibrating, testing, installing, repairing, modifying, and maintaining instruments and instrumentation systems for measuring, regulating, and computing physical quantities such as movement, force, acceleration, displacement, stress, strain, vibration or oscillation frequency, phase and amplitude, linear or angular velocity, voltage, current, power, impedance, etc. Examples of such instruments and equipment are: gyro, optical, photographic, timekeeping, electrical, metered, pressure, and geared instruments, test equipment, and navigation, flight control, and fuel totalizing systems. The work requires knowledge of electrical, electronic, mechanical, optical, pneumatic, and/or hydraulic principles. Work that primarily involves fabricating and repairing electronic instruments should be coded to the electronic equipment installation and maintenance family, 2600.

WG-3306 Optical Instrument Repairing	WG-3359 Instrument Mechanic
WG-3314 Instrument Making	WG-3364 Projection Equipment Repairing
WG-3341 Scale Building, Install/Repair	

WG-3400   Machine Tool Work Family

This job family includes occupations that involve setting up and operating machine tools and using hand tools to make or repair (shape, fit, finish, assemble) metal parts, tools, gages, models, patterns, mechanisms, and machines; and machining explosives and synthetic materials.

WG-3414 Machining	WG-3422 Power Saw Operator
WG-3416 Toolmaking	WG-3428 Die Sinker
WG-3417 Tool Grinding	WG-3431 Machine Tool Operating

WG-3500 General Services & Support Work Family

This job family includes occupations not specifically covered by another family that require little or no specialized training or work experience to enter. These occupations usually involve work such as moving and handling material (e.g., loading, unloading, digging, hauling, hoisting, carrying, wrapping, mixing, pouring, spreading); washing and cleaning laboratory apparatus, cars, and trucks, etc.; cleaning and maintaining living quarters, hospital rooms and wards, office buildings, grounds, and other areas; and doing other general maintenance work, by hand or using common hand tools and power equipment. They may involve heavy or light physical work and various skill levels. Skills are generally learned through job experience and instruction from supervisors or, in some instances, formal training programs lasting a few days or weeks or longer.

WG-3502	Laboring	WG-3515	Laboratory Support Working
WG-3506	Summer Aide/Student Aide	WG-3543	Stevedoring
WG-3508	Pipeline Working	WG-3546	Railroad Repairing
WG-3511	Laboratory Working	WG-3566	Custodial Working
WG-3513	Coin/Currency Checking		

WG-3600 Structural & Finishing Work Family

This job family includes occupations not specifically covered by another family that involve doing structural and finishing work in construction, maintenance, and repair of surfaces and structures, e.g., laying brick, block, and stone; setting tile; finishing cement and concrete; plastering; installing, maintaining, and repairing asphalt, tar, and gravel; roofing; insulating and glazing.

WG-3602	Cement Finishing	WG-3609	Floor Covering Installing
WG-3603	Masonry	WG-3610	Insulating
WG-3604	Tile Setting	WG-3611	Glazing
WG-3605	Plastering	WG-3653	Asphalt Working
WG-3604	Roofing		

WG-3700 Metal Processing Family

This job family includes occupations which involve processing or treating metals to alter their properties or produce desirable qualities such as hardness or workability, using processes such as welding, plating, melting, alloying, annealing, heat treating, and refining.

WG-3702	Flame/Arc Cutting	WG-3720	Brazing & Soldering
WG-3703	Welding	WG-3722	Cold Working
WG-3705	Nondestructive Testing	WG-3725	Battery Repairing
WG-3707	Metalizing	WG-3727	Buffing & Polishing
WG-3708	Metal Process Working	WG-3735	Metal Phototransferring
WG-3711	Electroplating	WG-3736	Circuit Board Making
WG-3712	Heat Treating	WG-3741	Furnace Operating
WG-3716	Leadburning	WG-3769	Shot Peening Machine

WG-3800 Metal Working Family

This job family includes occupations involved in shaping and forming metal and making and repairing metal parts or equipment. Includes such work as the fabrication and assembly of sheet metal parts and equipment; forging and press operations; structural iron working, stamping, etc. Doesn't include machine tool work.

WG-3802	Metal Forging	WG-3819	Airframe Jig Fitting
WG-3804	Coppersmithing	WG-3820	Shipfitting
WG-3806	Sheet Metal Mechanic	WG-3830	Blacksmithing
WG-3807	Iron Working	WG-3832	Metal Making
WG-3808	Boilermaking	WG-3833	Transfer Engraving
WG-3809	Mobile Equip. Metal Mech.	WG-3858	Metal Tank & Radiator Repair
WG-3815	Pneumatic Tool Operating	WG-3869	Metal Forming Mach. Operating
WG-3816	Engraving	WG-3872	Metal Tube Making & Installing
WG-3818	Springmaking		

WG-3900 Motion Picture, Radio, Television, and Sound Equipment Operation Family

This job family includes occupations involved in setting up, testing, operating, and making minor repairs to equipment such as microphones, sound and radio controls, sound recording equipment, lighting and sound effect devices, television cameras, magnetic videotape recorders, motion picture projectors, and broadcast transmitters used in the production of motion pictures and radio and television programs. Also includes occupations that involve related work.

WG-3910	Motion Picture Projection	WG-3940	Broadcasting Equip. Operating
WG-3911	Sound Recording Equip. Operating	WG-3941	Public Address Equip. Operating
WG-3919	Television Equip. Operating		

WG-4000 Lens and Crystal Work Family

This job family includes occupations involved in making precision optical elements, crystal blanks or wafers, or other items of glass, polished metals, or similar materials, using such methods as cutting, polishing, etc.

WG-4005	Optical Element Working	WG-4015	Quartz Crystal Working
WG-4010	Prescription Eyeglass Making		

WG-4100 Painting & Paperhanging Family

This job family includes occupations which involve hand or spray painting and decorating interiors and exteriors of buildings, structures, aircraft, vessels, mobile equipment, fixtures, furnishings, machinery, and other surfaces; finishing hardwoods, furniture, and cabinetry; painting signs; covering interiors of rooms with strips of wallpaper or fabric, etc.

WG-4102	Painting	WG-4104	Sign Painting
WG-4103	Paperhanging	WG-4157	Instrument Dial Painting

WG-4200 Plumbing & Pipefitting Family

This job family includes occupations that involve the installation, maintenance, and repair of water, air, steam, gas, sewer, and other pipelines and systems, and related fixtures, apparatus, and accessories.

WG-4204	Pipefitting	WG-4255	Fuel Distribution Systems
WG-4206	Plumbing		Mechanic

WG-4300 Pliable Materials Work Family

This job family includes occupations involved in shaping, forming, and repairing items and parts from non-metallic moldable materials such as plastic, rubber, clay, wax, plaster, glass, sand, or other similar material.

WG-4351	Plastic Molding Equip. Operating	WG-4370	Glassblowing
WG-4352	Plastic Fabricating	WG-4371	Plaster Pattern Casting
WG-4360	Rubber Products Molding	WG-4373	Molding
WG-4361	Rubber Equipment Repairing	WG-4374	Core Making

WG-4400 Printing Family

This job family includes occupations involved in letterpress (relief), offset-lithographic, gravure (intaglio), or screen printing; including layout, hand composition, typesetting from hot metal type, platemaking, printing, and finishing operations.

WG-4402	Bindery Work	WG-4422	Dot Etching
WG-4403	Hand Composing	WG-4425	Photoengraving
WG-4405	Film Assembly-Stripping	WG-4441	Bookbinding
WG-4406	Letterpress Operating	WG-4445	Bank Note Designing
WG-4407	Linotype Machine Operating	WG-4446	Bank Note Engraving
WG-4413	Negative Engraving	WG-4447	Sculptural Engraving
WG-4414	Offset Photography	WG-4448	Siderographic Transferring
WG-4416	Platemaking	WG-4449	Electrolytic Intaglio Platemaking
WG-4417	Offset Press Operating	WG-4450	Intaglio Die & Plate Finishing
WG-4419	Silk Screen Making & Printing	WG-4454	Intaglio Press Operating

WG-4600 Wood Work Family

This occupation includes jobs involved in blocking, bracing, staying, and securing cargo for shipment by land, sea, or air. It requires skill in construction, placing, and installing wooden blocks, wedges, bracing, structures, and other staying devices, as well as skill in securing items using wires, ropes, chains, cables, plates, and other hardware.

WG-4602	Blocking & Bracing	WG-4618	Woodworking Mach. Operating
WG-4604	Wood Working	WG-4620	Shoe Lasting Repairing
WG-4605	Wood Crafting	WG-4639	Timber Working
WG-4607	Carpentry	WG-4654	Form Block Making
WG-4616	Patternmaking		

WG-4700 General Maintenance & Operations Work Family

This job family includes occupations which (1) consist of various combinations of work such as are involved in constructing, maintaining and repairing buildings, roads, grounds, and related facilities; manufacturing, modifying, and repairing items or apparatus made from a variety of materials or types of components; or repairing and operating equipment or utilities; and (2) require the application of a variety of trade practices associated with occupations in more than one job family (unless otherwise indicated), and the performance of the highest level of work in at least two of the trades involved.

WG-4714	Model Making	WG-4741	General Equipment Operating
WG-4715	Exhibits Making/Modeling	WG-4742	Utility System Repair/Operating
WG-4716	Railroad Car Repairing	WG-4745	Research Laboratory Mechanic
WG-4717	Boat Building and Repairing	WG-4749	Maintenance Mechanic
WG-4737	General Equipment Mechanic	WG-4754	Cemetery Caretaking

WG-4800 General Equipment Maintenance Family

This job family includes occupations involved in the maintenance or repair of equipment, machines, or instruments which are not coded to other job families because the equipment is not characteristically related to one of the established subject-matter areas such as electronics, electrical, industrial, transportation, instruments, engines, aircraft, ordnance, etc., or because the nature of the work calls for limited knowledge/skill in a variety of crafts or trades as they relate to the repair of such equipment, but not a predominant knowledge of any one trade or craft.

WG-4802	Musical Instrument Repairing	WG-4839	Film Processing Equip. Repair
WG-4804	Locksmithing	WG-4840	Tool & Equipment Repairing
WG-4805	Medical Equipment Repairing	WG-4841	Window Shade Assembling,
WG-4806	Office Appliance Repairing		Repairing
WG-4807	Chemical Equipment Repairing	WG-4843	Navigation Aids Repairing
WG-4808	Custodial Equipment Servicing	WG-4844	Bicycle Repairing
WG-4812	Saw Reconditioning	WG-4845	Orthopedic Appliance Repairing
WG-4816	Protective/Safety Equip. Fab.	WG-4848	Mechanical Parts Repairing
WG-4818	Aircraft Survival/Flight Equip.	WG-4850	Bearing Reconditioning
WG-4819	Bowling Equipment Repairing	WG-4851	Reclamation Working
WG-4820	Vending Machine Repairing	WG-4855	Domestic Appliance Repairing

WG-5000 Plant and Animal Work Family

This job family includes occupations involved in general or specialized farming operations; gardening, including the general care of grounds, roadways, nurseries, greenhouses, etc.; trimming and felling trees; and propagating, caring for, handling, and controlling animals and insects, including pest species.

WG-5002	Farming	WG-5034	Dairy Farming
WG-5003	Gardening	WG-5035	Livestock Ranching/Wrangling
WG-5026	Pest Controlling	WG-5042	Tree Trimming and Removing
WG-5031	Insects Production Working	WG-5048	Animal Caretaking

WG-5200 Miscellaneous Occupations Family

This job family includes occupations which are not covered by the definition of any other job family or which are of such a general or miscellaneous character as to preclude placing them within another job family.

WG-5205	Gas and Radiation Detecting	WG-5221	Lofting
WG-5210	Rigging	WG-5222	Diving
WG-5220	Shipwright	WG-5235	Test Range Tracking

WG-5300 Industrial Equipment Maintenance Family

This job family includes occupations involved in the general maintenance, installation, and repair of portable and stationary industrial machinery, tools, and equipment such as sewing machines, machine tools, woodworking and metal working machines, printing equipment, processing equipment, driving machinery, power generating equipment, air conditioning equipment, heating and boiler plant equipment, and other types of machines and equipment used in the production of goods and services.

WG-5306	Air Conditioning Equip. Mech.	WG-5334	Marine Machinery Mechanic
WG-5309	Heating and Boiler Plant Mech.	WG-5335	Wind Tunnel Mechanic
WG-5310	Kitchen/Bakery Equip. Repairing	WG-5341	Industrial Furnace Building & Repairing
WG-5312	Sewing Machine Repairing		
WG-5313	Elevator Mechanic	WG-5350	Production Machinery Mechanic
WG-5317	Laundry/Dry Cleaning Equip. Repairing	WG-5352	Industrial Equipment Mechanic
		WG-5364	Door Systems Mechanic
WG-5318	Lock & Dam Repairing	WG-5365	Physiological Trainer Mechanic
WG-5323	Oiling & Greasing	WG-5378	Powered Support Systems Mech.
WG-5324	Powerhouse Equipment Repairing	WG-5384	Gas Dynamic Facility Installing/Repairing
WG-5326	Drawbridge Repairing		
WG-5330	Printing Equipment Repairing		

WG-5400 Industrial Equipment Operation Family

This job family includes occupations involved in the operation of portable and stationary industrial equipment, tools, and machines to generate and distribute utilities such as electricity, steam, and gas for heat or power; treat and distribute water; collect, treat, and dispose of waste; open and close bridges, locks and dams; lift and move workers, materials, and equipment; manufacture and process materials and products; etc.

WG-5402	Boiler Plant Operating	WG-5423	Sandblasting
WG-5403	Incinerator Operating	WG-5424	Weighing Machine Operating
WG-5406	Utility Systems Operating	WG-5426	Lock and Dam Operating
WG-5407	Electric Power Controlling	WG-5427	Chemical Plant Operating
WG-5408	Sewage Disposal Plant Operating	WG-5430	Drawbridge Operating
WG-5409	Water Treatment Plant Operating	WG-5433	Gas Generating Plant Operating
WG-5413	Fuel Distribution System Operating	WG-5435	Carton/Bag Making Machine Operating
WG-5414	Baling Machine Operating	WG-5438	Elevator Operating
WG-5415	Air Cond. Equip. Operating	WG-5439	Testing Equipment Operating
WG-5419	Stationary-Engine Operating	WG-5440	Packaging Machine Operating

WG-5444	Food/Feed Processing Equip. Operating	WG-5478	Portable Equipment Operating
		WG-5479	Dredging Equipment Operating
WG-5446	Textile Equipment Operating	WG-5484	Counting Machine Operating
WG-5450	Conveyor Operating	WG-5485	Aircraft Weight & Balance Operating
WG-5454	Solvent Still Operating		
WG-5455	Paper Pulping Machine Operating	WG-5486	Swimming Pool Operating
WG-5473	Oil Reclamation Equip.Operating		

WG-5700 Transportation/Mobile Equipment Operation Family

This job family includes occupations involved in the operation and operational maintenance of self-propelled transportation and other mobile equipment (except aircraft) used to move materials or passengers, including motor vehicles, engineering and construction equipment, tractors, etc., some of which may be equipped with power takeoff and controls to operate special purpose equipment; ocean-going and inland waterway vessels, harbor craft, and floating plants; and trains, locomotives, and train cars.

WG-5703	Motor Vehicle Operating	WG-5736	Braking-Switching & Conducting
WG-5704	Fork Lift Operating	WG-5737	Locomotive Engineering
WG-5705	Tractor Operating	WG-5738	Railroad Maint. Vehicle Ops.
WG-5706	Road Sweeper Operating	WG-5767	Airfield Clearing Equip. Ops.
WG-5707	Tank Driver	WG-5782	Ship Operating
WG-5716	Engineering Equip. Operating	WG-5784	Riverboat Operating
WG-5725	Crane Operating	WG-5786	Small Craft Operating
WG-5729	Drill Rig Operating	WG-5788	Deckhand
WG-5731	Mining/Tunneling Mach. Operating		

WG-5800 Heavy Mobile Equipment Mechanic

This job family includes occupations involved in repairing, adjusting, and maintaining self-propelled transportation and other mobile equipment (except aircraft), including any special-purpose features with which they may be equipped.

WG-5803	Heavy Mobile Equip. Mechanic	WG-5823	Automotive Mechanic
WG-5806	Mobile Equip. Servicing	WG-5876	Electromotive Equip. Mechanic

WG-6500 Ammunition, Explosives, & Toxic Materials Work Family

This job family includes occupations involved in the manufacturing, assembling, disassembling, renovating, loading, deactivating, modifying, destroying, testing, handling, placing, and discharging of ammunition, propellants, chemicals and toxic materials, and other conventional and special munitions and explosives.

WG-6502	Explosives Operating	WG-6511	Missile/Toxic Materials Handling
WG-6505	Munitions Destroying	WG-6517	Explosives Test Operating

WG-6600 Armament Work Family

This job family includes occupations involved in the installation, repair, rebuilding, adjusting, modification, and testing of small arms and artillery weapons and allied accessories. Artillery includes, but is not limited to, field artillery, antitank artillery, antiaircraft weapons, aircraft and shipboard weapons, recoilless rifles, rocket launchers, mortars, cannon, and allied accessories. Small arms includes, but is not limited to, rifles, carbines, pistols, revolvers, helmets, body armor, shoulder-type rocket launchers, machine guns, and automatic rifles.

WG-6605	Artillery Repairing	WG-6641	Ordnance Equipment Mechanic
WG-6606	Artillery Testing	WG-6652	Aircraft Ordnance Systems Mech.
WG-6610	Small Arms Repairing	WG-6656	Special Weapons Systems Mech.

WG-6900 Warehousing & Stock Handling Family

This family includes occupations involved in physically receiving, storing, handling, and issuing supplies, materials, and equipment; handling, marking, and displaying goods for customer selection; identifying and condition classifying materials and equipment; and routing and expediting movement of parts, supplies, and materials in production and repair facilities.

WG-6902	Lumber Handling	WG-6912	Materials Examining & Identifying
WG-6903	Coal Handling	WG-6915	Store Working
WG-6904	Tools and Parts Attending	WG-6941	Bulk Money Handling
WG-6907	Materials Handling	WG-6968	Aircraft Freight Loading
WG-6910	Materials Expediting		

WG-7000 Packing and Processing Family

This job family includes occupations involved in determining the measures required to protect items against damage during movement or storage; selecting proper method of packing, including type and size of container; cleaning, drying, and applying preservatives to materials, parts, or mechanical equipment; and packing, equipment, parts, and materials.

WG-7002	Packing	WG-7009	Equipment Cleaning
WG-7004	Preservation Packaging	WG-7010	Parachute Packing
WG-7006	Preservation Servicing		

WG-7300 Laundry, Dry Cleaning, & Pressing Family

This job family includes occupations involved in receiving, sorting, washing, drying, dry cleaning, dyeing, pressing, and preparing for delivery clothes, linens, and other articles requiring laundering, dry cleaning, or pressing.

WG-7304	Laundry Working	WG-7306	Pressing
WG-7305	Laundry Machine Operating	WG-7307	Dry Cleaning

WG-7400 Food Preparation & Servicing Family

This job family includes occupations involved in the preparation and serving of food.

WG-7402	Baking	WG-7407	Meatcutting
WG-7404	Cooking	WG-7408	Food Service Working
WG-7405	Bartending	WG-7420	Waiter

WG-7600 Personal Services Family

This job family includes occupations concerned with providing grooming, beauty, or other personal services to individuals, patrons, guests, passengers, entertainers, etc., or attending to their personal effects.

WG-7603	Barbering	WG-7641	Beautician
WG-7640	Bus Attending		

WG-8200 Fluid Systems Maintenance Family

Includes occupations involving repair, assembly, and testing of fluid systems and components of aircraft, aircraft engines, missiles, and mobile and support equipment. These fluid systems store, supply, distribute, and move gases or liquids to produce power, transmit force, and pressurize, cool, and condition cabins.

WG-8255	Pneudraulic Systems Mechanic	WG-8268	Aircraft Pneudraulic Systems Mechanic

WG-8600 Engine Overhaul Family

This job family includes occupations concerned primarily with the manufacture, repair, modification, and major overhaul of engines (except where covered by another job family) including the disassembly, reassembly, and test phases of engine overhaul programs.

WG-8602	Aircraft Engine Mechanic	WG-8675	Liquid Fuel Rocket Engine Mech.
WG-8610	Small Engine Mechanic		

WG-8800 Aircraft Overhaul Family

This job family includes occupations concerned primarily with the overhaul of aircraft, including the disassembly, reassembly, and test phases of aircraft overhaul programs.

WG-8810	Aircraft Propeller Mechanic	WG-8862	Aircraft Attending
WG-8840	Aircraft Mech. Parts Repairing	WG-8863	Aircraft Tire Mounting
WG-8852	Aircraft Mechanic	WG-8882	Airframe Test Operating

WG-9000 Film Processing Family

This job family includes occupations that involve processing film, for example, operating motion picture developers and printers; cleaning, repairing, matching, cutting, splicing, and assembling films; and mixing developing solutions. Does not include processing work that requires specialized subject-matter knowledge or artistic ability.

WG-9003	Film Assembling and Repairing	WG-9055	Photographic Solution Mixing
WG-9004	Motion Picture Mach. Operating		

Appendix D
Agency Skills Index

Individuals interested in government employment seldom know where to begin their job search. Larger agencies offer employment in a wide range of occupations and many smaller agencies use a diverse cross section of skills and trades.

This index captures 28 departments and agencies plus various independent government organizations. After locating the organizations that utilize your skills, education, and background, review the earlier chapters for specific guidance on how to complete your federal style résumé and apply for jobs.

Skills and occupations are listed alphabetically and agencies or departments that utilize these skills follow each listing. An asterisk precedes the agency that is the largest employer for a skill. The total number of federal employees within each occupation is identified in parentheses following each entry.

This list is not complete. A broad cross-section of occupations are presented to steer you in the right direction. If a related occupation is identified it is highly probable that your skills will also be required by that agency. Agencies other than those identified for each skill or occupation may offer employment in small numbers for a specific occupation. Many agencies hire small numbers of employees within a series or group. These agencies are not on this list.

The purpose of this list is to steer you to the agencies that offer the greatest opportunities and chance of employment. However, don't overlook any agency in your job search, especially those within your commuting area. Identify local agencies in your phone book under "U.S. Government" in the blue pages of the white-pages phone directory and Appendix B, to review our agency directory.

Use this index to locate federal agencies and departments that are seeking your skills, academic major, or related field of study for entry level jobs.

ABBREVIATIONS LIST

ALL	All Agencies	FAA	Federal Aviation Administration
ATC	Architect of the Capitol	FBI	Federal Bureau of Investigation
CIA	Central Intelligence Agency	FCC	Federal Communications
DOA	Dept. of Agriculture		Commission
DOC	Dept. of Commerce	GSA	General Services Administration
DOD	Dept. of Defense	HHS	Health & Human Services
DOE	Dept. of Energy	HUD	Health & Urban Development
EDU	Dept. of Education	NAS	NASA
DHS	Dept. of Homeland Security	OPM	Office of Personnel Management
DOI	Dept. of the Interior	SBA	Small Business Administration
DOJ	Dept. of Justice	SMI	Smithsonian Institution
DOL	Dept. of Labor	TRE	Dept. of the Treasury
DOS	Dept. of State	USI	U.S. Information Agency
DOT	Dept. of Transportation	VA	Veterans Administration
EPA	Environmental Protection Agency		

*   The largest employing agency

( )   The number in parentheses represents the total number employed.

The total employment number may represent a WG Family or GS Group. For example, Family 5300 has 23 individual occupations listed in Appendix D. The total employment is distributed among all 23 occupations.[1]

SKILLS / OCCUPATIONS

ACCOUNTING / AUDITING ACCOUNTING TECHNICIAN GROUP GS-500
* DOT, ALL (126,258)

ADMINISTRATIVE / CLERK TYPIST / CLERICAL / SECRETARY GROUP GS-300
* DOT, (367,403)

AGRICULTURAL GS-1145/46/47/48
*DOA (1,040)

ADVERTISING
DOL

AERONAUTICAL ENGINEERING SERIES GS-861
NASA, *DOD, DOT, DOC (9,386)

AIR CONDITIONING/HEATING REPAIR FAMILY WG-5300
TRE, *DOD, DOA, DOJ, DOI, DOC, HHS, DOT, ATC, GSA, DHS, SMI, VA (9,737)

AIR TRAFFIC CONTROLLERS GS-2152
*DOT-FAA, DOD (22,406)

AIRCRAFT OPERATIONS (PILOTS) GS-2181 INCLUDES COPILOTS
*DOD, DOT-FAA, DHS, DOJ, DOI, DOA, DOE, NASA (2,907)

AIRCRAFT OVERHAUL FAMILY WG-8800
*DOD, NASA, DOJ, DOI, DOA, DHS (13,174)

---

[1] Excerpted from *Occupations of Federal White-Collar & Blue-Collar Workers* & OPM's Employment Cubes on http://www.opm.gov   .

AMMUNITION, EXPLOSIVES WORK FAMILY WG-6600
*DOD, GSA, DOJ, DHS (3,057)

AMERICAN HISTORY GS-170
National Archives & Records Administration

ANIMAL SCIENCE GS-487/700
DOA (103)

ARCHEOLOGY GS-193
*DOA, DOD (1,112)

ARCHITECTURE ENGINEERING GS-808
*DOD, DOJ, DOI, DOA, HHS, HUD, DOT, DOE, GSA, TVA, DHS, VA (1,351)

ART SPECIALIST GS-1056
*DOD, DHS, HHS (32)

ASTRONOMY & SPACE SCIENCE GS-1330 *NASA, DOD (105)

AUDITING GS-0511
*DOD, ALL AGENCIES (9,820)

AUTOMOTIVE MECHANIC WG-5823
*DOD, ALL (2,688)

BAKING WG-7402
*DOD, DOI (60)

BANKING GS-1160, GS-0570
DOA, Farm Credit Administration
DOT, Office of the Comptroller
Federal Reserve

BARBERING WG-7603
*VA, DOD (45)

BIOLOGICAL SCIENCES GS-400 GROUP
*DOA, DOI, DOD, HHS, DOC, EPA, NASA, VA, DHS (68,990)

BOILERMAKER WG-3808
*DOD (155)

BORDER PATROL AGENT GS-1896
*DHS, (20,337)

BOTANY
*DOA, DOD, DOI (416)

BUDGET CLERICAL & ASSISTANCE GS-561 *DOD, ALL (2,195)

BUILDING MANAGEMENT GS-1176
*GSA, DOD, DOJ, DOC, HHS, DOL (336)

BUSINESS & INDUSTRY GROUP GS-1100 *DOD, ALL (78,284)

CARPENTRY WG-4607
*DOD, ALL BUT DOS & DOL (1,429)

CEMENT FINISHING WG-3602
*DOD, DOI (43)

CEMETERY CARETAKING WG-4754
*VA, DOD (612)

CHEMICAL ENGINEERING GS-893
*DOD, DOI, DOA, DOC, DHS, DOJ, DOI, NASA (945)

CIVIL ENGINEERING GS-810
*DOD, MOST AGENCIES (10,494)

CLERK TYPIST GS-205
ALL (390)

CLINICAL PSYCHOLOGY GS-180
DOJ, Bureau of Prisons

COMPUTER GROUP GS-332/5 and GS-2210 ALL (78,233)

CONTRACTING GS-1102
*DOD, ALL (25,069)

COOK WG-7404
*DOD, DOJ, DOI, DOA, HHS, VA (4,110)

COPYRIGHT GROUP GS-1200
*DOC, DOA, DHS, DOD, DOJ, DOI, DOE, NASA (5,750)

CORRECTIONS OFFICER GS-007
*DOJ, DOI (17,866)

CRIMINAL INVESTIGATION SERIES GS-1811 *DOJ, ALL (44,574)

CRYPTANALYSIS SERIES GS-1541
DOJ (20)

CUSTODIAL WORKING WG-3566
*VA, ALL (10,649)

DECKHAND WG-5788
*DOD, DOJ, (218)

DENTAL SERIES GS 680/1/2/3
*DOD, HHS, VA (5,536)

DIETITIAN & NUTRITION GS-630
*VA, HHS, DOD, DOA, DOJ, DHS (1,803)

DISPATCHING GS-2151
*DOD, DOI, DOA, VA, GSA (777)

EARTH SCIENCE
DOD, Defense Intelligence Agency, Defense
Mapping Agency

ECOLOGY GS-408
*DOI, DOA, DOD, DOC, DOE, EPA (1,092)

ECONOMICS GS-110/119
*DOL, ALL AGENCIES (4,150)

EDUCATION/TRAINING GS-1700
*DOD, ALL AGENCIES (39,984)

ELECTRICAL ENGINEERING GS-850
*DOD, ALL BUT HUD, OPM, USI & SBA
(3,383)

ELECTRICIAN WG-2805
*DOD, ALL BUT DOE, DHS (4,180)

**ELECTRONIC EQUIPMENT
INSTALLATION & MAINTENANCE
FAMILY WG-2600** *DOD, DOT, HHS, DOI,
DOE, DOA, DOC, TVA (12,821)

ELECTRONICS TECHNICIAN GS-856
*DOD, DOT-FAA, DOS, DOT, DOJ, DOI, DOA,
DOC, HHS, DOE, EPA, GSA, USI, NASA, VA
(8,274)

ELEVATOR MECHANIC WG-5313
*Architect of the Capitol, DOD,
HHS, VA, DOC, DOJ, DOI, DOT, VA (51)

ENGINE OVERHAUL FAMILY WG-8600
*DOD, DOI, DHS, VA (3,484)

ENGINEERING PSYCHOLOGY
Consumer Product Safety Commission

ENGLISH
Federal Trade Commission
DOL, DOD, DOT, USI

ENTOMOLOGY GS-414
*DOA, DOD, HHS, EPA, DOI (599)

ENVIRONMENTAL ENGINEERING GS-819
*DOD, TVA, DOE, HHS, DHS, DOT, DOI, DOJ,
DOA (2,692)

**EQUAL EMPLOYMENT OPPORTUNITY
GS-0260** *DOD, ALL AGENCIES (2,298)

EQUIPMENT OPERATOR GS-350
*DOD, MOST AGENCIES (493)

EXPLOSIVES OPERATING WG-6502
DOD, DOA (819)

FARMING WG-5002
*DOA, DOJ, DOI (31)

FACILITY MANAGEMENT GS-1640
*DOD, TVA, DOJ, DOI, DOC, NASA, HH, DHS
(1,592)

FINANCIAL ADMINISTRATION GS-501
*DOD, ALL AGENCIES (13,810)

FINGERPRINT IDENTIFICATION GS-072
*DOJ, DHS, DOD (434)

FIRE PROTECTION GS-081
*DOD, VA, DOE, NASA, GSA, HHS, DOS,
DOT, DHS, DOC (9,121)

FISH BIOLOGY GS-0482
*DOI, DOC, DOA, DOD, DOE (2,466)

FOOD INSPECTION GS-1863
*DOA (3,929)

FOOD TECHNOLOGY GS-1382
*DOA, DOC, HHS, DOD (158)

FOREIGN AFFAIRS GS-130
*DOS, DHS, DOS, DOE, DOD, DOC (3,823)

FORK LIFT OPERATOR WG-5704
*DOD, DOC, GSA,DOT, VA (325)

FORESTRY GS-460
*DOA, DOD, TRE, TVA (2,841)

FUEL DISTRIBUTION WG-5413
*DOD, DOI (895)

**GENERAL ADMINISTRATION, CLERICAL,
& OFFICE SERVICES GS-300** ALL (286,894)

GARDENING WG-5003
*VA, DOD, DOJ, DOI, DHS, DOA, DOC, HHS,

DOT, GSA, VA (543)

GENERAL MAINTENANCE & OPERATION WG-4700 *DOD, ALL (15,678)

GENETICS GS-440
DOA, HHS, DOI, DOC (458)

GEOCHEMICAL ENGINEERING
Nuclear Regulatory Commission

GEODETIC TECHNICIAN GS-1374
*DOC, DOD (44)

GEOGRAPHY GS-150
*DOI, DOC, DOD, DOA, DOE, DOT (635)

GEOLOGY GS-1350
*DOI, DOD, DOT, DOA, EPA, DOE, DOL, TVA (1,518)

GUARD GS-085
*DOD, TRE, DOJ, DOI, DOC, HHS, DOT, TVA, VA, GSA, USI (3,363)

GUIDE GS-090
*DOI, DOD, DOA (857)

HEALTH GROUP GS-600
*VA, HHS, DOT, DOJ, DOA, DOS, NASA, DOD (189,526)

HISTORY GS-170
*DOD, DOJ, DOI, DOA, DOT, TRE (714)

HORTICULTURE GS-437
*DOA, DOI, DOD, VA (100)

HOUSING MANAGEMENT GS-1173
*DOD, DOI, HHS, DHS, HUD, VA (1,630)

HUMAN RESOURCE MANAGEMENT GS-0201 *DOD, ALL AGENCIES (20,586)

HYDROLOGY GS-1315
*DOI, DOD, EPA, DOA, DOC, DHS (2,451)

ILLUSTRATING GS-1020
*DOD, DOI, DOJ, DOA, DOC, VA, DOT, DOE (283)

IMPORT SPECIALIST GS-1889
* DHS (990)

INDUSTRIAL EQUIPMENT MECHANIC WG-5352

*DOD, TRE, DOI, DOA, VA, HHS, TRE, DOT, GSA (1,172)

INDUSTRIAL HYGIENE GS-690
*DOD, DOL, DHS, DOI, DOA, HHS, DOE, EPA, GSA, TVA, VA (1,370)

INSURANCE EXAMINING GS-1163
*DHS, DOD, DOT, DOE (36)

INTELLIGENCE GS-132
*DOD, DHS, DOS, TRE, DOJ, DOI, DOC, DOT, DOE (4,732)

INTERNAL REVENUE AGENT GS-512
TRE (13,581)

INTERNATIONAL RELATIONS GS-131
*DOD, DOT, DOE, DOS, DOA, DOC (221)

INVENTORY MANAGEMENT GS-2010
*DOD, ALL (4,895)

INVESTIGATION GROUP GS-1800
*DHS, ALL AGENCIES (162,158)

LABORING WG-3502
*DOD, ALL (3,632)

LANDSCAPE ARCHITECTURE GS-807
*DOA, DOI, DOD, VA, TVA (454)

LAND SURVEYING GS-1373
*DOI, DOD, DOA, DOE (409)

LANGUAGE SPECIALIST GS-1040
*DOJ, DOD, DOC, DOS, TRV, HHS, USI, NASA (917)

LAUNDRY WORK WG-7300
*VA, DOD, DOJ, DOI, DOS, HHS (1,221)

LEGAL GS-900
*TRE, ALL (59,622)

LIBRARIAN GS-1410
*DOD, ALL (1,226)

LITERATURE
DOL

LOAN SPECIALIST GS-1165
*DOA, HUD, DOI, DOA, DOC, VA, SBA (4,646)

LOCK AND DAM REPAIR WG-5318
*DOD, DOI, DOT (427)

LOCKSMITHING WG-4804
*DOD, VA, DOI, DOC, DOJ, HHS (258)

LOGISTICS MANAGEMENT GS-346
*DOD, ALL AGENCIES (3,933)

MACHINE TOOL WORK FAMILY WG-3400
*DOD, ALL BUT DOL & DOS (4,722)

MAIL & FILE GS-305
*TRE, ALL (6211)

MAINTENANCE MECHANIC WG-4749
*DOD, ALL AGENCIES (10,207)

MANUAL ARTS THERAPIST GS-637
VA (32)

MARINE CARGO GS-2161
DOD (71)

MARKETING
DOC, DOD, TRE

MATERIALS ENGINEERING GS-806
*DOD, NASA, DOI, DOA, DOC, TRE, TVA, GSA, DOE, DHS (850)

MASONRY WG-3603
*DOD, VA, NASA, GSA, DOT, HHS, DHS, DOJ, DOI, DOE (336)

MATERIALS HANDLING WG-6907
*DOD, ALL AGENCIES (8,479)

MATHEMATICS GROUP GS-1500
*DOD, ALL (15,404)

MEATCUTTING WG-7407
*DOD, DOA (1,254)

MEDICAL GROUP GS-600
*VA, ALL (189,526)

MEDICAL EQUIPMENT REPAIR
WG-4805 *VA, HHS, DHS, DOD, DOJ (175)

MEDICAL OFFICER GS-0602
*VA, MOST AGENCIES (23,691)

MEDICAL TECHNICIAN GS-0645
*VA, DOD, HHS, DHS (2,050)

MESSENGER GS-302
*HHS, DOD, DHS, VA, TVA (22)

METAL PROCESSING FAMILY WG-3700
*DOD, DOA, DOJ, DHS, DOI, DOT, VA (4,360)

METALLURGY GS-1321
*DOD, TRE, DOI, DOC, TVA, DOE (71)

MICROBIOLOGY GS-403
*HHS, VA, DOD, EPA, DOI, DOA, DOC DOJ, DHS, DOJ, DOE (2,290)

MINE SAFETY & HEALTH GS-1822
*DOL (1,218)

MOBILE EQUIP. SERVICING WG-5806
*DOD, DOJ, DOI, DOA, GSA, VA, TVA, DOE, DHS (379)

MOTION PICTURE, RADIO, TV WORK
WG-3900 *DOD, DOI, HHS (41)

MOTOR VEHICLE OPERATING WG-5703
*DOD, ALL 5,740)

MUNITIONS WORK WG-6500
*DOD, DOA (1,831)

MUSEUM CURATOR GS-1015
*DOI, DOD, Smithsonian, DHS, HHS, DOT, DOC, DOA (319)

MUSEUM SPECIALIST GS-1016
*DOD, DOI TRE, DOS, DOC, DOJ, HHS, DHS, Smithsonian (383)

MUSIC SPECIALIST GS-1051
*DOD, DOT (13)

NAVAL ARCHITECTURE GS-871
*DOD, DOC, DOT, DHS (749)

NUCLEAR ENGINEERING GS-840
*DOD, TVA, DOE, DOC, DOI, DOS (2,014)

NUTRITION
DOA, VA

NURSE GS-610
*VA, HHS, DOD, TRE, DOS, DOJ, DOI, DOC, DOA, DOT, DOL, DHS, NASA (51,714)

OCCUPATIONAL THERAPIST GS-631
*VA, HHS, DOD, DOI (849)

OFFSET PHOTOGRAPHY WG-4414
*DOJ, DOD, DOI, DOT (19)

OPTOMETRIST GS-662
*VA, DOD, DOT (681)

**OUTDOOR RECREATION PLANNING
GS-023** *DOI, DOA, DOD (606)

PACKAGING GS-2032
*DOD, DOS, DOT (167)

**PAINTING & PAPERHANGING GROUP
WG-4100** *DOD, ALL (4,147)

**PACKING & PROCESSING GROUP WG-
7000** *DOD, DHS, DOJ, DOC, DOT, HHS, GSA,
VA (1,238)

PARALEGAL SPECIALIST GS-950
*DOJ, ALL (4,225)

PARK RANGER GS-025
*DOI, DOD (6009)

PATENT ADMINISTRATION GS-1220
*DOC (138)

PATHOLOGY TECHNICIAN GS-646
*VA, HHS, DOD (443)

**PERSONNEL MANAGEMENT GROUP
GS-200** *DOD, ALL (37,309)

PEST CONTROL WG-5026
*DOD, VA, DOA, DOI, GSA (279)

PHARMACOLOGY GS-0405
*HHS, DOD, DOA, DOJ, VA (430)

PHOTOGRAPHY GS-1060
*DOD, ALL (627)

PHYSICAL SCIENCE GROUP GS-1300
*DOD, ALL but DOE, OPM USI (28,001)

PHYSICS GS-1310
*DOD, HHS, DOE, DOC VA, (2,302)

PIPEFITTING WG-4204
*DOD, DOJ, HHS, DHS, VA, DOT (2,633)

PLUMBING WG-4206
*DOD, MOST AGENCIES (904)

POLICE GS-083
*DOD, DOC, DHS, DOT, DOJ, VA, TRE, DOI,
HHS, GSA (12,291)

PROCUREMENT GS-1106
*DOD, ALL (1,935)

**PSYCHOLOGY AIDE & TECHNICIAN
GS-181** *VA, DOD, HHS, DOT (596)

PSYCHOLOGY GS-180
*VA, ALL (4,382)

PUBLIC AFFAIRS GS-1035
*DOD, ALL (4,101)

PURCHASING GS-1105
*DOD, ALL (2,905)

**QUALITY ASSURANCE, INSPECTION,
& GRADING GROUP GS-1900**
*DOD (11,743)

RAILROAD SAFETY GS-2121
*DOT (466)

RAILROAD REPAIRING WG-3546
*DOD, DOI (45)

RECREATION AIDE & ASSISTANT GS-189
*DOD, DOI, DOA, VA, (1,543)

**REHABILITATION THERAPY ASSISTANT
GS-636** *VA, HHS, DOD (752)

RESPIRATORY THERAPIST GS-651
*DOD, VA, HHS, DHS, DOJ (512)

ROOFING WG-3606
*DOD (59)

SAFETY ENGINEERING GS-803
*DOD, DOI, VA, TVA, DOL, HHS, DOT, DOE,
DOC, GSA, NASA (465)

SALES STORE CLERICAL GS-2091
*DOD, VA (5,010)

SECURITY GUARD GS-085
*DOD, MOST AGENCIES (3,636)

**SEWAGE DISPOSAL PLANT OPERATION
WG-5408** *DOD, DOJ, DOA, VA, DOI (317)

SHEETMETAL MECHANIC WG-3806
*DOD, DOA, DOJ, HHS, DHS, VA DOE, TRE
(6,795)

SHIPWRIGHT WG-5220
*DOD (853)

SIGN PAINTING WG-4104
*DOD, DOI, VA (114)

SMALL ARMS REPAIR WG-6610
*DOD, DOJ, GSA (478)

SMALL ENGINE MECHANIC WG-8610
*DOD, DOI, (68)

SOCIAL SERVICES GS-187
*DOD, VA, DOI, HHS, DHS, DOA (647)

SOCIAL WORK GS-185
*VA, DOD, HHS, DOJ, DOI, DOT, DHS (6,116)

SOIL CONSERVATION GS-457
*DOA, DOD, DOI, DOE (4,517)

**SPEECH PATHOLOGY & AUDIOLOGY
GS-665** *VA, HHS, DOD, DOI (1,257)

SPORTS SPECIALIST GS-030
*DOD, DOJ, DHS, DOI, VA (492)

STATISTICIAN GS-1530
*DOC, ALL (2,915)

SUPPLY GROUP GS-2000
*DOD, ALL (30,494)

SURVEYING TECHNICIAN GS-817
*DOI, DOD, DOA, DOC (376)

TAX EXAMINING GS-592
TRE (11,677)

**TECHNICAL WRITING & EDITING
GS-1083** *DOD, ALL (969)

TELEPHONE MECHANIC WG-2502
*DOD, VA (414)

TELEPHONE OPERATING GS-382
*VA, DOD, DOJ, DOI, DOA, DOC, DOL,

HHS, GSA (782)

TOOLMAKING WG-3416
*DOD, DOJ, DOE, NASA (464)

TOXICOLOGY GS-0415
*HHS, DOD, DOA, DOI, VA, DOC, DOE (203)

**TRANSPORTATION GROUP
GS-2100** *DOT, ALL (42,248)

**TRANSPORTATION MOBILE EQUIPMENT
MAINTENANCE FAMILY WG-5800**
*DOD, ALL EXCEPT DOS & DOL (16,581)

UNITED STATES MARSHAL GS-082
DOJ (839)

UTILITY SYSTEMS REPAIR WG-4742
*DOD, MOST AGENCIES (1,729)

VETERINARY SCIENCE GS-700
*DOA, HHS, DHS, VA (2,768

VOCATIONAL REHABILITATION GS-1715
*VA, TVA, DOL, DOI, DOJ (530)

WELDING GS-3703
*DOD, DOA, DOJ, DOE, DOI, DHS, VA, (2,444)

WILDLIFE BIOLOGY GS-0486
*DOA, DOI, DOD, DOE (2,471)

WILDLIFE MANAGEMENT GS-485
DOI (669)

WOOD WORK GROUP WG-4600
*DOD, MOST AGENCIES (2,411)

WRITING GS-1082
*DOD, ALL (1,173)

ZOOLOGY GS-410
*DOI, DOD, DOA, DOC, HHS (58)

Index